WINGS OF WAR

Tiger Squadron, the fiercely proud story of Royal Air Force No. 74 Squadron, is author Ira Jones's loving description of how the RAF—often outnumbered and usually ill-equipped—prevailed against steep odds in two world wars. "Taffy" Jones scored 40 victories as a member of No. 74, nicknamed the Tiger Squadron, in the First World War; and he remained in close contact with it from his RAF command position in the Second. Whatever he flew, from the Sopwith Pup to the Supermarine Spitfire, he epitomized the aggressive RAF spirit.

Jones entered the First World War in 1915 as a mechanic, delighted that his five-foot-five-inch, 126-pound frame had been spared the rigors of the infantry, but impatient to engage in combat with the dreaded "Hun." (Jones's diary entries were often written in the aftermath of a battle in which he had lost a friend, and "Hun" is among the mildest terms he uses to refer to the Germans.) His restless zeal and his passionate desire to meet the enemy soon earned him a chance to fly over the lines as a radio operator. Later he was chosen for pilot's training and earned a commission, an outcome far beyond the dreams of the young man who had flunked his school exams because he was more interested in rugby and fighting.

In March 1918, Jones was posted to the just-forming No. 74 Squadron, where he flew and fought with some of the greatest names in the history of air combat, including the inimitable Major Edward "Mick" Mannock, a 73-victory ace whose hatred of the Germans exceeded even Jones's own. Blind in one eye and the most combative of all the top aces, Mannock exulted in every kill and he taught his men to fly with wild abandon. As it happened, he suffered the fate he had wished most on his enemies, dying when his own aircraft was shot down in flames.

Jones's vivid diary descriptions of combat form the heart of *Tiger Squadron*. On one afternoon, for example, his patrol attacked twelve German scouts. "A grand schemozzle followed for about five minutes," he wrote. "I then engaged the leader at 75

TIME-LIFE BOOKS INC., ALEXANDRIA, VIRGINIA 22314

yards' range from above and behind. This E.A. [enemy aircraft] got on its back and went down vertically from about 5,000 feet, when his wings collapsed and he crashed."

After the Armistice, Jones remained in the RAF. He then flew with the British Relief Force against the Bolsheviks and carried out other peacetime duties. In 1936 he retired, only to be recalled when World War II began in September 1939. He was 43—old for a combat pilot then—but he succeeded in getting back into the cockpit of a fighter briefly as commander of No. 7 Bombing and Gunnery School. He sent such promising pilots as Flight Lieutenant Adolph "Sailor" Malan to join No. 74 Squadron, which carried on its World War I tradition by distinguishing itself over Dunkirk, during the Battle of Britain, and subsequently throughout the war. Jones himself made some combat sweeps during the war, but his primary assignments included working directly for Lord Beaverbrook, minister of aircraft production, in dispersing planes after their manufacture.

In addition to *Tiger Squadron*, Jones wrote two other books, one a biography of Mannock, *King of the Air Fighters*, and an autobiography entitled *An Air Fighter's Scrapbook*. In 1960, at age 65, Jones died following an accident at home. The old pilot would have been the first to appreciate the irony of surviving so many air battles only to die after a fall from a ladder.

Walter J. Boyne

This volume, like every book in Wings of War, has been reproduced photographically from an original edition. It thus preserves the authenticity of the original, including typographical errors and printing irregularities.

TIGER SQUADRON

Eich annwyl fab
Ira /.

"TAFFY"

W/CMDR IRA JONES. D.S.O. M.C. D.F.C. M.M.

O.C. 53 O.T.U. 1941-
O.C. 54 O.T.U. 1940

THE AUTHOR

A portrait sketch by Cuthbert Orde

TIGER SQUADRON

The Story of 74 Squadron, R.A.F.,

in Two World Wars

BY

WING COMMANDER
IRA ("Taffy") JONES
D.S.O., M.C., D.F.C., M.M.

W. H. ALLEN

LONDON

1954

Made and printed in Great Britain
by the Camelot Press Ltd., Southampton, for the
publishers, W. H. Allen & Co., Ltd., Essex Street,
London, W.C. 2.

CONTENTS

I GRATEFULLY ACKNOWLEDGE THE very kind assistance given to me by the following in the preparation of this book:

My wife
Captain CUTHBERT ORDE
Dr. T. M. DAVIES, C.B.E., M.R.C.S., L.R.C.P.
Mr. BOB THOMAS (Bridgend)
Mr. J. C. NERNEY, I.S.O. ⎫ Air Historical Branch
Miss SYBIL BROWN, I.S.O. ⎭
Group Captain FRED SOWREY, D.S.O., M.C.
Wing Commander NEVILLE BLOND, C.M.G., O.B.E.
Wing Commander DONOVAN (O.C. Flying, 53 O.T.U., Llandow, April, 1942)
Squadron Leader LEIGHTON MOBRAY ⎫ of
Mr. LESLIE FISHER ⎬ Cardiff
Miss THELMA HARDING ⎭
Mr. GOMER EVANS, J.P. (Llanybri, Carmarthen)

I wish especially to acknowledge the invaluable assistance given in the writing of this book by my fellow-Welshman, JACK THOMAS.

ILLUSTRATIONS

Photos by courtesy of Air Ministry and other sources.

The rank and decorations of the pilots sketched by Captain C. Orde are those at the time the drawings were made.

FOREWORD

THIS IS THE story of the greatest fighter squadron of all time.
That it is also my own story is purely incidental.

I had the luck to be posted to 74 (Tiger) Squadron on its
formation in March, 1918. I maintained my close association
with it through the hottest fighting of two World Wars.

During the War of 1914–18, the offensive spirit of the Royal
Flying Corps, and later of the Royal Air Force, was the pride of
Britain and the despair of her foes. In the darkest hours, outnumbered and outgunned, the dour tenacity, the will to conquer,
of pilots and observers never weakened. They ended the war as
masters of the skies. And their high tradition was most honourably maintained by their sons in World War II.

In 1918, when the air war was at its peak, it was Tiger Squadron
which led the fighters who put paid to the Kaiser's ambitions.
At the end of the Battle of Britain, which tore the guts out of
Goering's Luftwaffe and settled once and for all Hitler's dreams
of invasion and conquest, it was again the Tigers who headed
the gallant Hurricane and Spitfire squadrons.

The supreme fighting aces of the two world wars—Captain
Edward (Mick) Mannock, V.C., D.S.O. and two bars, M.C.
and bar, in 1918; Group Captain Adolph ("Sailor") Malan,
D.S.O. and bar, D.F.C. and bar, during the Battle of Britain—
were both men of Tiger Squadron.

It was my privilege to know and fight with these brave men
and a thousand less famous but no less gallant comrades.

During more than twenty years in the Royal Flying Corps and
Royal Air Force I whiled away off-duty hours by keeping a
diary. It is with the help of those notes and a good memory that
I now write this story.

If my own experiences are inextricably woven with the tale,
they will, at least lend authority to the account. I flew every
type of single-seater fighter from the Sopwith Pup, with a speed
of 106 m.p.h., to the 400 m.p.h. Spitfire. I fought more "dog-
fights" than I can remember; and the Air Ministry, in 1919,
credited me with forty official victories. Unofficially, I tacked my
Spitfire on to offensive sweeps over northern France in 1941
and shared the thrill of that incredibly fast fighting.

From my first solo I have always been frightened when I felt myself airborne. I have never left the ground without uttering a short prayer for a safe return, but the unsafeness of my landings had become an R.A.F. legend. In point of fact, I have crashed twenty-nine times. I have handled the Dornier DOX 12-engine flying boat. I have flown as a passenger with air vice-marshals and sergeants. I have been the first passenger with many pilots less airworthy than I care to remember.

In one forced landing, the plane was surrounded by angry Arabs, intent on our blood. My pilot, Flying Officer Neville Vintcent, achieved the distinction of being the first ex-Cranwell cadet to be awarded the D.F.C. as a result of his courage in this "dust-up."

In 1919, I flew miles over the Bolshevik lines in north Russia, where a forced landing meant death. I have landed on an aircraft-carrier, been catapulted, and carried out practice jumps with early, far-from-perfect types of parachute.

But this book was not planned as a personal "line-shooting" operation. Its only heroes are the air fighters of yesterday who built the R.A.F.'s great traditions. If it inspires one fledgling "erk" to emulate their gallantry, it will have achieved its purpose.

Book One

BUILDERS OF THE TRADITION

I

THE ROYAL FLYING CORPS, Naval and Military Wings, was formed on May 13, 1912, with a strength of seven aircraft and even fewer qualified pilots.

Like most new weapons, the aeroplane was greeted with little enthusiasm by any general or admiral, except Lord Fisher. Wedded to the horse and the battleship, the "top brass" could see no future for this man-made, clumsy imitation of a bird.

The Naval Wing, later to be known as the Royal Naval Air Service, had to fight particularly hard for its existence. Though men like Commander Rumney Samson[1] and Commander Arthur Longmore[2] had proved its potential usefulness in sea warfare, the stubborn admirals refused to take it to their bosoms. Ironically, it was these same crusted shell-backs who, after World War I, fought desperately to separate the Fleet Air Arm from the Royal Air Force.

The generals, while critical, were more sympathetic towards the Military Wing, particularly after the 1912 manœuvres, when the little band of pilots proved the potential value of the aeroplane for reconnaissance even in stormy weather.

When, in the middle of August, 1914, the Royal Flying Corps accompanied the British Expeditionary Force to France—the first national air force to fly to a war overseas—it was accepted that reconnaissance would be its main task; any other duties, such as bombing and air fighting, would be mere sidelines. As a result, the sixty-three wood and fabric aircraft were ill-equipped for combat. Revolvers, rifles, carbines, duck guns, steel darts, inferior type bombs and grenades were the weapons provided. The only Lewis gun in the Corps was literally smuggled to France.

Before war broke out, it had been decided that the military aeroplane must be slow, since it was thought that reconnaissance could be carried out more effectively if the plane were travelling slowly over the enemy's territory. Besides which, the observer

[1] Later, Air Commodore.   [2] Now Air Marshal Sir Arthur Longmore.

could write his report on the way back from patrol and have it ready for delivery on arrival!

The problem of high wind velocity, which sometimes blew the slow, cumbersome British Experimentals, Farmans, Bleriots and Avros backwards, appears to have been completely overlooked.

Today the supreme factor is speed. All types of aircraft, especially fighters, must be as fast as possible, and able to climb to great heights with virtually the speed of a rocket. Most aircraft which went to war in August, 1914, cruised at about 65 m.p.h. and took ten minutes to climb to 3,000 feet!

It was soon realised in those early days that a slow aeroplane could not live long in war, and that its length of life could be increased only by arming it better than its opponents. Consequently, a frantic race began between designers on both sides to improve performance and armament.

Inevitably, the balance of power tilted from time to time, but even when the weight was most heavily against us, the gallantry and offensive spirit of our pilots and observers remained unimpaired. They carried out their missions, whatever the odds against them. Often the effort, costly in casualties, required prodigious resolution, but there were no complaints, and it must be recorded that German airmen seldom displayed similar resolution when casualties were heavy. Nor did their successors show to better advantage during the Battle of Britain in World War II. Their morale fell as losses rose. To quote the vernacular: "They could dish it out, but they couldn't take it."

Curiously, it was with the destruction of the Zeppelin that our pilots' minds were most preoccupied at the beginning of World War I. General Henderson, who commanded the R.F.C. in the field, was asked by his airmen if it were their duty to ram a "Zepp" and destroy it. When he replied that it should be attacked only with the weapons at their disposal, some of the pilots were obviously disappointed.

The first reconnaissance under war conditions took place on August 19, 1914, from Maubeuge Aerodrome. The area reconnoitred was the German right wing in the direction of Brussels and Louvain and the B.E. aircraft at once proved its value.

It was from the air observers that General French first heard of Von Kluck's ambitious enveloping movement, which was aimed at wiping out our "contemptible little army," and which culminated in the retreat from Mons. Air observers reported Von Kluck's wheeling movement to the south-east on August 31. Instead of encircling and taking Paris, he attempted a second

Builders of the Tradition

Sedan—an error in strategy which probably cost the Germans final victory. And it was the air observers who reported on September 4 that Von Kluck's army was crossing the Marne, information which decided General Joffre to deliver the counter-stroke that was the turning-point of the war.

Joffre was liberal in his praise of the British airmen. "The precision, exactitude and regularity of the news brought in by them are evidence of the perfect training of pilots and observers," he wrote.

Our aircraft kept constant observation on the Germans during the retreat. Hustled from landing-ground to landing-ground, the efficiency of the squadrons nevertheless remained unimpaired.

Sir John French recorded: "Their skill, energy and persever-ance have been beyond all praise. . . . Fired at constantly both by friend and foe, and not hesitating to fly in every kind of weather, they have remained undaunted throughout."

So, early in the campaign and under great difficulties, the newly-born Air Arm proved its value to the Commander-in-Chief and received the highest congratulations. A good begin-ning, which was to end in proud achievement. But it was a time of improvisation and expediency.

While the R.F.C. was concentrated at Maubeuge, rifles were fitted in the aeroplanes, and, since our troops were continually firing on their own aircraft, a Union Jack shield had to be painted on the underside of the lower wings of every machine to make it more easily recognisable.

One of our aircraft was shot down by British infantrymen and the pilot killed. On another occasion, the petrol tank of a Bleriot was pierced by a rifle bullet. Luckily, the hole was within the pilot's reach, and plugging the spouting petrol with his finger, he managed by skilful flying to reach the aerodrome safely.

On August 22, 1914, Sergeant-Major Jillings, of 2 Squadron, acting as observer to Lieutenant Noel on a reconnaissance of Mons-Ath-Lessines, spotted a regiment of Uhlans to the east of Lessines. As the aeroplane circled above the enemy, Jillings felt a sharp blow in the backside. The reconnaissance continued, but Jillings soon began to feel some pain, and something warm trickled down his leg. He shouted to his pilot and the machine was flown back to the aerodrome, where it was confirmed that the sergeant-major had become the first of seven thousand British airmen to be wounded in the war.

It was on this same day that the first enemy aeroplane was

B   17 seen. Captain Charles Longcroft, a Welshman, in a B.E. and Lieutenant Louis Strange, an Englishman, in the Farman which mounted the only Lewis gun in the Corps, took off and gave chase. But the Hun had too much start and they were unable to engage him. Nevertheless, the failure had its consolation, for it had given practical meaning to the pre-war Flying Corps dictum: "A fixed determination to attack and win is the surest road to victory."

The very first air battle over the British front took place during the morning of August 25, 1914. A Taube monoplane was sighted in the vicinity of the Foret de Mormal, and it was chased to the ground by Lieutenants Harvey-Kelly and Mansfield, who were armed only with revolvers. They landed near the Taube, but the Germans escaped into a wood and got away. The enemy plane was burned by one of our cavalry patrols before Mansfield or Harvey-Kelly could intervene and only a few charred souvenirs could be flown back to the R.F.C. mess.

This combat, the prelude to air fighting on a scale then undreamed of, proved that the successful co-operation of aircraft with ground troops depended entirely on air supremacy, which could be gained only by aggressive tactics.

During the retreat from Mons, the R.F.C. shared to the full the hardships of the Army. For the most part, all the squadrons were concentrated on single aerodromes, usually stubbled fields, from which the stooked corn had to be removed to allow the machines to land.

Many and varied were the adventures of airmen in these pioneer days. Typical was that of one pilot who lost his way, and landed near to some troops to ask for guidance. They turned out to be Germans. He escaped by the skin of his teeth.

On September 1, while the Corps was located near Jeully, a signal was received ordering all transport to depart immediately dusk fell. One light tender was to be left behind for any pilot and mechanic whose aeroplane refused to fly. All night long, with the sounds of the German advance drawing ever nearer, the pilots and mechanics guarded their machines with rifles and revolvers until all were got safely away.

Lieutenants Dawes and Freeman,[1] of 2 Squadron, were on reconnaissance many miles over the enemy lines when their aircraft began to give trouble. There was nothing for it but to land, and as the machine finished up against a tree Dawes and Freeman dived for the cover of a wood, one jump ahead of Hun

[1] Later Air Chief Marshal Sir Wilfred Freeman.

infantry and cavalry units. For hours they lay in the under-growth, listening to the noises made by the search-parties, and when darkness fell, they started their ten-mile trek back to the British lines. Every now and then they froze in their tracks as a German outpost loomed up ahead, but the sentries were too busy celebrating their victorious advance to notice the fugitives, who, footsore and weary, reached the Aisne as dawn broke. They flopped down in a ditch to sleep, only to be jolted awake by the crashing bark of a nearby Hun battery. Moving forward cautiously, they found Uhlans patrolling the road which ran parallel with the river bank. Then, to add insult to injury, British gunners began plastering the neighbourhood with shrapnel. The two men swam the river and at last found friendly territory, but before they eventually rejoined their squadron they had been missing nearly three days.

Typical of the "fluid" state of war was the mission allotted to two members of 5 Squadron on the morning of the Battle of Le Cateau. Haig's Corps had not taken up its assigned position and Lieutenants Borton[1] and Small were given the delightfully vague order: "Find Sir Douglas Haig and give him this dispatch." The pilot of an accompanying machine, equipped with wireless, was instructed to send a message back to Headquarters as soon as Haig was found. Twice the searching plane landed near our retreating troops to try to get a lead on Haig's movements, and since the only suitable field was in the 1,000 yards of no-man's-land separating our positions from the Hun, the experience was not without its excitement. At last the pilot found a cavalry patrol which knew where Haig was, and the dispatch was delivered, but during all this time the plane had been under heavy rifle and gun fire from the Germans. Crouching low, the pilot bolted across no-man's-land and climbed into the cockpit while lead whizzed all round him. As he taxied the aircraft to a position for take-off, a detachment of Uhlans galloped on to the field and two riders were within yards of the plane as it finally staggered into the air.

On September 7, the squadrons returned to Pezarches—the first move forward since the retreat. A battle had been fought on the field used as the aerodrome and small one-man trenches had to be filled in before the machines could land. Five days later the squadrons moved up to Fere-en-Tardenois and barely had they checked in when a heavy storm blew up. It played havoc with the aircraft, which, of course, were all out in the open. Many

[1] Later Air Vice-Marshal.

were turned over on their backs, like so many swatted flies, others blown right across the field. One was seen to leap about 30 feet in the air, crash down on another, and become locked with it in a hopeless tangle. Dawn broke on a scene of indescribable chaos and before long enemy planes came over to view the damage. One was brought down by rifle fire. The pilot was killed, but his officer observer landed the aircraft safely, which all agreed was a pretty good effort.

During the German retirement the art of aerial bombardment was born. Hand grenades, petrol bombs, and steel darts with fluted tails and sharp points were dropped over the enemy's horse lines and troops. A canister holding about 250 darts, 5 inches long and $\frac{3}{8}$ inch in diameter, was fixed under the fuselage of the aircraft, and when the observer pulled a wire, the tin opened and the darts showered down.

On the evening of September 13, an observer reported that the Germans were digging in along the length of the Chemin des Dames, and this proved to be the beginning of the formidable trench system, extending eventually from the Belgian coast to the Swiss frontier, which was to baffle Allied generals for four miserable years. By now the aeroplane had superseded the cavalry in taking on the heavy, exacting burden of all tactical and strategical reconnaissance. Tactical reconnaissance was confined to the battle area and to a depth of five to six miles behind the most forward enemy troops. Strategical reconnaissance, beginning where tactical reconnaissance left off, produced information which assisted the Commander-in-Chief to forecast the enemy's intentions, and as early as September 13 the Royal Flying Corps had come into its own, for Sir John French reported that our airmen had gained "something in the direction of the mastery of the air." Their tactics for dealing with enemy aircraft, he said, were to "attack them instantly with one or more machines."

Now began the Battle of the Aisne, and we tried out aerial photography and wireless co-operation with the artillery. At first, the results were not successful enough to impress the Army Staff, but as the war progressed so did the camera and wireless set become indispensable. It was soon apparent that the increasing number, depth and boldness of our aerial reconnaissances had the German High Command seriously worried, and orders were issued to their airmen to attack our aircraft on sight. It was the signal for the real war in the air to begin. Huns daring to challenge our pilots to mortal combat were met joyfully more than halfway. Often our men had to take up the challenge unarmed, and in lieu of weapons, they devised the charging tactic. They would scream down on the nose of a Hun plane as if to ram it, and usually the enemy pilot was unnerved completely. At least two planes were forced by such tactics to land in our territory. The heroes of these unorthodox exploits were Lieutenant Norman Spratt,[1] of 5 Squadron, and Lieutenant Medlicott, of 2 Squadron. The latter, accompanied by Lieutenant H. B. Russell[2] as observer, actually jockeyed his opponent back from over German territory.

Later in the war, Lieutenant Medlicott, accompanied by Lieutenant Whitten Brown as observer, was forced to land in the enemy lines, and the pair were captured. Medlicott became famous for his numerous, determined attempts to escape, and eventually, he was shot and killed by a sentry.

On September 22, 1914—a month to the day on which Sergeant-Major Jillings[3] had been wounded—Lieutenant G. W. Mapplebeck,[4] of 4 Squadron, spotted a German plane while flying on reconnaissance. He immediately engaged, but in trying to get to close quarters he was dangerously wounded in the thigh and belly. In great pain, and weakened by loss of blood, he flew his aircraft back to the aerodrome and made a three-point landing. He was the first British airman actually to be wounded in an air fight.

The dogged tenacity of mortally wounded pilots has become legendary in the story of British airmen in two world wars. The tradition was set by the first air V.C., Lieutenant Rhodes Moorhouse, who, though almost shot to pieces, brought his plane and his observer safely home. He was followed by Sergeant Mottershead, the only non-commissioned airman to win the V.C. during World War I, who brought his observer back to our lines in a blazing plane rather than be taken prisoner.

In due course it became clear to our High Command that if our aircraft were to be effective fighting machines they would have to be armed with machine guns, and that meant in effect that a new type of aeroplane for combat must be evolved.

As none of our designers could invent a device which would enable a machine gun to be fired through the revolving propeller, the choice of a new machine fell upon the "pusher," an aircraft in which the pilot and gunner sat in front of the engine and

---

[1] Later Group Captain.   [2] Later Group Captain.
[3] Later Group Captain.   [4] Killed.

propeller. There was an unlimited field of fire and view forward, and the pilot manœuvred the aeroplane while the gunner did the shooting. It was towards the end of September, 1914, that the advance guard of the "pusher fighters" arrived in France. They were Maurice Farman Shorthorns, mounting Lewis guns. Their tendency to remain stationary when headed into a strong wind, coupled with the continual jamming of the Lewis guns, hardly made for success.

Nevertheless, at this period, many tactical lessons were learnt: among them, the value of the sun and clouds as aids in surprise attacks; the importance of closing to within 100 yards of the enemy before opening fire; the vital necessity of attacking from the enemy's blind spot; and the importance of sticking to the enemy until he was shot down or dived for home. Above all, the necessity for speed was clearly demonstrated.

The sluggishness of our aircraft in adverse weather made them easy targets for the ground defences, and pilots and observers often found it necessary to fly unarmed in order to gain height. The strong prevalent westerly winds, which cut down speed, gave our pilots continuous nightmares.

Faster machines, single-seater scouts—Bristol monoplanes and 80-h.p. Le Rhones, with a speed of 100 m.p.h.—began arriving in France in September, 1914. The original allocation was one aeroplane per squadron for fast scouting duties, but their usefulness as fighters was soon recognised, and they were detailed for escort and protective work. They had to be ready to take off at a moment's notice to attack any marauder, and, since the Hun had numerical superiority at this time, they were kept pretty busy. Scout pilots were armed, at first, only with revolvers or rifles, it having been found that the mounting of a machine gun greatly reduced the performance of the aircraft. However, various tests and experiments showed that the Lewis gun would work equally well when stripped of its radiator casing and cooling fins, and this reduction in weight and wind resistance so altered the whole situation that every available gun was brought into use.

Originally the gun had been mounted at an angle, to ensure that the bullets would not collide with the propeller, but it was an arrangement that made accurate shooting impossible, because it compelled the pilot to manœuvre his plane in one direction and fire in another. Later on, a new method was tried, and this proved much more practical. Instead of being placed at an angle, the gun was fitted to the centre section of the top wing and was fired forward and over the propeller by a cable that ran from the gun to the side of the pilot in the cockpit. This method worked particularly well with some of the later fighters, such as the Nieuport Scouts, whose pilots achieved greater accuracy of fire by training the nose of the aeroplane on the target. The gun was so fixed and sighted that the pilot's line of sight coincided with the line of fire. One big disadvantage, though, was the difficulty of changing the 47-round drum of ammunition on the gun, while still maintaining control of the aircraft. The astonishing experience of Captain Louis Strange, flying a Martinsyde Scout, illustrates vividly what could happen to any pilot in those crazily experimental days.

While Captain Strange was at grips with an Otto over Menin it became necessary to change the ammunition drum. As often happened, the pilot found that the empty one was more than usually difficult to move and, to get both hands to it, he put the control column between his knees. While he was heaving at the drum, however, the control column slipped forward and before Captain Strange could guess what was in store for him, his machine turned over on its back. At the same moment the pilot's safety belt snapped and he was tossed right out of the cockpit. By a miracle he managed to retain his grip on the Lewis gun and, dangling in space, he clung on desperately as the machine dropped away, spinning slowly and upside down. Not until the machine had reached 6,000 feet towards destruction did Strange, in a last despairing attempt, manage to swing his legs back into the cockpit, where, by juggling the control column with his feet, he actually succeeded in righting the aircraft and dropping back into his seat, which by now had also become loose. Somehow, by superb courage and skill, Captain Strange got the Martinsyde back to his aerodrome and landed safely. When the plane was examined it was found that every instrument had been broken in the mishap and that all loose fittings, even to the pilot's cushion, had fallen out.

Many airmen met sudden death by falling out of their machines during World War I. Such accidents chilled the blood of friend and foe alike. The victims, with arms and legs spread-eagled, would drop away, twisting and turning, as they hurtled towards certain death. Astonishing as it may appear, the issue of parachutes to flyers had been vetoed and only balloon observers were deemed to be really in need of them.

It is part of an old story of how the R.A.F. had to wait nearly twenty years before its first pilot was able to save his life by parachute, and I remember only too well the agonising days that went before—days when I saw my friends and comrades plummeting to their deaths in their flying crates of wood and fabric, while defeated Huns were able to bale out and float safely to earth.

My habit of attacking Huns dangling from parachutes led to many arguments in the mess. Some officers, of the Eton and Sandhurst type, thought it "unsportsmanlike" to do it. Never having been to a public school, I was unhampered by such considerations of "form." I just pointed out that there was a bloody war on, and that I intended to avenge my pals.

Incidentally, Ernst Udet, the German ace credited with having accounted for sixty-six of our aircraft, once told me he had had to use his parachute soon after he had shot down his fourth plane.

The non-provision of parachutes was by no means the only "gripe" that rankled in the minds of many of our airmen when the end of World War I came. During the "peace years" it became increasingly clear that too many armchair pilots were reaching the dizzy heights of promotion in the R.A.F. Discontent among the pilots who had done the actual air fighting was rife. It was more than injustice to have to listen to the B.B.C.'s fulsome praise of certain senior officers on the day the R.A.F. came of age in April, 1939, without a single mention being made of aerial giants, such as Mannock, Ball, McCudden and their like. Yet they were in every way the true builders of the Tradition.

2

I T W A S N O T until 1915, when the Germans were winning, with the help of the Fokker, the first round in the struggle for air supremacy, that I got into the fighting. The curious thing is that if my first boyhood ambition had been realised, I should never have seen the inside of an aircraft. As a child, I lived with my mother in St. Clears, a village on the Tenby road, eight miles out of Carmarthen. I was educated at Glasfryn Council School and the Queen Elizabeth Grammar School, Carmarthen, where I failed all my examinations because I wasted my time in fighting and playing rugger.

In 1912, when the *Titanic* struck an iceberg and sank, I was just sixteen. The story of the disaster shocked and thrilled me, and I read and re-read every newspaper account, fascinated by the heroism of the young radio operator who stayed at his post, sending out S.O.S. signals until the seas poured into his cabin and engulfed him.

I told my mother: "That's the job for me. I'm going to be a wireless operator. The sea's the only life." But she had other plans. When I left school, she found me a post as junior clerk in the local land valuation office. It was a safe job with a pension at the end of it. That, in her eyes, was worth any amount of sea-going nonsense.

The head of the office, Major de Rees, commanded the 4th Welch Territorials, and it seemed to me it might be good policy and good fun to join the regiment. If I couldn't be a wireless operator, week-end soldiering offered at least some prospects of excitement. I was hardly the build for an infantryman. I stood 5 feet 5 inches, and weighed less than nine stone, and my long-barrelled Lee-Enfield, with the bayonet fixed, was taller than I was. It was hard to slope arms without poking out the eye of the next man in line. Still, I enjoyed every minute of my service with the unit.

My other relaxation was Rugby football. I played regularly as scrum half for Carmarthen Harlequins, then rated the best second-class team in Wales. These pursuits made clerking bearable for some eighteen months, but by the end of 1913 I could stick my desk no longer. As far as I was concerned, it was going to be wireless operating or nothing. Somehow, I talked my mother round, and she agreed to let me take a course at the British School of Telegraphy in London, although it involved considerable financial sacrifice. Early in 1914 I set out for London.

Though Britain remained calm, internationally things were warming up. Already there was serious trouble in the Balkans and a major war seemed on the cards. If it came, I wanted to be in on it. As a trained wireless operator I should stand a good chance.

I sat for my second-class Postmaster-General's Certificate in the last week of July, and went back to St. Clears to await the result. A few days later, on August 4, war was declared. As an active Territorial, I immediately reported to Carmarthen Barracks, but when the adjutant heard that I had my second-class wireless certificate and expected to sit for my first-class ticket in a few weeks' time, he said: "Go back to London and complete your course. We'll call you if we need you. I don't think you need worry. It will all be over by Christmas."

I got my first-class certificate in October. To the Postmaster-General, I was now a fully-fledged operator. I could send and receive messages at the required rate of twenty-two words a minute. That seemed to me only half the battle. There was still no word from the 4th Welch. I decided to pass the time of waiting for my call-up by taking a course in the erection and maintenance of wireless stations, and by April, 1915, I had passed my first examination on the technical side and was ready to sit for my final. That was how matters stood when one lunchtime I was pulled up by a recruiting sergeant while strolling down Whitehall. He was a burly, red-faced character, with protuberant, watery blue eyes, vinous nose and moustachios waxed to long needle-points. His great chest, bisected by the broad red sash of his office, was hung with rows of medals. Red, white and blue streamers fluttered at each side of his cap. He looked like a prize-winning dray horse at a May Day parade.

"Young feller," he boomed. "Don't you know there's a war on?"

"I've heard about it," I said.

"Well, w'y aren't you in uniform?"

"I'm in the 4th Welch Territorials, and I'm waiting to be called up," I explained.

That seemed to disappoint him, but his expression quickly brightened. " 'Ere. W'y wait?" he asked insinuatingly. "The recruitin' office is only a step away, in Great Scotland Yard. 'Ow about comin' along an' takin' the shillin' *now*?"

On the spur of the moment, I asked: "Any vacancies in the Royal Flying Corps?"

He stared at me as if I'd asked for a commission in the Prussian Guards. "The Flyin' Corpse?" he repeated. "Now wot the 'ell d'you want to join them for?"

I replied: "I'm a qualified wireless operator. And I'd like to fly."

His face lit up. "Blimey! You're just the boy we're lookin' for. You come along o' me!"

We must have looked a comical pair—the giant turkey-cock of a sergeant, and all 5 feet 5 inches of me, in bowler hat and reach-me-down "civvies," almost trotting to keep pace with his parade-ground strides. I didn't care. I was bursting with pride. Already, in imagination, I was a dare-devil pilot, shooting my first Hun down in flames.

It wasn't to be so simple as that though. I signed on, and took the King's shilling. Then, still in "civvies," I was turned loose to go and sit for my final wireless examination. Five weeks went by before I was called to the colours, and then not as a pilot, but, a very raw recruit, to put in a fortnight's "square-bashing" at Farnborough Depot.

Flying seemed very far away. I put in weary hours, peeling spuds on cookhouse fatigue or sitting polishing my buttons and trying to forget the agony of feet blistered by new ammunition boots. Once initial training was over, however, I was posted to 10 Squadron, R.F.C., at Netheravon, as air mechanic first-class, on wireless duties.

The squadron was equipped with B.E. 2C two-seater reconnaissance biplanes, capable of a top speed of about 65 m.p.h. and a maximum altitude of some 6,000 feet. The only offensive weapons they carried were the revolvers of the pilot and observer. My work was to fit the aircraft with wireless transmitters. Even to be in the cockpit of a grounded machine gave me a big thrill. Long after my official job was done, I would sit there, visualising myself at the controls, soaring over enemy territory amid a storm of bursting "Archie" shells. Somehow, I *had* to get into the air.

Among the squadron N.C.Os. was Sergeant Baldwin, a genial, long-service type who adopted an almost fatherly attitude

Tiger Squadron

towards us youngsters. On my second day on the station I nerved myself to approach him.

"Do you think you could possibly wangle me a flight, Sergeant?" I asked.

Frowning, he affected to consider the point. At last, he said: "I'll see. The planes have got to be flight-tested every day. Maybe I could persuade one of the officers to take you up. Any particular fancy?"

I was in no doubt about that. There was one man who seemed to my hero-worshipping eye to be a god among gods. He was Captain William Mitchell[1]—a well-built, dapperly-uniformed flyer who strode about the aerodrome with an air of supreme confidence. Always cheerful, yet with more than a hint of underlying toughness, he was a pilot second to none, and he symbolised everything I ever longed to be. The idea of flying as his passenger was almost unimaginable. But somehow I got the words out.

"Do you think I could go up with the officer with the ginger hair?" I asked.

Baldwin wagged his head slowly. "Can't make no promises, sonny. I'll see what I can do. You'd better be messing around in the hangar when he's getting ready to go up to-morrow morning."

I could hardly wait. Such matters as sleep, breakfast and early morning parade were unendurable delays, but at last I managed to reach the hangar, and began to fiddle about with quite imaginary adjustments. My mates viewed this gratuitous zeal with the deepest distrust, but all the time I was covertly watching Sergeant Baldwin's movements. When I saw him go over to Captain Mitchell, my heart almost stopped beating. They spoke together briefly. Baldwin turned and came striding towards me. He winked and smiled. I knew it was O.K.

"Report to Captain Mitchell," Baldwin said. "He's willing to take you up."

I dropped the screwdriver I was holding and fairly hared across the tarmac. As I halted in front of the Captain, my hand shot up in the smartest salute I could achieve.

"Air Mechanic Jones, sir!"

Captain Mitchell looked down at me with a grin. "Your first flight?" he asked understandingly.

"Yes, sir."

"Well, hop in that machine over there."

I don't remember getting into the cockpit. I only snapped out of my dream when the engine roared and, at last, incredibly, the

[1] Later Air Marshal Sir William Mitchell.

28

aircraft was rolling over the grass and lifting into the air. For about fifteen minutes we circled the aerodrome. Leaning over the side of the observer's cockpit I watched, fascinated, as the patch-work pattern of the fields unrolled beneath us. I saw men like ants walking on the ground. I looked up into the limitless blue kingdom of the sky. And I prayed: "Oh, God, please let me do this for ever."

It was all over too soon. The machine went into a long glide, touched down, bumped gently, then ran slowly to a halt in front of the hangar. Reluctantly, still under the spell, I climbed out of the cockpit.

Captain Mitchell's eyes gleamed with some secret joke. But all he said was: "Enjoy it?"

I could hardly stammer my thanks.

Nos. 10 and 11 Squadrons left Netheravon for France that day. No. 11 Squadron, the first fighter squadron of the R.F.C., was equipped with Vickers two-seaters, and although these machines were too slow to bring the enemy to action, they could hold their own in actual combat.

On the day 10 Squadron, the squadron to which I was attached, became operational, July 25, 1915, the first Victoria Cross was won for air fighting. Captain L. G. Hawker, of 6 Squadron, flying a Bristol Scout armed with a Lewis gun, shot down two enemy two-seaters, one in flames and the other down and out of control. Six days later another V.C. went to Captain J. A. Liddell, of 7 Squadron. Badly wounded in a fight over Bruges, he flew his seriously damaged R.E. 5 back to a Belgian aerodrome near Furnes. He died of his wounds a month after-wards.

It took us three days to get from Havre to our base at Choques, near Bethune. We rumbled in lorries over the interminable, straight French roads. Through the lines of poplars in full leaf we could stare at fields apparently untouched by war. We seemed to be getting nowhere. Then, in the late afternoon of July 25, somebody said: "There's the aerodrome!" Eagerly we looked over the side of the lorry. On the left of the road was a bare black patch of cinders, about 300 yards square, fringed by three canvas hangars. There was not a plane in sight, nor a figure moving. Even in the bright sunshine, the place looked forlorn and deserted.

Over a bank of trees behind the aerodrome shone the white turrets of an ancient chateau—the first I had seen outside picture books. This, I discovered later, was to be Squadron H.Q. and officers' mess. The lorries rolled on past the aerodrome, turned right down a narrow lane and came to rest in the yard of a tumbledown farm. The farmer, his wife, and their pretty, sixteen-year-old daughter waved and cheered from the door of the house as we pulled in. The daughter's greetings were returned with particular fervour.

I had visions of a nice quiet bed in a room under that lichened, overhanging red roof. Instead, we were marched off in flights to the different outbuildings. My billet that night was a palliasse on the floor above the cow byres. It was clean enough, but somewhat strongly scented.

Dumping our kit, we got busy immediately on the job of going into occupation. The aircraft flew in from another aerodrome within a couple of hours of our arrival. By nightfall, 10 Squadron was fully operational. Next morning, after breakfast, I was taken by wireless tender to 16 Squadron, stationed at La Gorgue, near Lestrem, about ten miles from Choques. There I was to undergo a fortnight's course in battery-and-aircraft communication.

No. 16's commanding officer was Major "Stuffy" Dowding, a lean, dark man with a tendency to undue solemnity. I was to find him a very good type, completely lacking in "side." Often he would come and sit by me as I operated my receiver, and talk to me, if not as an equal, at least like a human being.

Wireless communication in those early days was really a rag-time affair. My receiver consisted of a crystal, a cat's whisker and a simple inductance coil, enclosed in a small wooden box. My aerial was a 60-foot length of wire, slung between two 20-foot sectional masts. The artillery spotting plane was fitted with a battery-powered, spark-type transmitter, operated by a buzzer key fixed on the right-hand side of the observer's cockpit. The limit of effective transmission and reception was about ten miles.

Before a "shoot" started, the spotting plane would circle the aerodrome and tap out a code message: "Are you receiving me?" When the ground operator received it, he would take off his headphones, rush out of the wireless hut and lay out white strips of cloth on the ground. This signified: "Receiving you, loud and clear."

At the end of the fortnight's course, the wireless tender took me up to Fosse 7 at Annequin, a couple of miles from the Hohen-zollern Redoubt, where I was to be attached to 10 Siege (8-inch howitzer) Battery, commanded by Major Collingwood. From now on, my job would be to keep in contact with the aircraft from 10 Squadron detailed to act as battery spotter over the Redoubt.

The observer's job was to note the fall of our shells and transmit the location of the bursts back to the battery. Ensconced in a corner of the C.O.'s dug-out, I received the messages and shouted them over to Major Collingwood, so that he could adjust the range of his guns. I remained with 10 Siege Battery for three months. Then, following a further three months with 2 London Heavy Battery on the same front, I was taken back to 10 Squadron for a rest. I did not know it, but I was soon to be promoted to air-gunner and observer—an unusual honour to be bestowed on an air mechanic at that time.

After a week of routine duties at Choques, the old urge to fly got too much for me. Seeking the aid of Sergeant Baldwin once again, I asked him: "Do you think you could get Captain Mitchell to try me out as an observer?"

"That's a bit of a tall order," he said. "Write out your application. I'll see Captain Mitchell gets it."

I was on tenterhooks for several days. Every time I passed Captain Mitchell I looked hopefully for some reaction which would tell me what my chances were. Apart from his usual friendly smile, he showed no particular awareness of my ambitions. It was now January, 1916. The weather was cold and wet. Flying, never pleasant, was often quite impossible. It seemed to me I had better forget the whole thing. Then one morning Baldwin told me: "You're wanted. Captain Mitchell's office—at the double!"

The order was superfluous. I was already heading at speed for the back of the hangars. The Captain was sitting at a plain deal table in the cubby-hole he called his office. "Ah, Jones," he said. "I've spoken to Major Burke. He has considered your application. I am to take you up and try you out on a shoot. Sure you feel confident enough?"

"Positive, sir."

"Right! I'll take you up directly after lunch."

I went out of the office treading on air. Sergeant Baldwin was waiting in the hangar. He was almost as excited as I. "How did you get on?" he asked anxiously.

I could only grin.

After lunch I went to the stores and drew out an observer's leather coat, helmet and flying boots. I felt the entire flight was watching as I walked out to the aeroplane. A mechanic was warming up the engine. He gave me a friendly "G'luck!" as I climbed into the observer's cockpit. Captain Mitchell came strolling nonchalantly across the cinders. How I envied the careless ease with which he took the controls! He throttled back, shouting: "All right in front?"

I put up my thumb, the way I had seen observers do it. We took off, and I prayed fervently that there would be no slip-up. As we circled the aerodrome, I tapped out a message to the ground receiving station. "Are you receiving me?" I watched, with my heart in my mouth, for the signal accepting my message. Far below, a tiny figure ran out of the wireless hut and laid white "L" strips on the cinders. All well, so far. I gave my pilot the "O.K.," and he flew towards 10 Siege Battery. Once more I tapped out my call signal—this time to the battery wireless operator—and saw the "L" acknowledgment. I signalled: "Are you ready to fire?" The appropriate confirmation strips were laid out.

Captain Mitchell climbed to 3,000 feet and headed for the target, an intersection of German trenches on the Hohenzollern Redoubt. As soon as he saw us, the Hun opened up with everything he had. Before the first of our howitzers had gone into action, "Archie" bursts were ringing the plane. Captain Mitchell flew on, quite unperturbed. I cannot claim a similar detachment, but I managed to control the butterflies in my stomach by keeping my mind severely on the job. As each of the Battery's shells landed, I signalled back the position of the explosion.

After ten rounds had been fired, we called it a day and headed back to the aerodrome. On the homeward run, the pilot kept the plane twisting and turning in the most extraordinary evolutions. I thoroughly enjoyed myself. It was better than being on the Barry Island switchback railway. I did not realise the manœuvres were deliberately intended to make me airsick—a fatal flaw in many observers.

We touched down and taxied to the hangar. Climbing out of the cockpit, we stretched our cramped limbs. There was a little pause. Then Captain Mitchell grinned. "You'll do, Taffy," he said.

It was the accolade.

After my first war flight, I practised assiduously the art of spotting machines in the air. I used to spend hours, when on the ground, trying to pick out aircraft over the lines. Backing one's ability to see more planes in the air than the next man was a

Five phases in the service career of the Author.

Outside Dispersal Hut, 1940. Aubert; Treacy; Cobden; Byrne; Mayne; Mungo-Park; Smith; Measures; Freeborn; Mould and Hoare.

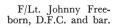

F/Lt. Johnny Freeborn, D.F.C. and bar.

Rochford, 1940. Richardson (killed); Mungo-Park (killed); Skinner.

MEMBERS OF TIGER SQUADRON

favourite pastime among mechanics. Having the natural advantage of long sight, and also the necessary patience and enthusiasm, I usually won any bets I made. This spotting practice stood me in good stead when, as a patrol leader, my life and the lives of my comrades were to depend primarily on my good eyesight. It is my proudest memory that, thanks to my highly trained vision, coupled with the fighting abilities of my team, my flight was never taken by surprise. Usually we surprised the enemy, instead. I can boast that I never lost a pilot.

Apart from doing his best to shoot down the enemy in combat, the chief duty of an air-gunner is to spot hostile aircraft in good time. It is a most difficult and onerous task. Even for a man blessed with long sight, an enormous amount of practice in the air is essential. An efficient gunner must never allow an aircraft to approach unseen within a mile. He must be able to spot a plane so far away that it looks no bigger than a fly. Nor is mere spotting enough. The machine must be recognised as friendly or hostile, and its type determined. All these details are necessary for deciding combat tactics.

For example, the pilot of a two-seater, fighting a single-seater, should always keep below his adversary to have an equal chance of obtaining a hit. Fighting another two-seater, he must try to get directly underneath his opponent, giving the gunner an almost vertical shot while remaining immune from retaliation (unless, of course, the enemy has an opening in the floor of the fuselage, through which he can fire downwards).

I completed my month's rest at Choques and returned to Annequin to resume my wireless duties. No. 10 Siege Battery had gone. The gun-site was now occupied by 13 Siege Howitzers, commanded by Major P. R. M. Collins. He was one of the finest, most "human" officers I have ever known. It is literally true to say his men almost worshipped him. The difference in morale between this battery and its predecessor was most noticeable. But, though happier, Annequin was still no place for a rest cure. Nos. 10 and 13 Batteries had the first 8-inch howitzers in France. The Germans hated them. And the fact that 13 Siege had a reputation for accurate shooting only made things worse. At the first salvo, a couple of Hun planes would come scooting over the area, trying to locate the battery by its gun-flashes. In a matter of seconds, several enemy batteries would open up with shrapnel in retaliation.

It was all highly unpleasant, though, for the first three months, the worst damage the opposition achieved was the occasional loosening of my aerial masts. When that happened, I had to hop out of the comparative safety of the dugout and, with the aid of a couple of gunners, re-erect the masts under a heavy shower of shrapnel. Since we had no steel helmets, the job had its moments.

The luck we had enjoyed was too good to last. One evening in May, 1916, the Hun spotter got our range, and the enemy plastered the gun-site with considerable skill and energy. Sitting by my receiver, listening to the whine, scream and rumble as shells of all calibres came over, I thanked Saint Marconi that my job kept me well under cover. Through the dugout entrance I could see, about 10 yards away, the crew clustered round No. 1 howitzer, reloading. Suddenly the air seemed to be ripped across by sound. The gun crew opened outwards like the fingers of a quickly spread hand and a rain of shrapnel tore into the ground. A really big fellow had burst directly overhead.

Two of the gunners came reeling towards the dugout. The striker and two other men lay sprawled in grotesque attitudes beside their gun. They were obviously badly wounded, I pulled off my headphones and dashed out to get them in. The striker was nearest to me. Like most gunners, he was a big man. Luckily, early Boy Scout training in Carmarthen had taught me the trick of the "fireman's lift." I grabbed his right arm, wriggled under his body and hefted him on to my shoulders. As I jerked him into position he yelled in agony. The arm I had seized had been almost cut away by shrapnel.

I half-dragged, half-carried him to the dugout and dumped him at the entrance. His two unwounded mates had recovered sufficiently to pull him inside. I went back and got another of the injured men. The third was brought in by men from No. 2 gun.

No. 1 howitzer being immobilised until crew replacements could be brought up, I now had little to do. I remained on the gun-site for a few days. Then the wireless tender arrived to take me back to Choques.

One of the first men I met on arrival at 10 Squadron H.Q. was Captain Mitchell. Holding out his hand, and looking at me quizzically, he said: "Congratulations, Taffy. I hear you've put up a pretty good show." I shook hands with him, but I honestly did not know what the devil he was driving at.

The following day, I was posted in orders to C Flight for training as an observer.

3

WHILE I WAS DELIGHTED by this opportunity I could have wished that I had been posted for training to some unit other than the one selected for me. The commander of C Flight, Captain Gordon Bell, was one of the most erratic characters in the R.F.C. Tall and spare in body, he had a florid face reminiscent of a pug-dog's mask. A rimless monocle seldom left his pale blue eye. Careless in dress, he always carried a cavalry cane, with which he swished his leg as he ambled about the aerodrome. To complete his oddness, he stammered badly.

He was a brilliant stunt pilot. The things he could do with a B.E. made the average flyer's hair stand on end. He originated the "tail slide," an evolution which consisted of flying into a strong wind, making a short dive, then pulling the aircraft up steeply and pulling the throttle back. The strength of the wind caused the machine to slip backwards and downwards at a terrifying angle and speed. It was a most unnerving sensation. I never knew another pilot who could do the stunt.

One of Bell's exploits became an R.F.C. legend. It happened at Netheravon in 1915. Bell was throwing his B.E. around, close to the ground, in his usual carefree fashion when something went wrong and he crashed.

Ordered to explain the pile-up, he put in the following report to his C.O.:

"Sir,—While flying in B.E. 2C No. X, I got into the backwash of a sparrow. The machine went out of control, and I crashed."

Since nobody could take him very seriously, he got away with it. On another occasion, a staff officer galloped up and found Bell's aircraft upside down in a tree. He asked, fatuously: "Have you crashed?"

Struggling to get out of the cockpit, his eyeglass still firmly in position, Bell replied: "N-n-no, you d-d-damn f-fool. I always l-l-land like this!"

My first meeting with this fabulous character almost ended

my career in his flight. I marched into his office, saluted smartly, and announced: "Air Mechanic Jones reporting, sir."

"Oh, y-yes," he said. "Y-y-you are c-coming to be t-t-trained as an o-observer."

Having re-developed a childhood stammer under the strain of working with the howitzer batteries, I replied: "Y-y-yes, sir." Bell shot out of his chair, took the monocle out of his eye, grabbed his cane threateningly, and in an awful voice said: "Y-y-you are not b-b-bloody w-well m-m-mimicking me, are you, J-Jones?" Now the more a stammerer hears another man stutter, the worse his own affliction becomes. Completely unnerved by this time, I could only gasp out: "N-n-no, sir."

Bell glared at me suspiciously for what seemed a couple of minutes. Then he said: "Y-y-you can g-go, now. I'll s-s-see you again."

The flight sergeant must have convinced him that my stammer was as genuine as his own, for he never referred to the matter again and went out of his way to be kind to me. My first few days with C Flight were spent on the machine gun range, studying the mechanism and peculiarities of the Lewis gun. Rectifying stoppages interested me, and I was flattered when the range sergeant said: "Taffy, you are much quicker than most of the officers."

I have been keen on shooting since I was a boy of fourteen. On the 4th Welch miniature range at Carmarthen Barracks I had proved myself well above the average with a ·22 rifle. This early training came in useful when I began my acquaintance with the Lewis gun. I concentrated on range practice so much more than the officer-observers that the sergeant nicknamed me "Taffy the Tiger." Coming off the range, one morning, I was told to report to the Squadron Commander's office, which was located in the saddlery room of the chateau's stables. I obeyed with some trepidation, but not without hope either. The Old Man had never shown any desire to see me before. Walking across the cobbled courtyard to the stables, I speculated upon the reason for this sudden call. Perhaps I was going to be made an observer or, better still, a pilot. Maybe I was even going to be recommended for a commission.

None of these guesses was correct. I had been sent for to be congratulated on being the first mechanic in the Squadron to be awarded a decoration. I had been given the Military Medal for carrying in the two wounded gunners.

The news certainly staggered me. I had thought only brave

men got medals. I had only done my obvious duty. Nevertheless, as I marched out of the office my undeveloped chest expanded proudly with every pace I took. According to the C.O., I was a blooming hero! A few weeks later, I was sent for again—this time to be told that his Imperial Highness, the Tsar of Russia had been pleased to award me the Medal of St. George, the Russian equivalent of the V.C. This was a greater surprise than the first.

Of all my decorations I always treasure these two the most, simply because they came so unexpectedly. Knowing only too well how unfairly many awards are made, I cannot think much of my later "gongs," even though they were of a higher distinction. Since men in war are expected to do their duty, there is no justification for decorations. Men who fail to do their duty should be punished. It's as simple as that.

From the moment I was posted to C Flight I tried to get in as much flying as possible, in order to qualify for my observer's wing. I was sick almost every time I got into the air, but my soap-bag concealed the evidence. Luckily, I never got sick while my plane was involved in a fight. If he's going to be any use to his pilot an observer-gunner has to be on top line, with body and mind at the peak of alertness. An airman lives by his wits in wartime. There are certain chances a flyer must take. His pilot may become a casualty or the controls may be shot away or the wings may crumple; worse still, the petrol may be set on fire. Any of these things may spell death. I was prepared to accept them. But the thought that my sickness at a critical moment might jeopardise my pilot's life as well as my own was a constant mental worry. I was between the devil and the deep blue sky. Had I admitted to anybody that I suffered from air sickness, my flying career would have come to an abrupt end. On the other hand, there was the question of playing the game with my pilot. Would I let him down badly if I were taken ill during a fight?

My eagerness to fly overruled my misgivings. I told myself speciously: "If we do get shot down, I'll die, too." Leaning on that flimsy argument, I continued as a gunner. Luckily, the Providence that looks after chumps looked after me.

When Gordon Bell could not use me as an observer, I was frequently instructed to report to other flights. Usually I went to B Flight, commanded by Captain O'Hara Wood, a gaunt, hawk-faced Australian who was in peacetime a celebrated tennis player. It was as his gunner that I experienced my first air fight.

37

Tiger Squadron

It happened on the afternoon of the day I heard I had won the Military Medal. We were on reconnaissance over Lille. Suddenly I spotted a Fokker diving on our tail. I rapped on the cockpit edge to attract O'Hara Wood's attention, and pointed. Then, as the Hun came in close, I gave him a couple of bursts. O'Hara Wood slewed the plane half round to starboard to give Jerry a difficult deflection shot. I fired again as he flashed underneath us. O'Hara Wood slipped to port, keeping the Fokker in view. I could see it doing an Immelmann turn (nowadays called a half-roll), intended to bring the machine back underneath us and give the pilot a quick burst at our unprotected belly. The German ace, Immelmann, was the first pilot ever to carry out this useful tactical manœuvre. In this case, it didn't come off. O'Hara Wood was too skilful a pilot to be caught napping. His swift evolutions completely baffled the Hun, while enabling me to keep the Fokker in view.

Now, there were four socket mountings on the B.E., intended to cover a wide field of fire. To get a shot at the enemy when his pilot was outmanœuvred, the observer had to keep changing the Lewis gun from one socket to another. If a plane got under your belly, none of the sockets was any good. You just couldn't get at him. Seeing this blighter, and being unable to do anything about it, was more than I could stand. I yanked the gun out of the rear socket, leaned over the right side of the cockpit and, holding the Lewis like a rifle, let go with a burst.

I had reckoned, however, without the recoil of the gun and the effect of the slipstream on an insecurely held weapon. Before I had let off twenty rounds, the gun slipped out of my gloved hands. I shall never forget the look of horrified surprise on O'Hara Wood's face when he saw our only gun sailing down past the Fokker. My own feelings were beyond description. To say I felt naked is understating the fact.

The Hun must have seen the gun whizz past him. I shall never know whether he was one of the rare enemy sportsmen or merely stunned by surprise. To our astonishment, he broke off the action. We never saw him again. All the way home, as my pilot slithered the aircraft from side to side to prevent a surprise attack, my thoughts were of the direst. Instead of the coveted observer's wing, I was much more likely to get a court-martial. To my relief, when O'Hara Wood got out of the plane he took one look at my woebegone face and burst out laughing. He did not allow the incident to affect our relationship, and continued to choose me as his gunner, even when officer observers were available. Nor were there any official repercussions. But it was a long time before the Squadron let me forget the day I invented a new form of battle tactics.

I qualified for my observer's wing in October, 1916. I wore it proudly, for it signified, at this time, that the owner had flown over the enemy lines. It was not a symbol of bravery. Like the pilot's brevet, it was sported by a few proved cowards. But, speaking generally, the wearer deservedly enjoyed a good reputation and rarely betrayed the confidence reposed in him.

Observers were usually officers seconded from the infantry and artillery. They were first attached to a squadron for a trial period. Then, if they liked the work and were suitable physically, they were accepted after passing a very elementary practical examination in Lewis gunnery, photography, wireless and artillery observation. It was a common jibe among infantry and artillery officers that a C.O. never allowed any but "duds" to transfer to the R.F.C. My experience in 10 Squadron and others assured me that the insinuation had a rich flavour of jealousy. Ninety-nine out of every 100 observers were real men, without a yellow streak, who could be relied upon to do their duty without flinching in the face of the enemy.

Showing a bold face to the Hun was only one test. To volunteer to fly with indifferent pilots was often a greater proof of courage. It is only those who have flown over the enemy's lines with "dud" pilots who will recognise the truth of this assertion.

Since the B.E. had no dual control, the observer's life was always in his pilot's hands. If the pilot were unskilled or pusillanimous in combat, the unlucky observer was helpless. If the pilot were killed, the observer could rarely do anything to avert his own death. He had to sit waiting as his machine hurtled earthwards to destruction. Looking behind him, he could see the dead pilot leaning forward on the control column, causing the plane to dive vertically. And with no parachute, he could do nothing but await his end.

On one tragic day in the life of 10 Squadron, Lieutenants Whitely and Foster collided over the aerodrome. Whitely and the two observers were killed instantly. Foster got away with only a sprained ankle. Such is the freakish luck of the air.

Observers always sat up and took notice when a new pilot joined the flight. One of them eventually would have to go up with him. The new boy's first flight, always a solo effort, was watched intently by officers and other ranks. If his landings were good, he had passed the first test. If they were not, the observers would retire to the mess to drink, without much confidence, their own continued health. Even if the landings were good, there was a greater test in store for the pilot, and this time it had to be shared with an observer. It was the acid test of doing one's duty in the face of and in spite of the enemy. Since it was difficult to judge by appearances how a newcomer would shape under fire, his first few flights over the German lines were anxious trips for his observer.

Appearances are often deceptive. I have noticed that big men rarely prove as brave as their build and manner would suggest, while smaller men seldom show cowardice. Most of the great air fighters in the two wars have been men of small or medium height. Typical in World War I were Ball, McCudden, Beauchamp-Proctor, Willy Coppens, Richthofen, Boelcke, Udet and Fonck. Similarly, I have noticed that no professional footballers or boxers became famous pilots or air fighters, while there was a wealth of Rugby Union footballers among the aces.

However, the big men seem to get on well in Staff jobs, and I suppose you can't have it both ways.

Undoubtedly, the ideal Air Force officer is the man who is both a good administrator and pilot. Names which spring to mind are John and Geoffrey Salmond, Tedder, Newall, Longcroft, Ludlow Hewitt, Longmore, Slessor, Jack Scott, D. S. Evill, Van Ryneveld, Brancker, Portal, Sholto Douglas, and the great little Samson, who at the age of forty-five, led a flight of Fairey IIIF from Cairo to Cape Town and back, setting an example to future senior officers which will be difficult to follow.

The aeroplane we flew in 1916, the B.E. 2E, was an improvement on the B.E. 2C, a product of the Royal Aircraft Establishment, South Farnborough. An exceptionally stable aircraft, it could fly in calm weather on a straight course without control by the pilot. In 1914, Sir Sefton Brancker, then a major, flew in a B.E. from Farnborough to Upavon without touching the controls, except on taking off and landing. The B.E. had been designed before the war for reconnaissance. At the outbreak of hostilities it was the best of its kind among the belligerents. It was a two-seater, with the pilot's cockpit in the rear. The designers never lauded its performance as a fighter; consequently, attacks made upon it in Parliament in 1916 and 1917 were totally unjustified.

The tragedy of the B.E. in France, especially during the spring of 1917, was not the fault of its designers. The whole British aircraft industry, and the Government departments behind it, failed to meet the demands of the High Command for an improved aeroplane in sufficient numbers to overwhelm and defeat the enemy's air forces. Before the war, Britain had refused to buy any of the products of the brilliant Dutch aircraft designer, Anthony Fokker. He threw in his lot with Germany, and in July, 1915, a new type of machine appeared on the Western Front. It was the Fokker E.I, "E" standing for *eindecker* or monoplane.

Powered by an 80-h.p. Oberursel engine, the Fokker E.I was the first fighter to be equipped with a machine gun firing through the propeller by means of a deflector plate device. In September, 1915, it was fitted with a synchronised gear which enabled bullets to pass through the propeller without hitting the blades. The rotation of the engine and the action of the gun were so attuned by the use of cam gears that the gun fired only when there was no blade in the path of the bullet. Since the propeller blades often rotated at more than 2,000 revolutions per minute, it was a remarkable invention.

Improved types of Fokker followed rapidly—E.II, E.III and E.IV, driven by a 160-h.p. Oberursel engine more powerful than any of ours. British squadrons were hopelessly outclassed. Debris of B.E. aircraft was scattered widespread behind the German lines. Unexampled bravery alone cannot achieve the initiative, which is the deciding factor in air warfare. Superior aircraft performance is also a vital necessity. The Fokker had that superiority over the B.E. With its synchronised gun gear, it was a fast, good-climbing, strong-structured, highly manœuvrable aeroplane—all essential qualities of an efficient fighting machine. When flown by such masterly, determined pilots as Boelcke and Immelmann, it was almost invincible.

By September, 1915, the Fokker had become such a menace that Colonel Brancker decided our reconnaissance aircraft must be accompanied by an escort machine from 11 Squadron (Vickers Fighters). Our losses increased to such an extent by the middle of January, 1916, that orders were issued for three fighters to escort all reconnaissance planes. Shortly afterwards the size of the escort was increased to six, and all units were ordered to practise formation flying. Thus, the effect of the arrival of the first genuine fighting aircraft was to lay the foundation of formation flying and to impose the use of protective escorts.

The tactics of the Fokker pilot were simple and deadly. He dived beneath his opponent, zooming up and firing as he did so. To avoid retaliatory fire, he did a very sharp turn, still keeping his plane beneath the enemy. Then he would climb away some distance and repeat the attack. In armament we were a long way behind the Germans. We had no synchronised gear (the Constantinesco) until the spring of 1917, though the Scarff-Dibowsky interrupter gear was fitted in the Sopwith 1½-strutters in May, 1916.

The machine gun arrangements in the British observer's cockpit were comical. Since we could not fire through the propeller, we had to resort to crude devices. We had four fixed mountings: one between the two cockpits, so that the gun could protect the machine from attack from the rear; one on either side of the observer's cockpit and another in the centre, so that the areas in front and to the sides of the aircraft were covered. To enable the gun to be fired upwards and forwards, a wire was stretched across the centre-section wing struts in such a way that the gun could not possibly be pointed low enough for the bullets to hit the propeller blades. During a fight the observer had to help the pilot by changing the position of the gun from mounting to mounting, so as to open fire on the enemy when he had out-manoeuvred our machine. It was a most exhausting performance.

Squadrons 11, 20 and 24 were chiefly responsible for ending the Fokker's mastery of the air. No. 20 Squadron, equipped with F.E. 2B (the last "pusher" two-seaters in France), arrived at the end of February, 1916. Employed on escort work, this was the first squadron to take formation flying seriously. It proved that co-operation and flying discipline could do much to counteract an enemy's superiority.

No. 24 Squadron also arrived in February, equipped with a new type of single-seater "pusher" fighter which was to prove a great success. This was the 86-m.p.h. D.H. 2, with a Vickers hand-operated machine gun fitted in front of the pilot's cockpit. No. 11 Squadron was re-equipped with the 110 h.p. Nieuport Scout, a very manoeuvrable French fighter with a speed of more than 100 m.p.h. and a Lewis mounted on the centre section of the top wing. It was with this aircraft that the great Captain Albert Ball began his illustrious career.

A boy of nineteen, born in Nottingham and deeply religious, Albert Ball truly regarded the war as a crusade against the powers of evil. He led the R.F.C. in its challenge to the mighty Fokker. Fighting like a tiger, setting a brilliant example to his comrades, he would tackle any number of Huns. He proved that determination and the will to conquer were the key to successful air fighting, and was the first British pilot to make a real business of shooting down Huns.

Builders of the Tradition

When the bloody battle of the Somme opened on July 1, 1916, the three fighter squadrons were strengthened by 22 Squadron (F.E. 2B), 27 Squadron (Martinsydes), 60 Squadron (Morane Scouts and biplanes) and 70 Squadron (Sopwith 1½-strutters).

The air war divided itself into three distinct phases, roughly coincident in time with the military phases. Up to the middle of July, the R.F.C. had the edge on the enemy. Although the German command knew the Somme offensive was impending, they made little or no effort to concentrate aircraft in the zone. They believed they could best relieve their armies on the Somme by continuing offensive operations at Verdun.

Before the first phase of the battle ended, powerful enemy air units had been allocated to the newly threatened area. The German First Army, which had been temporarily broken up, was resuscitated under the command of General Fritz von Buelow on July 19, with responsibility for the front from Peronne to Hannescamps. It took over from the right wing of the Second Army, which it had relieved. Its air units, totalling seventy-four aeroplanes, received a heavy reinforcement of sixty-six aircraft. Nor was this all. The new fighter squadrons of the First Army had been formed by concentrating single-seaters specially withdrawn from reconnaissance and artillery units. The nominal strength of these fighter squadrons was twelve aeroplanes each. When the second phase of the operations opened, therefore, the enemy air service was in a much stronger position to dispute our supremacy.

Throughout this phase, reinforcements continued to arrive. All the same, our superiority was not seriously challenged. The R.F.C. offensive and bombing formations had to fight harder, but they kept the upper hand, while the artillery and contact patrol aircraft continued about their daily work without being unduly worried by enemy fighters.

There were three main reasons for this state of affairs. The first was the determined offensive policy of the R.F.C., the deliberate object of which was to fight the air war far inside the enemy lines. The second was the continued reliance of the Germans on the "air barrage" or defensive policy, which relegated great numbers of their aircraft, unsuited for offensive fighting, but eminently suitable for offensive bombing, to useless patrols behind their own lines. The third was the superiority of British fighting aircraft, especially the De Havilland, F.E., Martinsyde and Sopwith 1½-strutters, over the now outclassed Fokker.

With the beginning of the third phase of the Somme battle,

in mid-September, the air war suddenly intensified. For this there were two important reasons. The first was a change in the German High Command and a drastic revision of policy. The second was the formation of new pursuit squadrons (*Jagdstaffeln*), equipped with fighting aircraft fitted with twin machine guns firing through the propeller and, from every other point of view, more efficient than any contemporary Allied machine.

The change in the German High Command took place on August 29, when Field-Marshal von Hindenburg succeeded General von Falkenhayn as Chief of the General Staff. Hindenburg, with General von Ludendorff as his Quartermaster-General, immediately stopped the offensive at Verdun and began massing reinforcements on the Somme. The German air units at Verdun and along the remainder of the Western Front were thinned relentlessly. The air concentration on the Somme reached its climax in mid-October, when more than a third of the whole German air service was flying in opposition to the French and British on the Somme front. Coincident with the change in the High Command came the new air fighters, Halberstadt and Albatross, armed with two fixed guns firing through the propeller and with a speed of a little more than 100 m.p.h.

The initiative for the formation of special pursuit squadrons rested with Lieut.-Colonel Thomsen, the German air commander. Every effort was made to get the best out of the new units. Pilots, hand-picked from among those who had already distinguished themselves with squadrons in the field, were given an intensive course at single-seater fighter schools in Germany, and at Valenciennes, and further training when they reached the *Jagdstaffeln* at the front.

Identified with the *Jagdstaffeln* was the personality of Oswald Boelcke. After brilliant work at Verdun, this officer had gone on a tour of the Eastern theatres of war, empowered to select personnel for the *Jagdstaffel* he was soon to command. Among the men he chose on the Russian front was Manfred Freiheer von Richthofen.

Boelcke's unit, *Jagdstaffel* 2, was formed at Lagnicourt on August 30, 1916, but the aircraft for the unit did not arrive until seventeen days later. On September 17, Boelcke led five of his pilots on their first patrol. They flew into a bombing formation of B.E. 2C of 12 Squadron, escorted by F.E. 2B of 11 Squadron. Without loss to themselves, they shot down two of the bombers and four escorts. Richthofen was one of the pilots who claimed his first British victim.

In spite of these formidable reinforcements, the enemy policy remained for the most part defensive. The R.F.C. was still able to fulfil the wide demands for co-operation which came from the ground forces, while Hun airmen made only sporadic appearances over the British lines. Our casualties, though heavy, were not disproportionate to the great amount of work carried out. Our fighting over the Somme taught us that an offensive policy is necessary at all times, that the defensive power of formation flying can do much to neutralise the effect of superior equipment, and that the maintenance of high morale is essential (I know of only one case of an airman being accused of self-inflicted wounds, and he was acquitted). Our enemy, Boelcke, by raising the general morale of his pilots, illustrated the supreme importance of personality and leadership.

The great Immelmann was shot down on June 18, 1916, by Corporal Waller, of 25 Squadron, acting as air-gunner to Lieutenant McCubbin in an F.E. 2B. There is a legend that Immelmann and McCubbin were at school together in Johannesburg, South Africa. If that were so, Fate is indeed cruel. Boelcke was killed when his plane collided with that of a brother pilot during a formation combat on October 28, 1916. His loss was the greatest the German air service suffered during the war. He was killed at a crucial point in the air war, when his pilots were gradually regaining their morale under his leadership. The R.F.C. showed its admiration for a gallant enemy when a wreath was flown and dropped over the German lines to be placed on his grave.

Immelmann and Boelcke were good sportsmen who fought with clean weapons. Often they showed real chivalry to defeated enemies who had been taken prisoner, even visiting them after capture, and, when permitted, taking them to the German mess for a final dinner before the ordeal of the prison camp.

4

THE MORE I FLEW as an observer, the more I liked flying. The yearning to handle the controls of my own aircraft was at times overpowering. O'Hara Wood apparently had a high opinion of my machine-gunning capabilities and general keenness. After we had concluded an interesting fight with a Roland two-seater, which we forced to run away with its tail under its fuselage, he suddenly asked me: "Wouldn't you like to be a pilot, Jones?"

"O-of c-course I w-would, sir," I replied eagerly.

"Well, I'll see what I can do for you," he said. "You're keen, and a good shot. You've got good eyesight and no nerves, as far as I can see. You're just the type to do well."

I could have danced for joy on the aerodrome cinders. It was the first hint I had been given that I might be recommended for training as a pilot—the apex of all my ambitions and dreams.

Many months rolled by before my dream became reality. In the meantime, my war consisted of a series of brief attachments as wireless operator to batteries hidden in orchards between La Bassée Canal and Vermelles. At intervals, returning to the Squadron for the official rest cure, I renewed the thrill of flying and fighting.

The war had been so varied and interesting that the whole of 1916 had passed before I noticed that I had had no leave since landing in France. This was the first year in my life during which I had not spent a single day in my beloved Wales. The realisation gave me a shock. I felt a sudden *hiraeth*. Air mechanics were not so lucky as officers in the all-important matter of leave. The latter got a furlough every three months or so. As a principle, this was correct for pilots and observers. The strain on their nerves was tremendous.

The feeling of isolation, the tension of concentrating on the control of an aircraft, are fatiguing enough in normal circumstances. When a pilot is flying over a battle zone, where death may lurk behind any cloud or in the cottonwool burst of an "Archie" shell, the strain is intensified beyond measure. Most men are not afraid of dying. Very few can remain unconcerned while awaiting that inevitable tap on the shoulder. The best the ordinary chap can do is to steel himself and hope to accept his call bravely.

It was the constant effort of outfacing death—the fear of being afraid—that shattered the nerves of many operational flyers. Hence, frequent leave was more than justified; it was essential. What I could not understand was why officers in "cushy" administrative jobs got leave more often than some air mechanics who were carrying out more arduous and dangerous duties. How many officers spent a year in France without leave?

My turn for Blighty came in the middle of January, 1917. I shall never forget the journey from Bethune to Calais. The weather was bitterly cold. The train was slower than any donkey-cart. Only the officers rode in coaches. Other ranks travelled in cattle-trucks, through which draughts like Polar ice-blasts blew continually. Long before dawn we were frozen to the marrow. The train stopped as soon as there was light enough to see, and the troops then climbed painfully from the wagons. In an effort to get circulation going, they stamped and rushed up and down and were thankful for the mugs of hot tea, with a strong flavour of grease, that were handed out and helped everybody to regain their spirits again. Though he loves to grouse, the British "Tommy" does not believe in being out of humour too long, especially on a homeward-bound leave train.

Flying in the winter months was a most trying business. At high altitudes the oil in the machine guns froze and they refused to work. There was always the risk of frostbite for pilot and observer. I used to cover my face with vaseline and try to muffle my face and hands so well that no part was exposed. Yet once, despite these precautions, I got a nasty spot of frostbite on my nose. As the war rolled on, anti-freeze oil was introduced to take care of the machine gun trouble, while improved flying helmets and goggles increased the airman's comfort and efficiency.

On returning from leave I was attached for wireless duties to First Wing Headquarters, commanded by Colonel Tom Carthew, D.S.O. Towards the end of March, 1917, we moved to Bruay, a mining village in the Lens district, where Major Charles Portal's 16 Squadron were preparing for the Battle of Arras. The air fighting during that battle, which began on April 9, went very badly for us. It is safe to say it was the darkest period in the history of the Royal Flying Corps in France. The German pilots, in their Halberstadts and Albatrosses, were gaining in morale and fighting efficiency. During the week preceding the battle we lost ninety-one aircraft, mostly B.Es., through enemy action.

In an attempt to replace these heavy casualties, half-trained pilots, some with less than ten hours' flying time, were sent out from Britain. It only made matters worse. In the first five days of the Arras offensive we lost seventy-five aircraft in air fighting, and another fifty-six in crashes on our own aerodromes. The Richthofen crews had a glorious time, and one of them, Werner Voss, who was a Jew, shot down twelve machines in this brief period. Among the enemy pilots I met after the war was the famous ace, Ernst Udet. He told me he considered Werner Voss the greatest fighter pilot the Germans ever had. I do not know whether he had ever dared to express that opinion to Hitler. Goering, of course, needed no telling. As a brother member of Richthofen's "circus," he knew Voss well.

Goering had no sense of humour. Sir Sefton Brancker, when I was his personal pilot, introduced me to the Reichmarshal in Berlin. We murmured the usual platitudes. Then Sir Sefton said: "I wonder if you two ever met in an air fight, Taffy."

"He wouldn't be here now, sir, if we had met," I retorted.

Brancker laughed loudly, but Goering did not. He was cold to me for the rest of the evening. Funnily enough, when, during the Schneider Trophy race at Calshot in 1929, Air Commodore Sidney Smith introduced me to another German ex-pilot, he asked me a similar question. I gave a similar answer—and that pilot also sulked. No humour.

At a Handley-Page dinner between the wars, I got tired of listening to the Nazi Air Attaché laying down the law to the Italian, French and Belgian Air Attachés. Interrupting his diatribe, I said: "We knocked hell out of your air force in 1918, and you can tell Hitler we'll knock hell out of the Luftwaffe if he starts a war."

The Hun strutted away in a hell of a huff. After the Battle of Britain, the French Air Attaché sought me out at Heston to shake my hand. "You were right, sir," he said earnestly. "The Royal Air Force has saved us. You cannot believe how happy I am. We will now win the war." We adjourned to the mess, arm in arm.

The Germans claimed that during the Battle of Arras they shot down four of our aircraft for every one they lost. Certainly the squadrons of the First Wing were being literally murdered by the new German fighters. Richthofen's Red Halberstadts

[*Air Ministry photographs*

THE EARLY BIRDS

From Top Left: De Havilland 2; F.E. 8 Fighting Scout.
F.E. 2d "pusher" Biplane; Nieuport 12 Scout.
Sopwith F.I. Camel; The Sopwith "Pup."

Top: No. 74 Squadron, April, 1918. Lewis; Roxburgh-Smith; Hamer; Stuart-Smith; Dolan; Clements; Bright; Skeddon; Coverdale; The Author; Cairns; Young; Caldwell; Everard; Mannock; Howe; Piggott; Atkinson; Giles.

Bottom: King George V congratulates "Taffy" Jones in France, August, 1918.

inflicted severe casualties on 16 Squadron. No. 10 and the others fared no better.

The wreckage of B.Es. was scattered everywhere behind and in front of the enemy lines. It was a pitiable sight. Nothing angers me more to-day than to see how the brave men who weathered that dreadful storm have been passed on the ladder of promotion. In other branches of the Services valour in the field usually leads to advancement. It has not always been so in the R.A.F.

We commenced the battle with offensive patrols operating twenty-eight miles behind the German lines. Within two days we had to reduce the distance to eight miles because casualties were so heavy. The question arose whether any useful purpose could be served by sending fighters alone for such great distances behind the lines. Had we any reason to suppose the enemy would be found there, actually behind his own aerodromes? Would he fight, if found? If not, our pilots could not bring him to action. They must rely entirely on finding him where he was in some way fixed by his operational requirements.

So, during the Arras offensive, and certainly during its early stages, our fighters were able neither to protect our own nor to interfere with the enemy's co-operation aircraft. If the Richthofen Circus did not take off, our pilots got no action.

The few flights I had were with a young and rather inexperienced Canadian pilot, Lieutenant Crow. About twenty-two years of age, he was of average height and build, with the rather pale, oval face that often denotes the killer. Always quiet and soft-spoken, he was a lovely fellow to fly with. He did not give a damn for Richthofen or his Circus, though you would think that butter would not melt in his mouth. As we were getting ready for our first flight together, he said: "Jones, any Hun you see, knock hell out of him."

The flight was not a tremendous success. We got to the German lines all right, but only to be greeted immediately with the chatter of machine guns. I looked over the side of the plane. There, beneath us, three red machines were having a wonderful time. Holes were appearing all over our aircraft, though none appeared to be hitting a vital spot. I could do nothing with my Lewis gun. The Huns were underneath us, and I could not fire downwards with any degree of accuracy.

Crow tried to take avoiding action. He was not a very good pilot. Bullets continued to turn our aircraft into a collander. No matter how Crow flung the machine about, he could not dodge that deadly stream of lead. Eventually he lost so much height that the Red devils were at one moment on our level, and the next above us. And all the time they kept up their accurate shooting. They were having a lovely time. It was a grand war for them. What a game! I realised that if my pilot did not do something sensational in the flying line, we were going to crash. I prepared for the worst—and it came.

There was a terrific jolt, and a crash that sounded like the end of the world. There was a confused sensation like being drunk on a runaway merry-go-round. More crashing, rending and crackling. Then all was silent. Crow and I got out of the wreckage as best we could. We shook ourselves and stared at each other dazedly. But not for long. Machine guns coughed and chattered. Mud spattered all round us. Looking up, we saw our hostile pals zooming and diving as if they were giving an air display.

We had crashed among our reserve trenches, so we promptly chucked ourselves into the nearest one to hand. The Huns then went home rejoicing. A few days later, Crow was shot down again—but this time in flames. He died, as he had lived, a very gallant gentleman.

Though No. 16 Squadron lost many fine fellows like Crow during the Battle of Arras, they never lost their morale. They had a great commanding officer, who flew and set his air crews a high standard of duty. He lived to become the trusted and popular Chief of the Royal Air Force in World War II, and afterwards to be honoured with the title of Lord Portal of Hungerford.

During the Arras offensive, new types of British fighter were sent into action. They were the two-seater Bristol Fighter and the single-seater S.E. 5 and Sopwith Camel. All had speeds of more than 120 m.p.h., and carried two machine guns. They were to regain air supremacy for the Royal Air Force, and before the end of the war to subjugate the German fighters completely.

The Hun was now to prove that when the odds were even, he lacked the offensive spirit and will to conquer of the British pilot. Even when he had numerical superiority, he would fight only over his own lines. Because of this lamentable trait in his character, he lost the initiative. In World War II, his successors showed the same pusillanimity. The Hun just cannot take a hiding and come back for more. He lacks the essential guts. On the morning of May 18, 1917, I was ordered to report to Colonel Carthew. "Jones, instructions have been received that you are to go to England on May 27," he said.

Builders of the Tradition

"What for, sir?" I asked anxiously.

He replied: "Commission, and learn to fly."

I cannot hope to recapture in words my feelings of that moment. The goal of my life's ambition—to fly alone and fight the Hun in the air—was in sight. That the path might still be rough and dangerous never occurred to me. I had often heard pilots say they had done only ten hours' flying before being sent on operational trips. I saw myself returning to France within a couple of months. I was to be unlucky. For one reason and another, I was in Britain for almost a year.

I left Bruay for 10 Squadron on May 22, and I remember seeing the burnt bodies of a pilot and observer, their identities then unknown, being taken out of the tender which was to take me to Choques. Looking down on the blackened, unrecognisable remains of what had so recently been two high-spirited youngsters like myself, I felt a dreadful bitterness and anger against the whole nation of conquest-hungry barbarians beyond the Rhine. I prayed fervently: "Oh, God! Please let me kill at least one German before I die."

When, more than a year later, I destroyed my first enemy in the air, I yelled with joy as the blazing plane went down. I remembered not only the charred body of the flying partner I had gone out to avenge, but the bodies of those two unknown airmen of Bruay, as I gloated over the roasting of the departing Hun. The twin spirits of prayer and revenge were always with me during my war in the air. I always prayed before and after a flight. The lust to avenge dead comrades was the secret of my success as a fighter. It was many years before I came to realise that prayer and revenge can have nothing in common.

As I left 10 Squadron on May 27 for Boulogne and Blighty, I ended almost two years' association with the personnel of as fine an A.C. squadron as ever registered a true "O.K." There were one or two "duds" among them, but most of the officers and men were of the salt of the earth. The pilots and observers in their antiquated B.Es. faced death and danger with a stoicism which has never been surpassed. The mechanics worked with cheerfulness and enthusiasm. Together, they made 10 Squadron one of the finest in a Corps famous for its spirit and bravery. As the tender began to move away from the aerodrome and my friends gave me a cheery shout and wave of farewell, I am not ashamed to say I found difficulty in keeping back the tears. My service in the ranks had been a fine experience. I count myself privileged to have had it.

Tiger Squadron

Like all wartime train travel in France, the journey from Bethune to Boulogne was slow and uncomfortable. As I was going home to learn to fly, I cared very little. The sea voyage, however, turned out to be even grimmer. It was only through the kindness of a hardy Highlander that my collapsed carcase survived to be taken ashore at Folkestone.

5

Sᴇɴᴛ ᴀѕ ᴀ ᴄᴀᴅᴇᴛ to Christ Church College, Oxford, I sat for my passing-out examination in the last week of July, 1917 and got through without difficulty. Some of the men I had met on the course were frankly envious when they heard I was to be posted within a week to a unit where I would be taught to fly. On the eve of my departure I strolled round to their rooms to sympathise with them, and to my surprise I found them all packing hurriedly. They had just been told they were to be commissioned without having to take the examination. And they were going to accompany me on the following day.

It seemed a bit unjust. While I had spent the summer evenings in my rooms, studying hard for the all-important examination, these loafers had been caressing the local flappers in punts along secluded Thames backwaters. Since that experience, I have never taken much stock in the fable of the grasshopper and the ant.

I was commissioned on August 1, and issued with a cheque for £25 with which to buy my kit. This allowance was nowhere near enough to satisfy the demands of the expensive Oxford tailors, but at least it enabled newly-commissioned officers to buy the bare necessities of their rank. That their uniforms were hastily made was damningly proved by the photographers, who were doing a roaring trade at the time. Five days later we fledglings were split into groups and posted to flying schools throughout the country. With my old friends, Van Ryneveld,[1] Saunders[2] and Thompson, I was sent to the training school at Northolt, near Uxbridge, Middlesex. There each pupil was introduced to an instructor who would be responsible for his training. I was lucky. I was allotted to Lieutenant A. G. Kiddie. This officer, a South African from Kimberley, was one of the most reliable instructors at the school, and it meant something, for during this period of the war it was commonly recognised

[1] The brother of General Sir Pierre Van Ryneveld. He was later killed in a Sopwith Camel.

[2] Now Air Marshal Sir Hugh Saunders.

that most pilots learned to fly in spite of their instructors. That reproach could never be levelled at Kiddie, a magnificent pilot who was gifted with the knack of imparting his knowledge to his pupils. Strangely enough, he taught many pilots who were to become members of the same squadron in France and, in fact, became a member of it himself. At one period he was junior to one of his old pupils—myself!

The aircraft used for elementary instruction was the Maurice Farman Shorthorn, commonly called the "Rumptie." It was a "pusher" type plane which had been used operationally in France in 1914–15, and was fitted with dual controls, instructor and pupil sitting side by side. The Rumptie was a fairly easygoing, caressing old crate, but many of the pupils found great difficulty in landing after their first solo. In the middle of the aerodrome was a large, square tarmac patch whose use I was never able to determine, but it certainly attracted the first-solo pupil like a magnet. I have seen dozens of men fly straight into it at an angle of 45 degrees for no reason that was apparent. Perhaps they wanted to boast later that they had made a tarmac landing. If so, it was a pity. Many did not survive to tell the tale.

My first solo came as a great surprise. One calm evening about halfway through August, I had been drifting about the sky with Kiddie, occasionally practising landings. When we touched down for the fourth time, my instructor climbed out of the cockpit. I thought he was getting out to examine the undercarriage, but to my astonishment he shouted: "Go on, Taffy. See what you can do by yourself. Don't forget your flying speed. Good luck!" I never realised how quickly a man's feelings could change. A few minutes earlier, I had been a happy, confident little airman, enjoying every second of the ride. Now, the blood seemed to race through my veins, my heart pounded and every nerve prickled. I knew I was up against it.

Steadying myself, I gently opened the throttle and pushed the joy-stick forward a little. Then, as the aircraft began to move, I opened the throttle wider. The engine roared its approval. As the horse-power developed, so the machine jumped along until it lifted into the air. Once off the ground, I sat gripping the controls in a daze. I knew neither where I was going nor why. Upward and upward climbed the Rumptie, following its own desire. Suddenly I realised that I was at 1,000 feet (then, to me, a great height, especially alone), so I began to pull myself together. At least I had taken off, which was more than some of my friends had been able to do.

However, I was not very happy. I knew I could not continue to fly upwards and in the same direction very much longer. I would have to turn. It took a superhuman effort to move the controls into the required position. When the evolution had been completed, I felt a very sick man. But I had achieved something. I flew for some minutes in what I thought was the direction of the aerodrome. Then I braced myself sufficiently to look down at the ground, and to my consternation the aerodrome was nowhere in sight. I was lost, it seemed. Visions of having to crash-land in some remote part of the country began to trouble me and I felt bewildered and helpless.

I could not make it out. While flying as an observer and during my training with Kiddie, I had always been able to keep in touch with the ground. The knowledge that I was in sole command of my aircraft and entirely responsible for its safety seemed to have unbalanced me completely. Cursing myself for an hysterical nincompoop, I continued to fly round in circles. Since I could not be far from Northolt, it was better to do so than to fly aimlessly. After a little while it occurred to me that perhaps the aerodrome might after all be directly beneath the aircraft. I peered anxiously over the side. It was!

I could see the big black square which had exercised its spell over so many unlucky soloists. Now it was fascinating me. Staring blankly, ominously, it seemed to be saying: "O.K., wise guy! This is the middle of the aerodrome on which you have to land. Come on down, and see if you can make it."

Having spotted the black patch, I was determined not to lose it again and gradually I widened my circle in order to get sufficiently far away to glide in and land. Once in position, I would pull back my throttle. But I was in the grip of fear, and try as I would I simply could not find the courage to pull it back. This was a terrible state of affairs.

For fully five minutes I flew around trying to pluck up the nerve to pull the throttle and eventually I worked myself into such a state that I suddenly shut my eyes and jerked it back. The abruptness of the movement caused the engine to give several loud reports. The noise so startled me that I promptly opened up again.

I broke out in a clammy sweat and my condition now bordered on panic. I knew that if I could not pull myself together, this was going to be my last flight. With a tremendous effort of will I managed to throttle back gently and to my unspeakable relief, the Rumptie began to glide in at its usual angle. Some 1,500 feet

55

beneath me was Harrow-on-the-Hill, so I put the nose of the aircraft in the direction of Northolt. Lower and lower I descended. Then, as I got closer to the field, I realised that I was under-shooting. Once more I gently opened the throttle and flew towards the aerodrome. About 20 feet up, just over the boundary hedge, I throttled back and glided in. The Rumptie, believe it or not, came to a standstill in the very centre of the black tarmac square and I had not the faintest idea how I had got there!

Kiddie was waiting for me by the hangar. He was smiling cheerily as he waved his arm. I knew that as far as he was concerned everything was all right. He praised my landing most flatteringly, and I thought it would be a pity to disillusion him. However, that evening in the mess, while standing him the large tankard of beer he so richly deserved, I casually suggested that it would perhaps be a good thing if he gave me a few more lessons in landing before I did my second solo.

He agreed, I thought, a shade too readily. Months later, in France, he told me why.

"Taffy, old boy," he said. "I knew at the time you had not the faintest idea whether you were on the ground or in China."

That is what I call a perfect instructor.

Having completed five hours' solo on the Farman Shorthorn, I was now ready for posting to a service-type aircraft. Luckily for me, Captain O'Hara Wood was then forming 74 T.D.S. at London Colney. Having heard that I was learning to fly at Northolt, he applied for me, and, accompanied by Van Ryneveld, I was transferred to the squadron at the beginning of September. I counted it a privilege to be with O'Hara Wood again. I knew he expected great things from me. I was determined not to let him down.

As the unit had just been formed, the camp consisted of one hangar, housing two Avro aircraft, and small wooden huts for the officers' mess. We were billeted in empty houses opposite a church on the far side of the adjoining aerodrome. The latter was the home of 56 T.D.S., which had three permanent houses and fifty pupils. I persuaded O'Hara Wood to ask for many of my old friends of cadet days. Soon sharing my sleeping quarters were Van Ryneveld, "Dingbat" Saunders, "Ruggles" Thompson, Billy Clarke and "Baldy" Paxton.[1]

Pupils at 74 T.D.S. could honestly claim that they had learned to fly in spite of their instructors, who came and went almost as often as their students crashed. During eight and a half hours'

[1] Later Air Vice Marshal.

flying instruction, I had no less than twelve instructors. To this circumstance, coupled with the poor quality of the teaching, I always attributed the weakness of my aerodrome flying. Many of the instructors were pilots who had been sent home because they were afraid of fighting. It was a great pity that they were not transferred to the infantry in France instead of being dealt with in this way. Frequently, they were given promotion and then given jobs in which they were worse than useless.

There were others who were totally unfitted to become instructors because they were too hasty-tempered, intimidating the trainees when they should have been encouraging them. In yet a third category came those who rushed their pupils into going solo, so that they could claim credit for having trained the highest number of pilots in a given period. I had to contend with one of these speed-merchants as soon as I started flying at London Colney.

When I had completed three hours' dual training—at the hands of seven instructors!—I was ordered to go solo in an Avro which had no revolution-indicator, compass or altitude meter. I refused. As I had never been allowed to work the engine controls, I thought it was quite wrong to ask me to go solo in an aircraft without a revolution-indicator. A compass was also a necessity, since there was always the possibility that I might get lost.

I was reported to O'Hara Wood, charged with disobeying orders—one of the worst offences in the Service. The instructor, as I had expected, had distorted the facts. It only took a few minutes to explain what had happened. O'Hara Wood, having listened to my side of the story, decided that the instructor concerned was completely unfit for his job. That evening, we had the great pleasure of drinking to his departure.

Because of the shortage of aircraft, it was not until early in October that the first of the large number of pupils went solo. The honour fell to "Dingbat" Saunders, who showed every sign of developing into a reliable pilot. He was followed by Van Ryneveld, Thompson and Clarke. As for me, though I acquitted myself all right in the air, my take-off and landings made onlookers shudder. Indeed, my tenth instructor, P. G. Scott, gave me up as hopeless. He did his best to have me posted to another school, where pupils were trained for slower, two-seater service machines.

I could never understand why men who were not up to standard at landing an aeroplane should have been sent, as a matter of policy, to learn to fly two-seaters. Surely it would have been fairer to allow the "dud" pilot to take a chance on injuring or killing himself than to make an innocent person share the same fate? Thanks to O'Hara Wood, I was allowed to carry on with single-seaters. To him must go most of the credit for any service I was later able to give my country. If I had been "flunked" at London Colney, I should never have gone to France as a fighter pilot. I was the last of the "Bœties" to go solo. My leg had been pulled to such an extent that I was determined to put up a good show.

The great day arrived on October 12. I took off in zigzag fashion and climbed steadily to 8,000 feet. Though I had never looped the loop, I had secretly discovered the essential movements of the controls. Now, shutting my eyes tightly and, holding my breath, I pushed the joystick forward until the wires screamed with fear. Then, gently pulling the stick back until it rested against my belly, I held it in that position until I heard the wires screech again. Quickly I pushed the stick right forward, held it a few seconds, and pulled it back to my belly. I was now able to open my eyes again. As the first sensation had really appealed to me, I did three more loops, enjoying each one more than its predecessor.

Though I had dropped down to 4,000 feet, an altitude usually regarded as somewhat low for stunting, I still wanted to impress my fellow pupils. So I went into yet another loop, but on this occasion the engine ceased to function during the upward part of the manœuvre, and when I got to the top of the loop, I found to my horror that I was parting company with the seat of the machine. My feet suddenly left the rudder and I gripped the joystick with both hands and yelled: "My God! I'm falling out!"

For a second, I thought the end had come. But while I was wondering frantically what to say to St. Peter, the aircraft made a sharp, violent movement. Before I knew what was happening, I was reposing tightly in the seat once more, and the nose of the crate was pointing earthwards. Somehow, I regained control of the machine, and, with my heart in my mouth, pulled it out of the dive. Then, since I was too frightened to do any further flying, I decided I had better go down and land.

On the way down I decided I would do an "S" turn, just in case my comrades had not been sufficiently impressed, with the result that I found I was undershooting and going straight for the boundary hedge. I pushed the throttle wide open, but nothing happened. Into the hedge I went, arse over elbow, and came to rest on the other side—upside down, at that! So ended my first solo in an Avro. It was my first crash, but not my last. Twenty-eight more were to follow before I said goodbye to flying.

The number of pupils at the school now totalled twenty-five, most of them Colonials. Notable among the newer arrivals were Lieutenant W. B. Giles, Lieutenant H. G. Clements, Lieutenant Dolan, Lieutenant P. F. C. Howe and Lieutenant C. L. Skeddon, who were later to distinguish themselves with 74 Squadron. Compared with 56 T.D.S. across the way, there was very little drinking, but the mess was a lively place, with sing-songs, ragging and general ribaldry a regular evening feature. The merriment became somewhat subdued in late November, when a Major Twiselton-Wykam-Feinnes took over the reins from O'Hara Wood. But it rose to a new peak a few months later, as the result of the arrival of an instructor named Captain Edward Corringham Mannock.

In the meantime, a few advanced pupils, including Saunders and Thompson, were posted to service units overseas, and the remainder of us were kept back to form 74 Squadron, which was shortly to be mobilised. We were very disgruntled, especially when the letters began arriving from Saunders and Thompson, now with the famous fighting 84 Squadron, commanded by Major Sholto Douglas.[1] They were, according to what they told us, having a great time in their S.E. 5, and certainly, their stories about the air fights made us hopping mad to get to France.

However, there were compensations for our lack of martial activity. We had some riotous evenings in London, and our favourite haunt was the Regent Palace Hotel. *The Maid of the Mountains*, with lovely Jose Collins, was playing at Daly's Theatre, and we enjoyed this musical comedy so much that we sat through it eight times. It was at the Regent Palace, at about 10.30 p.m., that I heard the air raid buzzers for the first time, and I have never seen the mood of a happy throng change so quickly. One moment, all was gaiety, the next, there was a stampede of shrieking creatures who had been transformed from apparent fairies into wild women. I followed the mob from the grill room into the foyer, where most of the hotel's customers had assembled. One "lady," pointing at me angrily, screeched: "You're in the Flying Corps. Why the hell aren't you up there, chasing those devils away?"

Van Ryneveld and I strolled across empty Piccadilly Circus

[1] Now Marshal of the Royal Air Force Lord Douglas of Kirkside.

and went down the steps to the Underground station. We wanted to check on the stories we had heard of the Tube shelterers—stories we believed to be wildly exaggerated. The reality astounded us. The platforms were crowded with people of all classes and conditions. Many were old and infirm. Some were obviously sick. There were mothers with children, and their presence was excusable. But there were also scores of able-bodied shirkers of both sexes, with cowardice indelibly written on their white and twitching faces. Many of these rats had come to stay the night. They were equipped with mattresses, rugs, thermos flasks and sandwich baskets. Some were already well tucked up in their blankets.

The scene was incredible. It made me wonder what would happen in another war, when the bombing would undoubtedly be on a much heavier scale. I had to wait a quarter of a century for my answer. In World War II, at the height of the "Blitz," I paid another visit to the Underground. Sure enough, the lily-livered fraternity—their ranks now swelled by excitable Continentals—still huddled in terror on the platforms, while the real Cockney showed his guts and endurance in the blazing city above.

At the beginning of January, 1918, a number of American airmen joined us to learn to fly. They were the first Yanks I had met. It was an enlightening experience. I had heard the usual derogatory stories, and had looked forward to their coming with some misgivings, but the twenty or thirty men who came to London Colney were fine fellows, the flower of their great nation.

They certainly knew how to shake and dispose of a fast cocktail, and they were not exactly allergic to the fair sex. But their two main objectives were to finish their flying training and get into the air fighting with the utmost possible speed.

The first contingent of Americans had crossed the Atlantic in September, 1917, and finally had been posted to the various training units in Britain. Our school was lucky enough to get such grand types as Ken Curtis (a wizard at the piano, and no mean caricaturist), Fred Stillman,[1] Alexander Roberts, Clarence Fry, H. G. Shoemaker, C. Matthiessen, W. V. Waite and A. F. Morrison. No. 56 T.D.S., across the road, had to put up with "the Three Musketeers"—Elliott Springs, Hal Hallahan and Grider.

The keenness of these warriors to go solo as soon as possible

[1] The late John Winant, American Ambassador in London during World War II, told the author of his friendship with Stillman.

resulted in many accidents. They accepted them without turning a hair or losing any of their innocent enthusiasm. Fred Stillman, a giant in stature and in heart, was a favourite in the mess. On February 7, 1918, while flying round the aerodrome in an Avro, he collided with the aircraft of a Canadian named Ellis.

I was standing outside the mess when it happened. Although the collision occurred about a mile away, I distinctly heard the crash as the planes met. Looking up, I saw the two machines gliding earthward, interlocked, from a height of 2,000 feet. A wisp of black smoke was trailing from the falling wreckage. A few seconds later, the aeroplanes were enveloped in flames. It was a ghastly sight. The floating furnace drifted towards the aerodrome, eventually coming to rest on the outskirts, not far from Radlett golf-course. I jumped into a car and stepped hard on the accelerator. When I got to the spot, Stillman was walking about, badly burned, but fully conscious. Poor old Ellis was still in the blazing aircraft. No doubt he had died before the planes touched the ground.

Stillman tried hard to make a joke of his injuries, but he was plainly much more badly injured than he thought. We got him to hospital as quickly as we could. I visited him there daily. He could not move. His body, arms and head were swathed in mummy-like bandages. Just three little holes had been left for his eyes and mouth. Yet to listen to his cheery talk, you would have thought he was in the best of health. And never was he more cheerful than on February 22, the night before he died. His great heart, no less than his wonderful strength and fitness, undoubtedly had much to do with the valiant fight he put up, though the end was inevitable. No body so badly burned could survive. May we all die as gallantly as he.

Because of the lack of proper instruction, crashes were frequent. We all became inured to them. My own first few solos usually ended in my crawling out of the wreckage of an inverted machine. Somehow or other, I never succeeded in hurting myself. On one occasion I got into a spin whilst flying a Sopwith Pup at a height of 200 feet, and only got out of it after I had hit the ground. It was then rather too late.

In order to qualify for our "wings," we had to do a cross-country flight, usually from London Colney to Northolt and Hounslow and back to the aerodrome. I had an incurable passion for landing across wind in my Sopwith Pup. The undercarriage of the sturdy little machine did not care for such treatment, I usually ended upside-down. I only completed my cross-country flight with the aid of Van Ryneveld, who led me round the course. At each aerodrome, he landed first, to show me the way to come in. I was very grateful when the ordeal was over.

With the exception of Captain Meredith Thomas,[1] the instructors stood aloof from the pupils. Maybe the fact that they called us "the Huns" had something to do with their attitude. In any case the officers' mess was divided by an invisible and insurmountable barrier. The instructors enjoyed many privileges which were denied to the pupils, and it wasn't surprising that the favoured treatment fostered discord. The pupils learned to hate their instructors, instead of looking on them as philosophers and guides. Captain Thomas was the one officer to whom we all went for advice, in the knowledge that it would be sympathetically given and full of wisdom.

On February 1, a new instructor arrived. He was a tall, lean man whose reddish, weather-beaten face was topped by dark brown hair. His eyes were blue and keen, and he had a ready smile. On the lapels of his dirty tunic he wore the badge of the Royal Engineers. His left breast was decorated with the well-worn ribbon and silver rosette of the Military Cross and bar. We shook hands, and it was then that I came under the spell of Captain Edward Mannock, the greatest patrol leader of any fighter force in World War I.

He had been back in England for only a month, having been sent home for a rest after destroying twenty-one enemy aircraft while flying a Nieuport Scout with 40 Squadron. Thirty years of age, as wild, irresponsible and impetuous as any of his compatriots in his native County Cork, Mannock yet had a dominating personality which influenced all those around him. Whatever he said or did compelled attention. Almost his first words to me were: "Taffy, I am home for a rest, and I am not going to allow any damned disciplinary rot to interfere with it."

We realised that here, at last, was an instructor after our own hearts. From that time on, our outlook on the life of flying and fighting completely changed. Mannock convinced us that with a little practice we could knock hell out of the best Hun. He was not a success as an instructor. He admitted that it was as much as he could do to fly himself. He was almost as bad as I at landing, and many were the occasions on which I had the pleasure of hauling him out from his wreckage.

Major Alan Dore,[2] late of 43 Squadron, took over command on St. David's Day, March 1. Shortly afterwards, 74 T.D.S.

[1] Now Air Marshal.   [2] Now Air Commodore.

became 74 Service Squadron. The change caused great excitement in the camp. There were seven instructors and thirty-two pupils in competition for twenty places in the Squadron, and every last man of them desperately keen to go to France with it.

On March 7, the Squadron was chosen. The three flight commanders were Captain Mannock, A Flight, Captain W. E. Young, B Flight, and Captain W. J. Cairns, O Flight. Young and Cairns had previously served in 19 Squadron. Each had a few Huns to his credit.

Mannock's flight comprised Lieutenant Roxburgh-Smith, one of the instructors, Lieutenant Hamer, late of 60 Squadron, Lieutenant Dolan, who had won the M.C. as an artillery officer, Lieutenant Howe, a South African, Lieutenant Clements, a Canadian, and Lieutenant Atkinson, a Scot.

In Young's flight were Captain Glynn, Lieutenant Kiddie, who had seen service in West Africa, Lieutenant Savage, a South African, and Lieutenants Piggott, Stuart-Smith and Bright.

Cairns drew Lieutenant Giles (wounded during a battle on the Somme while with the Somerset Light Infantry, and later an observer in 43 Squadron), Lieutenant Birch, an instructor, Lieutenant Skeddon, a Canadian, and Lieutenants Begbie and Jones.

Lieutenant Harry Coverdale, famous England and Blackheath rugby half-back, was to be gunnery officer; Lieutenant C. Mansfield, equipment officer; and Lieutenant G. Lewis, recording officer.

Although the selection might have been improved on slightly, on the whole the selectors could well be proud of their judgment. It was rather hard to part from men I had got to know and admire, especially R. P. Wilson from Fernie, British Columbia, Jimmy Cohen from Sydney, Bill Clarke from Pretoria, and the sons of Uncle Sam who had proved such good friends. Like the rest of the "surplus" pupils, they were immediately posted overseas with other units.

Most of the flyers chosen for 74 Squadron were sent to Ayr in Scotland for a course in aerial fighting. The school was commanded by the Welsh V.C., Colonel L. Rees, and among the instructors were the famous Major James McCudden, V.C., Captain Gerald Maxwell, late of 56 Squadron, Captain Atkinson, late of 29 Squadron, and one-eyed Captain Foggin, who was tragically killed a few months later in an accident in France.

The course was simple. The instructor showed the pupil what to do and what not to do during an air fight. Besides practising fighting, trainees were encouraged to throw their aircraft around with abandon, in order to gain the maximum confidence in the machines. It was an excellent course. Its teachings saved my life more than once in actual combat. At the end of it, every pupil had to appear before Colonel Rees and explain not only what he had learned, but what stunting he had carried out. To the latter question, one pupil replied: "I climbed up to 15,000 feet, sir, and zoomed."

No. 74 Squadron was to be equipped with S.E. 5 single-seater scouts. While at Ayr I did all my flying in this type of machine. Pupils who were to go to France with Sopwith Camels—rotary-engined, single-seater scouts with exceptionally fast manœuvreability—had to fly in that type. The accidents were many. I remember seven funerals in one week as the result of the right-hand turn when close to the ground. Owing to the gyroscopic action of the rotary engine, the turn to the right was always much faster. Also, if the pilot were not very careful, the aircraft had a tendency to drop its nose quickly and get into a spin. Dozens of inexperienced pilots were killed by this peculiarity of the Camel. Yet in the hands of a capable flyer like the South African Captain Armstrong, it was probably the finest manœuvrable machine produced by any combatant nation in World War I.

We got back to London Colney on March 8. The command had been changed while we were away. The new C.O. was Major Keith Caldwell, M.C.,[1] a New Zealander from Waikato, near Auckland. He was a big man, with jet black hair, swarthy complexion, deep-set blue eyes and a prominent chin which was a good index to his determined character. It was not necessary to speak with him to realise that he possessed an outstanding personality. He was already famous throughout the Royal Flying Corps as a great fighter and a dashing patrol leader. I had heard much about him when he was serving in Jack Scott's crack 60 Squadron, which boasted such well-known pilots as Ball, Meintjies, Chidlow-Roberts, "Zulu" Lloyd, "Nigger" Horn, Young and Frankie Soden. Jack Scott once said that, in his opinion, "Grid" Caldwell (he got the nickname because he called all aircraft "grids") had engaged in more fights for the number of times he had been in the air than any other pilot. When one remembers Scott's vast knowledge of air fighters, that was no mean tribute.

When all his pilots had returned, Caldwell gave us a talk in the mess on what he expected of us. His manner of speaking was

[1] Now Air Commodore.

straight and to the point. He told us that he had been given command of the Squadron, that we were being equipped with the finest fighting aircraft of the time, and that we were lucky in having three experienced flight commanders, especially Mannock, whom he had known in France. He said he was sure we should be a very happy family. When we got to the war, he expected every one of us to fight like hell. It must never be said that a pilot of 74 Squadron had failed to go to the aid of a comrade, no matter how daunting the odds. Finally, no patrol of the Squadron must ever be late in taking off.

I am proud to say that the Squadron never let him down.

From now on until we had received the full complement of nineteen, S.E. 5 aircraft were delivered almost daily. Each active pilot was given a plane, while the three reserve pilots practised on training machines. As much individual practising in live and ground gunnery as possible was put in, and formation flying was also carried out. Skeddon became very proficient at stunting in formation. His half-roll at the top of a loop was considered to be quite out of the ordinary in those days. Mannock was gratified by our enthusiasm, but not particularly impressed. At the Squadron's farewell dinner, complimenting us on our pretty evolutions, he reminded us soberly: "They will be no damned use to you when you get a Hun on your tail."

He was quite right. Stunting was of no earthly use to a pilot during combat. If he wanted to give the enemy the advantage, all he had to do was a loop, roll or spin. However, the exercise was of great help in enabling a young flyer to gain confidence in handling his aircraft. While we were waiting for orders to proceed overseas, the C.O. detailed Mannock to give us lectures on air fighting. And what delicious dishes of the offensive spirit they were! He was a forceful, eloquent speaker, with the gift of compelling attention. After listening to him for a few minutes, the poorest, most inoffensive pilot was convinced he could knock hell out of Richthofen or any other Hun. Since Mannock's experience of air fighting was extensive, his talks were most valuable. His first lecture on single-seater fighting began and ended with the axiom to which he rigidly adhered: "Gentlemen, remember. Always above, seldom on the same level, never underneath."

The Squadron lived up to that slogan. In eight months of war, its record was 140 enemy aircraft destroyed and a further eight-five sent down apparently out of control, as against a loss of fifteen pilots killed or taken prisoner. Mannock's claim for the infallibility of his axiom was justified. During one of his talks, he told us that Fokker had produced a good triplane fighter, which was much superior in manœuvrability to the S.E. 5. The latter, however, was much faster. Furthermore, while the triplanes were not very sturdy and sometimes had broken up in the air because of excessive diving speed, the stronger S.E. 5 delighted in a steep dive.

"When we get to the war," he said, "don't ever attempt to dog-fight a triplane on anything like equal terms in altitude. He'll get on your tail and stay there until he shoots you down. Take my advice. If you ever get into such an unfortunate position, put your aircraft into a vertical bank, hold the stick tight into your belly, keep your engine full on—and pray hard.

"When the Hun has got tired of trying to shoot you down from one position, he'll try another. Here's your chance, and you'll have to snap into it with alacrity. As soon as your opponent starts to manœuvre for the next position, put on full bottom rudder, do one and half turns of a spin and then run like hell for home, kicking your rudder hard from side to side, so as to make the shooting more difficult for the enemy. And keep praying!"

That sage bit of guidance not only saved my life, the first time I met a Hun; it also proved to me the wisdom of taking advice from a more experienced fighter.

On March 30, the Squadron left in formation for France. Our mascot, a black puppy dog named "Contact," was carried as passenger in Lieutenant Jones's aircraft. Near Rochford Captain Cairns had engine trouble. He fired a white flare (a green one meant "Carry on"), and we all landed on the aerodrome. A couple of hours later we took off for Lympne, where we found that the rest of the Squadron had already left for France. Since the sky was cloudless, with very little wind, we took off again about eleven o'clock for St. Omer, leaving Birch behind with engine trouble.

Since we were crossing the "Ditch" at 10,000 feet, I had no worries about engine trouble and was able to concentrate on the fascination of my first flight over the sea. The white-flecked expanse of water, dotted everywhere with miniature ships, looked like a child's table model, and was wholly delightful. It was not difficult to follow the canal from Calais to St. Omer. By noon, we had all landed at the aerodrome. But not all intact. As usual, I had turned upside-down, and my friend Giles had followed suit. "Contact" threw up.

That evening the Squadron paid what was to be the first of many visits to the town of St. Omer, and stayed the night at the

Hotel de Commerce. The following day, we flew to aerodromes in the vicinity of Dunkirk. A and B Flights landed at Capelle, the home of 215 Squadron. C Flight landed at Petit-Sans, where 211 Squadron became its hosts. This was the first day of the amalgamation of the Royal Flying Corps and the Royal Naval Air Service into one united service, the Royal Air Force.

Owing chiefly to a certain amount of jealousy among the senior officers of the R.F.C. and the R.N.A.S., there had been friction between the two branches since the beginning of the war. I was quite prepared, therefore, to put up with some unpleasantness as the guest of a R.N.A.S. squadron. To my astonishment, our hosts could not do enough for us. With the exception of one hasty remark by a non-combatant officer, we met with nothing but the utmost friendliness. Major Chris. Draper[1] and Captain Teddy Jerrard, who were visitors for dinner, went out of their way to be charming. They were the first members of the much-maligned R.N.A.S. I had met. Since that time, contact with such men as Air Marshal Sir Arthur Longmore, Commander Samson, Squadron Leader George Reid, Air Vice-Marshal Bill Norton, Air Vice-Marshal D. S. Evill, Flight Lieutenant Kinkead, of Schneider Trophy fame, and Flight Lieutenant "Bones" Brady has convinced me that there were as good fellows in one service as in the other. On the other hand, the biggest swine of a senior officer I ever met in the Royal Air Force was ex-R.N.A.S.

A and B Flights had the unpleasant experience of staying at an aerodrome that was bombed on their first night at Capelle. They were ordered, next day, to fly to the new aerodrome which we were taking over from Draper's 208 Squadron at Tetengham. The latter was known as the "tennis court" aerodrome, for it was very narrow and not very long. As I was not clever at landing my S.E. 5, it made me quite sick to look at it.

And now let the yellowing pages of my 1918 war diary take up the story. They were written in extreme youth, and often in circumstances of excitement or desperate weariness after battle. That must excuse their literary shortcomings. . . .

[1] Draper caused a national sensation on May 5, 1953, when he flew under fifteen Thames bridges in an Auster "to prove he was not too old at sixty-one."

6

APRIL 3, 1918.—All machines are being overhauled, ready for line patrol duty. Everyone is very keyed up and itching for a fight. We want to show "Grid" what we are made of. I often wonder, as I look round the mess, which of us will be the first to be killed. One of us must be, but no one shows any visible signs of caring. I hope it isn't Roxburgh-Smith or Stuart-Smith, as they are both married, with families. Old Rox is the oldest member of the Squadron—thirty-four years old. Mannock is next, aged thirty-three.

Mick [Mannock] is the life and soul of the mess, with his greetings of "All tickets, please," and "Please pass right down the lift, so that the Old Man can see the Hun." Kiddie, who is short, fat, with a podgy face, has earned the name of "Old Man" because of his staid bearing. Nothing ever worries him. That is why he was such a good instructor.

It is odd to find myself serving with three of my instructors—Kiddie, Birch and Roxburgh.

April 4.—Giles and I sighted our guns this morning. The others had done so already. Each pilot, with the aid of Harry Coverdale, the English Rugby international, sights his own. If we fail to shoot any Huns down it will be our own fault. This knowledge will relieve Harry of much loss of sleep! Some of the mess baggage has turned up mysteriously. No one seems to know where it came from or who brought it. Anyway, it's here, and that's the chief point. All kit for the officers' mess is missing still, and we have to borrow utensils from the men. But we don't care. We're in France, which is the main thing.

April 6.—We are getting very restless, hanging about waiting for orders to do something. Grid phones up 64 Wing (Colonel Osmond), each day, asking if we can start our patrols, but for some reason we can't get permission. This is bad for us. Too much like sitting in a dentist's chair. To while away the time we have all been practising shooting at a target in the sea. It is a good idea, as we can see by the splashing of the bullets if we are aiming straight. Of course, the target is stationary, so it is not much of a test of our ability. When we aim at the Hun he will not be so obliging, unless he is fool enough to dive away from us instead of turning. If he dives, he will be more or less a stationary target and easy to hit.

Grid has told us that he will never forgive any one of us who dives away from a Hun. Whoever does and gets away with it, he has promised to kick his backside all round the aerodrome. Grid, like most Aucklanders, has big feet!

Everyone in the mess has agreed to pool the wine bill. This is a good idea, and proves the good comradeship that exists. Skeddon (my half-section) and I are strict teetotallers. We are fond of native drinks called citron and grenadine, sweet but very tasty. One is yellow and the other red.

We prefer the citron, but when we dine at a restaurant we drink the grenadine, as its colour makes it appear that we are drinking red wine which most of the others are doing. The fellows try to induce us to take wine, but Caldwell says that it is a good show that we don't; which is typical of him. He is a great leader of men. I would do anything or go anywhere for him, and I am sure that all the others would follow suit. Mick says that he is the bravest man in the Air Force, and that he will frighten hell out of us when he is leading the patrols. This, coming from Mick, makes us wonder what we are in for.

Just heard that Porter, a great friend of mine at London Colney, has been shot down and killed. He was in 56 Squadron.

April 7.—Owing to dud weather, we have not done anything for the last few days until last night, when C Flight put in a line patrol from Middlekerke to Ypres. There was no excitement. We did not even see any Huns. Today, however, I had my first bit of fun.

Cairns thought that a line patrol was a bit dull with no enemy around, so he took us across the lines between Dixmude and Nieuport in order to introduce us to "Archie." Over Nieuport the first "Archie" burst was just behind my machine. I thought it shook it rather badly, so I had a look round. Imagine my surprise when I saw a big hole in the fabric behind my seat, where the locker was.

I did not mind very much, but I wondered if poor old Contact was all right, as I had taken him up as my passenger, so that he could say he had flown during the war. I could see that the cover of the locker had a hole in it, and I was scared that Contact might fall out. This was at the beginning of the patrol, and I decided to carry on, as I considered it was the thing to do.

The patrol lasted one and a quarter hours, and by the time we got back to the aerodrome the fabric was torn a great deal. As soon as the machine touched the ground on landing, the fuselage broke in two. Out jumped Contact, as fit as a flea, much to my joy. My machine was the first casualty in the squadron, and I am proud of the fact. I am a firm believer in the motto, "Start badly, end well."

While flying over Nieuport I looked out to sea towards Ostend. I wondered in which part of that vast water poor old Dick Watson had been drowned.

Walters, one of the South Africans in A Squadron rugger team at Winchester, was killed this morning in an R.E. 8 near Poperinghe. He was a great little fellow, and the fact that his home is so far away makes his death all the sadder.

April 10.—We exchanged aerodromes with 29 Squadron yesterday. Our new home is not far from Poperinghe (commonly known as "Pop"), and is called La Lovie. 29 Squadron pilots don't think much of Tetengham, and less of our squadron. Clem overheard some of them say that we were a ragtime crowd, no discipline, but that we had a cracker of a C.O.

We don't think much of their C.O., anyway, and as for our discipline—they're talking tripe. One word from Grid, and the thing is as good as done. Certainly we cut out as much as possible the empty but deceptive type of discipline—"Yes, sir," "No, sir." "Three bags full, sir." We're a fighting squadron. We've come out to fight, and by our achievements as fighters we want to be judged, not by whether we wear breeches and puttees or slacks.

Met Ross and Read (South Africans), who were with me at Hursley Park. They are doing well in 29 Squadron. Also came across "Ginger" Osbourne, who is with 21 Squadron, flying R.E. 8. He tells me that the R.E. 8 is nicknamed "the flaming wafer," because it always bursts into flames when it crashes. Most of the pilots have got the wind up over it. It is as unpopular as the old Camel.

Pilots are very funny about machines. We damn a machine wholesale, often even when we have not flown one of the type. For example, all the King's horses and all the King's men couldn't induce me to fly either a Camel or an R.E. 8. An aeroplane is like a woman. Give her a bad name, and she's damn' lucky if she ever finds a lover.

Builders of the Tradition

There are strong rumours that the Huns have made an attack on the Portuguese front, and that they have captured Armentières and are advancing towards Kemmel, Bailleul, Merville, Estaires and Bethune. I can't believe it, and have bet Skeddon two to one in quids that this is not so. In the first place, I don't believe that there are any Portuguese in the trenches. They're all working in the lines of communication, helping the Chinks, as far as I know.

Skeddon and I went over to Abeele Aerodrome nearby, to see my old squadron, No. 10. They are equipped with Armstrong Whitworth two-seaters (commonly known as Ack W's). The C.O. is Keith Murray, a New Zealander from Auckland, and like Grid, he is a corker. I have never met a fellow with personality more prominently written all over him. When you look at him, you cannot resist saying: "There goes a *man*." Like Grid, he is worshipped by his squadron. No. 10 Squadron has indeed been lucky in its squadron commanders. Mitchell, Ward and Murray are names to conjure with.

My friend, Dunn, is now sergeant-major and, strangely enough, he is very popular as well as very efficient. He is a grand fellow. He was one of my "flag lieutenants" in connection with the Soldiers' Christian Association during my campaign of "saving souls." I think he is saddened by the knowledge that I no longer wear the mantle of Paul.

Many are the changes in the squadron, but the present pilots are as keen as the old bunch. Murray, like Grid, will have no duds. The brothers Norgarb, from Pretoria, are among us— stout lads and good rugger players. There is no doubt that rugger makes a man out of a boy better than any other game.

The old soldier, Joe Lawson, is still going strong and winning the same imaginary V.C. in his cups. He is a grand fellow in his own way. He told me he is quite content to remain in the squadron without changing rank until the end of the war, provided we win at last.

"My old woman will have to put up with it," he said with a malicious twinkle in his eyes. He's a naughty man, is Joe!

Had dinner at the R.F.C. Officers' Mess, "Pop," on the way back. The food was excellent. There is a heavy bombardment going on in the Ypres area, as I write. I am beginning to wonder if I have lost my bet with Skeddon. The rumour of a Hun advance strengthens with every hour. I can't believe it, though. It seems incredible that we could lose Armentières.

April 11.—It is true that Armentières has been taken. Damn the

Tiger Squadron

Huns. We'll knock hell out of them yet. 74 Squadron is going into action to-morrow! We left La Lovie this morning for Clamarais North Aerodrome. It is the last word in aerodromes. The staff officer who chose it obviously never had any intention of trying to land an S.E. 5 on it. I hope he got the O.B.E. It is "L" shaped, on the slope of a hill; measures about 300 yards by 150 yards; it is boundaried by a 10-foot hedge, and on one side are tall trees. What a hope I've got of not writing off my bus soon. Most of the other fellows are windy, too. We've got up a sweep on who will crash first. I've drawn Mick and, oddly enough, Mick has drawn me. Which is quite fair. Mick may be a crack shot, but he "ain't no good" at landing an S.E. 5!

We're in XI Wing, which is commanded by Colonel Pierre Van Ryneveld. No. 54 Squadron (Camels), who are sharing our aerodrome, speak very highly of him. Major R. S. Maxwell, commanding No. 54, looks the same type as Mick. He is lean and tall, with a slight stoop and a weather-beaten face, full of vitality. He walks about in a dirty tunic, with his M.C. ribbon indistinguishable. His squadron love him. He is a great fighter and has a charming personality.

Lieutenant Howe, who was an observer in 10 Squadron, and who was with Legget when they shot the Aviatik down over the aerodrome in 1916, is in the Squadron. So are "Digger" Moore, who was with me at Oxford, and Roy Royston, the famous young actor. Royston, I am told, is full of guts. He loves low strafing, for which he was recently awarded the M.C. They appear to be a full-out crowd, and it is easy to see why, when they have such a fizzing C.O. I'm very struck with Maxwell. He's the goods, I should say.

We are all so keyed up, waiting for to-morrow, our first day of real war. There was great competition among the flights as to who should carry out the first patrol, so lots were drawn for the honour. Cairns won. We are very bucked in C Flight, as we hope to shoot down the first Hun for the Squadron.

Cairns is a topping fellow, but he does not strike me as being a good patrol leader. In our practice flights against A and B Flights at London Colney he rarely saw our opponents soon enough. Mick always huffed him. From my experience as an observer, I know how important eyesight must be to a leader. He must shield his flight from surprise attacks; otherwise, casualties will occur and the morale of his flight will drop. We are hoping for the best, however. Skeddon and I have a bet as to which of us will shoot down the first enemy.

Mick is fed up to the teeth that he has not won the toss. Maxwell says that there are bags of Huns about and that they are quite aggressive, so to-morrow will be the day of days. There are two great questions in my mind: "Who will be the first fellow to shoot down a Hun?" and "Who will be the first to be killed?" Personally, I have no premonition of death, but I have a sneaking idea that I may bag the first Hun. The first one I see I am going for, if the odds are in my favour. It is up to Cairns to get me into the position.

I am writing this before going to bed. Most of the other fellows have gone into St. Omer to have dinner at a restaurant nick-named "George Robey." There is a nice mademoiselle there who is sweet on Mick. I did not go, as our patrol is at 6 a.m. and I want to be on top line in the morning. A wide awake pilot will always crack a sleepy one in an air fight, so let's hope that the Huns I meet to-morrow are having a party to-night!

April 12.—The day of days has arrived, and is now almost over.

Butler, my Cockney batman, called Skeddon and me (we are sharing a hut) at 5.30 a.m. The weather was cloudy, but the visibility was particularly good. After a cold sponge-down and a cup of tea and some biscuits, we donned our sidcot suits and strolled across to the aerodrome, about 200 yards away. Butler came with us to wish us luck.

Cairns, Giles, Birch and Begbie were already standing by their machines. As there were ten minutes to go, we were not late. Cairns told us that he was going to cross the line over Merville and work up towards Ypres over the salient. Everyone was bursting with keenness, each thinking of the Hun he was going to down and no one of the possibility of death or, worse, a breakfast of black bread and sausages in the enemy's lines.

Caldwell, Mannock and Coverdale were also present to see us off. The first- and last-named were there for obvious reasons. Mick turned up to ask us not to disturb the Huns, in case they were not there when his flight were on patrol. He's a rascal!

We were off the ground punctually at 6 a.m. Twenty minutes later, we were crossing the lines between the Forêt de Nieppe and Merville, which was now the front line of trenches, thanks to the aggressiveness of the enemy troops and the pusillanimity of the Pork and Beans (the Tommy's name for our gallant allies, the Portuguese!) As we crossed, I looked at my altimeter. I was amazed to find we were at only 6,000 feet. This was a ridiculously low height, I thought, as the clouds were quite 10,000 feet. From my observer's experience I knew that the enemy's "Archie" was fairly good at this height, while there was every prospect of the Huns attacking us from above.

It was not long before the "goods" arrived. And they were not wrapped up in a brown paper parcel.

Archie bursts soon bounced our machines all over the sky, while two miles away and about 2,000 feet above us and approaching was a large fleet of biplanes, led by a triplane. I watched them for a second or two, wondering whether they were our machines or Huns. We were approaching each other rapidly.

I dashed up to Cairns, waggled my wings to attract his attention and then pointed to the oncoming aircraft. He signalled back: "O.K." I returned to my position at the tail of the flight, on the right flank. We were flying in the customary "V" formation, with Skeddon and Birch on the immediate right and left of Cairns. Behind them were Begbie and Giles, and behind Giles was myself. This position of honour was given to me because of my exceptionally good eyesight. It was up to me to warn Cairns of any Huns sneaking up from the rear or any other angle. (In World War II, the rear upper flight of section did this work, informing the leader over radio-telephone.)

When Cairns continued to fly towards and underneath the approaching machines, I naturally assumed they were comrades. But the triplane puzzled me. As I couldn't recognise the type of the others, I became more and more anxious.

I remembered Mick's advice to us all during one of his many lectures. "When we get to the war," he had said, "don't ever attempt to dogfight a triplane on anything like equal terms as regards height, otherwise he will get on your tail and stay there until he shoots you down."

Were they Huns? I couldn't make up my mind. But as they came on fast, the black Maltese crosses on their wings soon settled the question. It was months since I had seen any. How pretty they looked! And what pretty machines! They were all colours. Black, red, bright blue, dark blue, grey, yellow—all the colours of the rainbow. It never struck me they were aeroplanes flown by men, possibly crack pilots of the German Air Force. Men whom I knew as Huns; death-dealing gentlemen, possibly smothered in Iron Crosses and Orders *pour la Merite*. They looked more like a rather beautiful flock of birds. But I was soon awakened from my reverie.

Cairns, as soon as he saw the machines, turned sharply left to get away from them as they dived to the attack. Skeddon and

Birch went with him and Begbie and Giles, by crossing over positions, managed to turn fairly quickly, too. But I, being so far behind, was left standing so to speak.

The Hun leader[1] soon took advantage of the gap between me and my flight, and brought his flight into it. He himself was soon on my tail, firing bullets of sweet welcome to 74 Squadron. Wisely, I kept my head and immediately put my machine into a vertical bank. I held the stick tight into my belly, kept my throttle wide open, and—prayed hard, as Mick had advised.

It did not take me long to realise that the gentleman who was doing his best to kill me was an old hand at the game. A sure sign of experience is that a pilot reserves his ammunition and only fires in short bursts. He knows that if he is aiming straight, a burst of twenty is as good as a burst of 200 and much more economical. A pilot has only about 500 bullets in all. It is foolish to use them up when he knows his aim is not good, just on the off-chance that an odd one may hit his opponent. Once he has used all his ammunition, he is defenceless.

Mick had warned us to be careful of the Hun who fired in short bursts. "On the other hand, if the Hun is firing long bursts at you, you can bet your bottom dollar that he is windy, and probably a beginner," he said. "Fight him like hell. He should be easy meat."

This guy on my tail was so close that I could easily discern his features. He had a small, square face, and a puggish little nose. Like myself, he wore no flying cap or goggles. His machine was painted red and black, the nose and tail red, with wings and fuselage black. He was flying superbly. He seemed to slither round me. Round and round we waltzed in what my opponent must have thought was a waltz of death—for me. This morbid aspect of the situation, luckily, never occurred to me.

Of course, I could see the big idea. The leader was to shoot me down, while his ten companions prevented anyone coming to my help. Some of them kept above and on the north side, the side where Cairns and his company had pushed off, while the remainder kept on the west side of me at various heights, so that I would have to run the gauntlet of their fire if I made a dash for it.

As we waltzed round, I kept on repeating to myself: "Keep cool, Taffy. He can't hit you. His bullets are going behind." I could see the paths of his bullets, because he was using tracers.

[1] Baron von Schleich, a Bavarian with thirty-six victories. I met him in London after the war, and checked his log-book. A very nice chap!

This fact encouraged me to keep cool. I had no desire to have a burning bullet roasting my guts, especially before breakfast.

Occasionally I swore at the top of my voice, telling him to do his damnedest, and calling him names which reflected gravely on his morals. He could not hear me, but it gave me satisfaction and acted as a temporary stimulant to my sorely tested courage. While he flew close to my tail but did not fire, I didn't mind very much; but whenever I heard the kak-kak-kak of his guns and saw the strings of flame behind me, I felt a little anxious that a stray bullet might find its mark.

Every now and then my attacker would zoom up, and a couple of his comrades would make a dive-and-zoom attack, hoping I would get out of my vertical bank. I wasn't having any. I knew of this old trick from past experience. Once they got me out of the vertical bank, the gent on my tail (he may have been Richthofen, Udet or any other of the star Hun turns, for all I knew) would have soon put paid to my account.

After a while, I feared that unless I got out of the mess quickly, Fate might step in and stop my engine, or, worse still, put a stray tracer through my petrol tank and send me down to Hunland in a blaze of glory.

That would be a glorious death for an airman, but it was not one I wanted on my first patrol. I wanted to kill a couple of Huns myself first.

As I whizzed round (there is no other description), I kept my eye on the big grey mass of trees about five miles away—the Forêt de Nieppe. I knew that those trees were in our territory. It was a consoling thought, but I could not make up my mind when to make my dash.

The triplane kept on nagging at me with his bullets. So did his companions. The longer I stayed as their guest, the more attention they paid me. Occasionally, two or three would have a crack together. The seconds passed like years, and the minutes like eternity. The tension grew until, in desperation, having given up all hope of anyone coming to my rescue, I decided to make a bid for home as soon as the triplane did his next zoom.

The old devil was then about 25 yards behind. I watched him carefully. He seemed to be grinning as I looked at him over my left shoulder. As soon as I saw him start to zoom up to change his position, I obeyed Mick's instructions and put on full bottom rudder. My machine did a turn of a spin and when I came out of it I found my machine was facing east instead of west. Another spot of bottom rudder turned her round westward, and there in front, a few miles away, was my landmark, the Forêt de Nieppe.

But between me and my objective were half a dozen Huns, black and red Huns, light blue and dark blue Huns, grey and yellow Huns, hungry and angry Huns, just waiting for me to come their way. So their way I went, accepting their challenge like a mad bull charging a gate. It was my only way to safety. It was now or never, so, barging through the middle of them, looking neither to left nor right—as I had often done through a rugger scrum when cornered—I went for home like hell, "kicking my rudder from side to side to make shooting more difficult for the enemy and—praying hard."

It was a grand thrill, that run for my lines. I knew by the incessant barking of the enemies' guns that hundreds, if not thousands of death-dealing bullets were chasing the little body that I love so much.

Occasionally during my mad skelter, I looked over my shoulder to see whether I was gaining on my opponents. To my joy, I could see that I was. But the bullets were still faster. It was not until I was well clear of the enemy, half a mile away, that I knew I was safe. It was wonderful to see my little S.E. gaining distance on the triplane and the Pfalz, and to listen to the fading rattle of the enemies' guns as my aircraft gradually forged ahead. I crossed our lines just on the north of the forest, right down on the carpet, and fortunately my enemies did not have the courage to follow me. They were probably windy of being caught in a trap by the rest of my flight.

I continued flying low as far as Hazebrouck before climbing and looking around for Cairns. I soon spotted him over Bailleul, still flying at about 6,000 feet and coming south. I climbed up and joined my flight over Merville again.

Then an extraordinary thing happened to me. During the affair with the enemy I had remained perfectly calm and not in the least windy. Suddenly, reaction set in. I started going hot and cold all over and momentarily lost control of myself. I decided I was no use as an airman, that I could never cross the lines again, and that I would inform Grid of the fact as soon as I landed.

I was simply terrified of the prospect of another flight over the lines. I felt convinced that I was a rank coward. I was so frightened that I wanted to nestle up close to Giles, but my loss of self-control was so complete that I was too frightened even to open my throttle to go closer. Visions of meeting those Huns again nearly made me desert my formation—a coward—as a few others in the Service had done. Thank God, I overcame the temptation.

That was the beginning of my recovery. A few minutes later I was ready to knock hell out of all the Huns in the air. What an extraordinary business, though. Psychological, I suppose. When we landed and my machine was examined, there was not a single bullet-hole in it. Grid and Mick gave me a good pat on the back, which pleased me as much as getting away from the Huns.

This little show has given me great confidence in my machine and in my own ability to hold my own against any Hun. When I told Grid this, he said: "Of course, you are better than those sods, the Hunnerinoes, but don't get over-confident. It's the first month, not day, that counts, Taffy." I shall remember this.

My little show (I can't call it a fight, as I was on the defensive the whole time) has increased my compassion for the hunted deer, hare, and even the roguish Reynard. Ten to one is not much sport to the one!

Mick and his flight were delighted to hear that we had not destroyed a Hun. They went on their first patrol at 8.25 a.m., full of buck and beans. When they returned, an hour and a half later, we knew they had been up to some dirty work. They were all firing Very lights of all colours, and diving and zooming at the sheds where we stood waiting their arrival.

Every one of them was very excited when they got out of their machines. It appears that the air was still full of Huns when they got over the lines. Mick had led his flight to the attack on a packet of Albatross Scouts over Merville at 13,000 feet, and he and Dolan had each succeeded in crashing an enemy. The first Hun was persuaded to go down by Mick's bullets. So to him, as we all expected, goes the honour of having destroyed the first enemy credited to the Squadron.

Later in the day, A Flight crashed another Albatross Scout, coloured black and yellow, which fell near the Bois de Phalempin. Mick, in his report, has said that "the whole flight should share in the credit of this E.A.," although all the fellows who were with him say that it was he who shot it down. This is just what I expected of Mick. He has done it to give his flight a little encouragement. I think Cairns and Young will do the same when the opportunity arises. Our flight commanders are good value.

The C.O. and Young also destroyed an Albatross Scout apiece, while C Flight tried hard to bag a two-seater on our second patrol at 14,000 feet over Ploegstreet Wood, but he got away from us. Dud show.

I nearly got a two-seater, though. We met him over Zillebecke Lake, a few miles east of Ypres returning from our lines at 17,000 feet. I was sneaking under his tail when he spotted me, and his observer opened fire. I was then 500 yards behind him. He immediately stuck his nose down and dived steeply, with his engine full on, in the direction of Roulers. I continued to dive after him, and at 10,000 feet he pulled out of the dive, no doubt thinking I had given up the chase.

As soon as I opened fire, he again dived steeply. Down and down we went, and he pulled out of his dive at about 7,000 feet. I gave him a long burst this time, and he now started spiralling down. I continued firing, and his observer returned the compliment.

Down and down we continued until, eventually, he landed in a large field about a quarter of a mile south-east of Roulers, near a road, railway and canal. As he was apparently all right, I fired my remaining bullets at him and then came home on the carpet.

What a trip it was! Hell was let lose all the way. "Archie" bursts, flaming onions, and bullets fairly buzzed around. I thought my number was up and was terrified that a formation of Hun scouts would spot me. I grudged every second of that run home. Occasionally I had to alter my course in order to put the "Archies" off. It was a grim business, but my luck was in.

I crossed the lines at Ypres. Never has that devastated town invoked so many cheers from anyone as it got then from me. I would gladly have got out of my machine and kissed the ruined Cloth Hall, had it been possible. It was such a glorious feeling to realise I was back safely.

Chasing the Hun was great fun. Mannock was cross that I had followed the enemy down so low. It must never be done, he says. All the Flights did three shows each, patrols of one and a half hours. Everybody felt pretty tired at the end of it. Clements, who developed a splitting headache on his last patrol—due to continuous high flying, I think—crashed on landing and wrote his machine off. I, too, was in the wars when my crankshaft broke during the evening patrol. We were then between Armentières and Lille, at 17,000 feet. Suddenly there was a cloud of smoke and the machine quivered. Slowly my propeller stopped, and so, I might almost say, did my heart. What a plight I was in! Far over enemy lines, while all around were bags of hungry Huns!

79

Tiger Squadron

Cairns and the flight protected me until I crossed the lines. It was an uncanny business. I could hear the roar of their engines, the violent detonation of the "Archies" (not the muffled noise one hears when the engine is running), and even at times the cannonade of the artillery. On my way down, I tried to think what I had done to deserve all this bad luck. Skeddon escorted me back. His face was wreathed in smiles as he came alongside. He put up a couple of fingers at me. I replied by thumbing my nose at him. He got the final laugh, watching me go head over heels as I tried to land in a ploughed field not very far from the aerodrome.

Grid says I'm a hoodoo. Mick goes even further. He says that the sooner I'm shot down in flames, the better.

Well, today has been a great day for the Squadron. Naturally, A and B Flights are very bucked at having shot down machines on their first patrol. Cairns is a little despondent, but the remainder of the flight are not. We all did our best. We could do no more. The boys who drink rightly uncorked the champagne bottles tonight, and we had speeches from the Hun-strafers. Mick, in particular, made a good speech. He has a flair for it. He gave all his flight, especially Dolan, a pat on the back. That we must kill as many Huns as we can, without being killed ourselves, was his main theme. Grid's theme, on the other hand, was: "Kill the sods, the Hunnerinoes, at all costs. Anywhere and everywhere!"

Grid got so close to his Hun to-day that, had he been carrying a stick, he could have put him out with a whack on the head. He's a fighter, all right.

There was an awful mess-up in Clamarais South Aerodrome just at dusk to-night. Machines started arriving from advanced aerodromes, as if in panic. Some belonged, I hear, to 98 and 20 Squadrons. A couple of Bristol fighters crashed and burst into flames. Two pilots were killed and one observer injured. It was a horrible sight to see the machines ablaze. Skeddon and I, who watched them land, decided that perhaps we wouldn't like to be burned to death, after all—glorious death though it seemed.

Norgarb, from 10 Squadron, landed at Clamarais to-night. He told me the old squadron had been hard hit during the past few days. Ground strafing.

To-night, an Order of the Day was put up in the mess. The mechanics are fitting bomb racks to our machines. In future we are going to carry some 20-lb. Cooper bombs on every patrol.

No. 54 Squadron have two machines missing. One was seen to

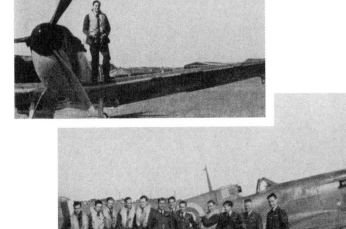

Top: At dispersal hut: Kirk; Ricalto; Glendinning; Nelson: Aubert; Smith; Boulding; Szcesny; Malan; Brezezina; Mungo-Park; Mould; St. John; Skinner; Hilton and Franklin.

Centre: P/O H. M. Stephen, D.S.O., D.F.C. and bar.

Below: Tiger pilots waiting to "scramble."

53 O.T.U. LLANDOW, NO. 8 COURSE

Back Row (Left to Right): P/O R. D. May; Sgt. G. B. Murray; Sgt. T. Lindsay; Sgt. S. O. Simpson; Sgt. J. L. Liggett; Sgt. A. N. Cresswell; Sgt. N. C. Todd; Sgt. G. W. Andrews; Sgt. C. B. Briggs; Sgt. E. G. Enright; Sgt. J. N. Dean; Sgt. R. J. Martin; Sgt. D. Linton.

Second Row (Left to Right): P/O C. P. Lloyd; Sgt. C. Brennan; Sgt. K. J. Wyllie; Sgt. C. C. Betts; Sgt. T. H. J. Williams; Sgt. D. J. McCrimmon; Sgt. N. V. Hobbs; Sgt. R. T. Hiskens; Sgt. H. L. Hargreaves; Sgt. V. P. Brennan; Sgt. W. E. Pearce; P/O G. W. Andrews; P/O W. G. Clark; P/O J. R. Sterne.

Front Row (Left to Right): P/O G. E. Caswell; P/O T. K. Robinson; P/O R. H. Whillans; Sqd/Ldr. A. J. A. Llewellin; W/Cdr. Ryder, D.F.C.; Gr. Capt. J. I. T. Jones, D.S.O., M.C., D.F.C., M.M.; Sqd/Ldr. B. Drake, D.F.C.; P/O V. O'Driscoll; P/O A. E. Drossaert; Sgt. L. J. G. Harmel; Sgt. J. Ester.

suffer a direct hit by a flaming onion. These flaming onions are most peculiar missiles. They resemble a ball of flame and are fired so rapidly, one after the other, that they look just like a chain of fire balls. The nickname "flaming onions" is good. When I ran the gauntlet of the onion batteries this afternoon, I was very windy. I found great difficulty in judging whether they were coming or going, and how near they actually were.

I have no fear of Huns, but for "Archie" and flaming onions I have a profound respect. I'm told that one of our machines was hit by "Archie" at 20,000 feet the other day. This is not playing the game. The flaming onions have been reported as high as 6,000 feet, but I doubt it.

Moore and Bowen, of 54 Squadron, shot down a couple of high-flying Rumplers to-day, so this cancels their losses. But Mick says that two for two is not good arithemetic.

April 18.—My third birthday in France. Oh! for the fourth in good old Blighty.

Since my last entry we have had bad weather every day. No air fighting. A Flight were suddenly ordered on Tuesday afternoon to go on a ground-strafing stunt at Wytschaete. Ground strafing is the name given to the dangerous task of shooting up the ground forces.

Maxwell, to whom I have spoken about it, tells me his squadron hates the game. Everyone is shooting at the machine all the time, and as it is flying at a low altitude—below 1,000 feet—there is no chance of getting back to our lines if the engine is hit. Casualties are usually heavy on this job.

The Huns came through and captured Bailleul and are now trying to get a footing on Mount Kemmel. It was filthy weather—raining, and clouds down to 600 feet. Mick said on his return that it was raining shells around Wytschaete. Apparently both sides were putting up a barrage, and occasionally the pilots could actually see shells in flight. None of the fellows relished the job. No. 54 had one machine missing on the same stunt. Clem lost his way, as his compass started swinging. To steady it he flew a straight course for a few minutes. He suddenly spotted Armentières, which is now several miles behind the enemy lines, and had a most unpleasant trip back. He pinched a lot of buttons, I understand. "Pinching buttons" is a great game during ground strafing, and is very popular, but a little annoying to the cushions!

Yesterday, General Webb-Bowen visited the Squadron and congratulated the C.O. on our show on the 12th. Personally, I did not see him. I was on a ground-strafing stunt at the time.

To-day I went to St. Omer with Skeddon to see the captured Hanover and Albatross machines. The place to attack the Hanover is just below the tail, which is in the shape of a box. I should like to have flown the Albatross, which was a single-seater, so that I could find out what its little failings are. It is a pretty machine.

Several bombs fell in St. Omer the other night. The inhabitants are getting noticeably windy. Some of them are preparing to leave.

We're going to play a game of rugger against the Squadron to-morrow, if it is still wet.

April 19.—We beat up No. 54 at rugger. It was a grand game. Maxwell, their C.O., and Grid had some fun in scragging one another. All the juniors joined in, and this part of the game ended in a very just draw.

Our star turn was Coverdale. He seemed to score just when he liked. Although only about 5 feet 3 inches in height and rather lean, his wiry little figure played havoc with his bigger, more cumbersome opponents. He played for Blackheath.

C Flight did a patrol at 6 p.m. I was feeling a little sore and tired. I am not sure it is a good thing to play rugger and then have to fly soon afterwards. I dropped my bombs on Estaires, but did no damage. It was very cold at 12,000 feet to-night, for some reason.

My luck is right out. After half an hour's flying my engine seized and once more I had to be escorted back to my lines with a stationary propeller. Luckily, I was not bothered by any Huns; otherwise I don't suppose I should be writing this now. All this trouble is getting beyond a joke. However, I'm not worrying.

I managed to put the old bus down in Estree Blanche Aerodrome, which two ex-R.N.A.S. squadrons are sharing. My machine came to a standstill about 300 yards from the hangars, but one of the C.Os. named Bell, an Australian, refused to help. He informed me bluntly that he had "no bloody time for the R.F.C." I went to the other squadron (203) for help. The C.O. —Major Collishaw,[1] a Canadian—did everything he could for me, including returning me to Clarmarais in his touring car. What a difference between two C.Os. of the same service! As I suspected, Collishaw is worth fifty of the other guy. Collishaw flies and fights, and has a damn' fine squadron.

[1] Now Air Vice-Marshal. He was the first A.O.C., North African Tactical Air Force.

Builders of the Tradition

The "Archie" was particularly good to-night. There was a cloud layer at 13,000 feet, and this probably gave the gunner a better indication of our height than if there were no clouds. Anyway, some of his shots on my way back to our lines were uncomfortably close. I wonder why the Hun "Archie" bursts are black, while ours are pinkish.

Our squadron is a very happy family. We all pull together splendidly. I can't get the sad thought out of my mind that soon one of us must die. I feel it won't be me, and naturally I am hoping that it will not be anyone in C Flight, especially my flight partner, Skeddon.

Am very tired—so to bed!

April 20.—Collected my machine from Estree Blanche during the afternoon. New engine installed. The mechanics worked all night; they are grand fellows.

Collishaw has been a trump over this show. I shall not forget his kindness in a hurry. One of his flight commanders—Little by name and stature—was also very kind to me. He is a celebrated Hun-strafer and has a pocketful of decorations already. How many he'll have when the war ends, God only knows.

This evening Grid took Begbie and me over the lines. We crossed the lines north of Ypres, over Houthulst Forest, and made for Roulers. From there we flew south to Lille, and then re-crossed our lines over Nieppe Forest. We never saw a single Hun, but we got plenty of "Archie." How I hate it! Begbie got a few pieces through his plane. He neither looked nor felt any too happy on landing. Grid thought it was great fun. I didn't. He's got too much guts for me. But I like example from senior officers.

I did a lot of sleeping to-day. I'm feeling a little of the effects of yesterday's rugger.

April 21.—The black day has come at last. Begbie is dead.

To-day has been fine all day. Each flight has done three patrols. I did an extra one, as I was feeling rather full-out—7 a.m., 11 a.m., 2 p.m. and 5.30 p.m. On the last patrol the sky was lousy with Huns. Cairns led us to the attack on four Albatross Scouts over Armentières at 15,000 feet. Begbie and Giles remained above to protect us from surprise, while Skeddon, Birch and I followed our leader in the attack. After a little waltzing around one another, Cairns and Skeddon sent a couple down out of control. I had a crack at one of the boys, but to no purpose. He was as bad as I was, so we both sleep in peace to-night.

Having reformed after the scrap, we had a second scrap a little later. This one started against four Albatross Scouts. Our enemies were soon reinforced by about ten others and then started a real dog-fight. Fourteen to six are rather long odds, but we held our own valiantly for some minutes. The Huns, as usual, were highly coloured and were pretty to look at. The fight continued for about five minutes. It was fast and furious while it lasted.

We were waltzing around one another in a vicious circle, with machine guns spitting fire for all they were worth. Every now and then machines would whistle past one another so closely that one forgot the flying bullets. First Skeddon, then Begbie and a Hun missed me by inches during our mad manœuvres. I soon decided it was foolish to sit on an enemy's tail for long. There were surplus Huns about who were no doubt itching to get on mine if they had the chance, so I began snap-shooting. But try as I would, I could not bring down any of the pretty war birds. It was very annoying. Some of the targets looked so easy!

No doubt I, too, looked a snip to my opponents, who were continually having a go. It was a grand fight, though very frightening. Out of the corner of my eye, I could see the others setting on a target, and every now and then, an enemy would spin away and I'd wonder if he was hit. The exchanges were too ferocious to give more than a moment's thought to an enemy already lost to sight.

Suddenly there was a blaze in the sky nearby. I looked. It was Begbie's S.E. A sudden feeling of sickness, of vomiting, overcame me. Poor old Begbie, I thought. How terrible! The kak-kak-kak of a machine gun a few yards behind me warned me of my own danger. Poor Begbie had to leave us without a farewell wave. I had another peep at him as I flew near. A Hun was still at him, pouring more bullets into his machine. He was making sure of him, the dirty dog. While he pursued his victim, an S.E.—it was Giles—dived on his tail. There was a kak-kak-kak! and the Hun dived away, not to be seen again. I hope he was killed, too.

One by one, the Huns left the fight. Giles and I flew towards Begbie's machine, which was floating enveloped in flames. It was a terrible sight. I hope he followed Mannock's advice and blew his brains out as soon as he realised he was on fire. Perhaps the Huns saved him the trouble. I hope they will "do" me, if Fate decrees that I am honoured with a flaming chariot to my grave. Why have we no parachutes, like balloon observers? It is now 1918, and there is a rumour that German airmen have them.

None of us can tell if we got any Huns, as it was such a mix-up, so we have not put in any combat reports. Skeddon had a miraculous escape. A bullet actually passed through his flying cap and singed a groove in his hair. Amazing luck! His machine was shot about badly, and his engine seized up during the fight. He only got away by diving into a thick, black cloud. He crossed the lines at 4,000 feet, landing at Marie Capelle Aerodrome at the foot of Cassel Hill. His nerves are shaken. At the moment he is asleep. His body is twitching in a dream. No doubt he is fighting the battle over again, as I do every night.

Dolan shot down a two-seater this morning. He seems to be developing into an "ace" (as the French say). Good luck to him. Personally, I don't seem to be getting into the trick of things at all. But I am not worrying. There is plenty of time. Keeping alive is my main objective at the moment.

No. 54 has two machines missing. Maxwell sent down a couple out of control in retaliation. Still bad arithmetic, though.

Although this is a sad day for us, it is also a sombre day for the famous Richthofen Circus at Douai. The great Baron von Richthofen has been killed in our lines. Thank God for that. I cannot subscribe, however, to Mick's hope that he, too, died in flames. This flaming business is no fun. After all, air fighting is only a sport—a cruel one, admittedly, but not deserving such a penalty as being slowly burnt to death while suspended in the air. We must draw the line somewhere, and that is where I draw mine. I'm all out for killing the Huns, but I'm also against any form of Oriental cruelties.

There appears to be some doubt whether Richthofen was shot down from the air or from the ground. Anyway, the great thing is that he has destroyed his last British machine, which precludes any possible chance of my name being added to his bag.

At dinner to-night we drank to Begbie's memory, coupling with his name that of Richthofen—as Mick said, in the hope that he "was in flames, too."

Everyone was very lively in the mess after dinner, as we had Maxwell and his boys in to join us. We played "Hi-cockalorum" and other foolish games in an endeavour to keep up our spirits. "The death of anyone among us must never be allowed to affect our morale," Grid has decreed, so we are going to have a lively guest-night whenever anyone is killed, "by order." And quite right, too.

Perhaps those Huns fought as hard as they did to-day because of Richthofen's death. The spirit of revenge was in their breasts. Good enough! 74 Squadron will avenge Begbie, too, so we ought to have some good fighting to-morrow.

7

April 26.—The past few days have been dud weather. Only one flight patrol has taken place each day. Nothing very exciting happened as far as I was concerned, except that I had to return with a dud engine again last night.

Mick had added another Hun to his record. On the 23rd, on evening patrol, he came across a formation of thirty to forty of the enemy at 14,000 feet, east of Merville. Manœuvring his formation so that they attacked the Huns—all scouts—from above and behind, he engaged the rear member of the patrol— a pretty Pfalz with black body, white-tipped tail and silver-and-black chequered top planes. He pumped about 120 rounds into it at very close range. The poor old Pfalz was soon on fire. Clem said he watched it turn upside-down and descend vertically. Dolan watched it hit Mother Earth with a wallop near Merville. Mick was very sorry that it didn't go down sizzling. How he hates the Huns! He had a go at another couple, but to no purpose.

Clem said it was a wonderful sight to see so many highly coloured Huns flying in formation. Their black Maltese crosses looked most attractive. I wish I had been with them. Mick keeps his formations above the Huns all the time, exploiting his dive-and-zoom tactics. One of his flight, whom I'll call "Windy," left his formation to attack a two-seater. He said Mick gave him hell on landing and told him that if he left him again he'd shoot him down. I'm not sure he didn't mean it.

Richthofen, I have since heard, was shot down by a Captain Brown in a Camel. Apparently, the Baron was cracking up an R.E. 8. Brown saw him and went to the R.E.'s rescue. He didn't know it was Richthofen, of course. A bit of luck for him. He'll no doubt get a decoration for his effort. He certainly deserves one; for only yesterday, in St. Omer, I met a staff-wallah who has never flown in the war—and he sported a Military Cross! Mick, I think, hates our non-flying staff-wallahs more than the Huns. The Huns are at least *men* and worthy of their parentage, he says. He's not the only one who holds this view.

Builders of the Tradition

We are fortunate in having Van Ryneveld as our wing commander. He is a South African from Bloemfontein. He keeps a Camel at Clamarais South and is continually flying over the lines. Like the "live" wing commander he is, he likes to go and see for himself that his squadrons are carrying out his orders. Woe betide the squadron he catches doing a line patrol when he has ordered it to be on offensive patrol.

Oh, yes, there are some squadrons among us who shirk their duty occasionally. Depends on who is leading the patrol. It's the squadron commander's fault, of course. He probably does not lead them himself. A C.O. of a fighting squadron is no damned good unless he is of Grid's and Maxwell's stamp. A squadron is what its C.O. is, unless he happens to have three damned good flight commanders, like 56 Squadron had when they went overseas. But that was a freak squadron. The C.O. was given *carte blanche* powers to choose whom he wished. What squadron could be dud with such redoubtable fighters as Ball, Bowman, Meintjies, McCudden, Mayberry, Crowe, Maxwell and Rhys-Davids?

To make certain of success, a fighter squadron must be commanded by a fighting C.O., not an ink-and-blotting-paper type. Why Mick is not commanding one of those squadrons with dud C.Os. I don't know.

There's a good joke floating about. It concerns a very popular brigadier-general, who commands one of the brigades (not ours), and one of his fighting squadron commanders. This C.O.'s squadron was not doing at all well. The brigadier, who flies a lot himself, ordered the C.O. to lead his squadron patrols in future. The first patrol he commanded ended in fiasco. He soon lost himself and has not been heard of since, although no Huns were seen during the patrol! The squadron has now a fiery C.O., who was trained in a great school—56 Squadron. He is Major Geoffrey Bowman, known to his friends as "Beery"—not because he is fond of beer, but because of his florid complexion. He is going great guns.

The C.O. must set an example to his subordinates if he wishes to command their respect. Gold braid, crowns and stars count for nought in a service where each man has to fight for himself. The junior looks for a standard to live up to. If he doesn't get it, he looks down his nose at his senior.

April 29.—The weather the past few days has not been too favourable for flying. Skeddon and I have gone up of our own accord each day, but nothing doing. I was sorely tempted to have a go at a sausage [balloon]. Not being too sure of my way about yet, I restrained the desire. Grid said I was quite right. However, there is a fellow in No. 1 Squadron at Clamarais South, Captain C. C. Clark, who is a fair terror to enemy balloons. The other day he cracked three, one after the other. I was up at the time, and suddenly I noticed a parachute floating below a balloon which was going down in flames. That's the stuff to give 'em!

No. 1 is a jolly good squadron, doing great work with the S.E. 5. Captain P. S. Clayson and C. C. Clark are the star Hunstrafers. Clayson plays the game in the Mannock style, employing tactics to get the enemy formation into an unfavourable position before attacking it. Clark, on the other hand, is a second Grid. "The sods, the Hunnerinoes—crack them at all costs!" is his motto.

Although Grid's spirit appeals to me more than Mick's tactics, I cannot help feeling that Mick is working on the right lines. After all, we are here to kill without being killed, if we want to win the war. Yet the spirit of adventure which is inherent in me demands the thrill of a fight when and where the opportunity presents itself. "To hell with tactics," it thunders. Then the faint spirit of caution whispers: "Don't be a fool. Go steady. A dead man is no good to his country." I'm very puzzled and a little worried over this matter. I cannot make up my mind which path to take—Grid's or Mick's. Perhaps a little stroll each way will be my best policy for the moment. We'll see.

On the 27th, W. B. Giles and I went up in the afternoon. The clouds were down to 500 feet. We tried to climb through, but found they were too thick. We got the wind-up and decided to go down to the clear atmosphere again. We soon lost one another, and on the way down I was terrified of colliding with him. I had the vertical gust up.

My compass started spinning and my wires screeching, although my speedometer was only registering 60 to 70 m.p.h. and still dropping. Something was wrong. I acted on Kiddie's instructions: "If in doubt, centralise your rudder and joystick." In spite of my obedience to the technique of flying, I came out of the clouds in a headlong rush and was only able to pull up my machine just in time. I poked my nose out of the clouds to be greeted with a clatter of "Archie" bursts. It was easy to recognise that my presence was not welcomed. I soon discovered why.

Directly below me was the "Archie" battery, lying hidden in the corner of Ploegstreet Wood. Two guns were firing for all they were worth at point-blank range. Unfortunately, I had got rid of my bombs in my terror while in the clouds. God only knows where they fell, and I hope He won't tell. Anyway, it was sad to think they were gone. I would have liked to have presented them to my friends below. Especially would I have liked to have handed one out, all to himself, to the pot-bellied gentleman who was looking at me through a pair of binoculars.

I circled the battery once, gave it a hurried—very hurried—splash of bullets, then scooted along the carpet for Bailleul. I considered the contest was very unequal. When I crossed our lines I sang a *Te Deum* with gusto. I flew through a thick rainstorm from the lines to Clamarais, but I didn't worry. I was on the right side of the line, so to hell with the rain.

Giles was back before me. He had been more skilful than I. He is a sound old devil. No flies on him. Kiddie and he are very alike—sound and steady, if perhaps a little slow in the uptake occasionally. They are the type one knows will never let one down. Human Rocks of Gibraltar!

Had dinner last night with No. 1 Squadron. It was indeed a merry night. Alcohol flowed freely, but not too freely. No one was "opsted," yet most were a little mellow. There is not much drinking going on in the squadrons, as far as I can see. Personally, I cannot see how a fellow can fight for his life with a sore head and a sick stomach. There is no doubt in my mind that many fellows have been shot down as the result of dulled wits following a beano.

I do not intend to touch a drop of alcohol while the war is on. I'm told I miss a lot of fun by being a teetotaller. Perhaps I do; but what a man has never had he never misses, so why worry? Anyway, I've compromised with my beery friends by promising to "taste a drop" on Armistice Day, whenever that will be. I'm quite convinced that I shan't be killed. Were I superstitious, I should touch my head and whistle. But Grid has knocked the stuffing out of all superstition. We light three cigarettes with one match or lighter as a matter of principle. We walk under ladders, fly on Fridays the thirteenth, and defy any other established old wives' tales. This is the stuff! Superstition is mere humbug and makes cowards of us all. "To hell with it," says Grid. And so say all of us.

No. 54 Squadron left here this morning for Calais, where they are going for a well-deserved rest. Maxwell and his pilots have had a nasty gruelling, ground strafing, the past few weeks. We are sorry to see them go, as we got on so well together.

But who couldn't get on with a squadron commanded by Maxwell?

We are expecting No. 4 Australian Squadron to arrive here at any moment, so I am not writing any more to-day. I am going on a patrol soon. When I come back, I shall be entertaining the Aussies. I never knew that there were special Australian squadrons. I wonder why there are no special Canadian, South African or New Zealand squadrons. Or, to push the point home further, Irish, Welsh and Scottish squadrons!

There is a high-flying Hun on reconnaissance overhead. I can hear the faint "Archie" bursts, and a babble of voices outside. One thing is certain. I shan't bring him down. Neither will his greatest enemy, Major McCudden, V.C., who has shot down more than twenty of them on our side of the lines. Just imagine. The equivalent of a whole British squadron! He must be a master shot, like Mick. There's a rumour of his coming out again, so Grid says.

April 30.—I've got a lot to write about to-day. The Australians arrived yesterday afternoon from Bruay. This was the aerodrome I knew so well as a mechanic in April, 1917, when 16 Squadron was getting such a hiding from Richthofen's Circus.

The Aussies are a fine bunch of "Diggers." The C.O. is one McClaughry, not typically Australian. Rather short in stature, quiet of manner, and a teetotaller. The pilots strike me as being a full-out bunch. In particular, I liked the look of Cobby, "Bow" King and Watson—very full-out guys. If they can fight as well as they can knock back cocktails the Hun is in for a fine time. Richardson, Toronto's cocktail wizard, mixes what Grid has named the "74 Viper." By all accounts, it is the goods. A couple are guaranteed to blow your head off. These Aussies make them appear to be made of milk and water.

Forty-nine sat down to the repast in our 70 feet by 25 feet wooden hut. After the meal, the revelry went on until midnight. We're going to get on well with this squadron, I can see.

Did three shows yesterday and had several holes in my machine from "Archie." C and A Flights dropped thirty bombs on the Hun lines near Wyschaete and got "Archie" to beat the band. Nine machines returned well holed. I hate this damned "Archie." I feel that perhaps, after all, I may buy a packet from it. It appears to have an attraction for my machine.

The show of the day was done by Mick and his flight, accompanied by Glynn. Mick found ten enemy scouts floating around the Dickebusch area, a few miles south-east of Ypres. Having got above, he attacked them from the east, taking them completely by surprise. He put fifty rounds into one, going up as near as 20 yards to it. Mick makes no bones about pressing his attack home. The enemy burst into flames and quietly fell to pieces. Dolan, Mick's protégé, simultaneously cracked another scout. It fell to earth in pieces. Dolan is developing into a star turn at this game. Glynn observed a triplane which belonged to the party approaching from behind and trying to get above him. Glynn zoomed upwards, turned towards the tripe and had a go at him with both guns. He must have killed the pilot, for Mick and Dolan saw it dive vertically into the ground. "This fight was good arithmetic," says Mick.

"Dad" Roxburgh also had a good show with an L.V.G. two-seater. On returning from the big fight, Mick saw this machine near Dickebusch Lake, apparently carrying out artillery co-operation duties. He dived with his flight to attack it. Mick's gun jammed after firing a couple of rounds, so he pulled away. Dolan and Rox then dived hell for leather at it. Just when Rox was getting his bead on it, Bolo swung across his bows, putting him clean off, apart from frightening the life out of him. Dolan was diving too steeply, overshot, and missed his target badly.

The Hun pilot was flying his machine very well, turning it into a steep bank, so that his observer had the maximum field of fire at his disposal. "Dad," however, sneaked up under his tail. His first burst of fire put the gunner out of action. The pilot then spiralled downward, with his engine apparently off. "Dad" stuck to him, firing the whole time. At last, the machine crashed in a shell-hole.

"Dad" had followed it down to the ground, quite forgetting in his excitement that he was now a few miles over the lines. The noise of "Archie" and the crackle of machine guns soon brought home to him the necessity of making a bee-line for home. Fortunately, he had kept his bearings. Looking west, he saw a red Very light (in this case, a signal from the leader to re-form) dropping gently in the distance. After a thrilling, dodging, zigzag run, he eventually joined up with Mick and Bolo, and he realised how lucky he had been to get away with it.

His machine, on landing, was found to have a fair-size hole in the left lower plane, a bullet hole in the main spar of the upper plane, the bomb lever nearly shot away, and three bullet holes in the fuselage. The old S.E. is as strong as a lion. Everyone has great confidence in it, which is of great importance to morale.

Roxburgh pushed out a champagne boat on the strength of

this show. Everyone drank to the toast: "Here's to your health, Dad. May you have many more such experiences." The champagne was obviously appreciated. I wonder if I am missing much by being a teetotaller.

A most extraordinary thing happened last night to Zulu Savage. Just about dusk he was returning from a patrol, when suddenly some of the mechanics saw his machine dip its nose at about 200 feet and dive straight into a field adjoining the aerodrome.

He was pulled out of the wreckage unconscious, and has been taken to a hospital between here and St. Omer. The doctors think he must have fainted, for he is not wounded. I've been to see him this afternoon. He says he remembers nothing about the crash. He is not badly cut about, and says his sorest spot is his right buttock.

So Begbie was to be the first death and Zulu the first injured pilot. I wonder who will be the first to be wounded, and the next to be killed. Dismal conjectures though they may appear, I am in no way morbid. I know someone has to die next. I'm just wondering who it may be. I have no feeling that it is going to be me. But who knows? What I hate is the thought of being taken prisoner. Peter can open his Golden Gates—but not the Kaiser. How we hate his guts! He should hear us paying our respects to him as we drink our morning tea before the dawn patrols. What blasphemies!

Dolan did another star turn to-day. Mick will have to look to his laurels. Skeddon and I were looking for Huns, Ypres way, in the afternoon, when we noticed a fight going on over Poperinghe. By the time we got down from 18,000 feet to the scene of action the Hun had been shot down. Dolan was circling round and round him. Great show!

Dolan, Mick and Split-pins took a trailer out to bring the machine in. When they got to it, the Huns were shelling the area with mustard gas. This did not deter them. With the aid of a few mechanics and some Tommies, they got it on the trailer. As they were drawing away, the enemy got a direct hit on the trailer, completely messing the party up. Two of the Tommies were killed, but none of the mechanics. The trailer had been blown to glory. The lorry with the mechanics in it was untouched and got safely away, the driver putting up a good show.

Dolan is developing into a corker. He has no fear. He goes, like Grid, bald-headed for every Hun he sees. If he doesn't meet with any bad luck, he will soon be one of our aces.

Builders of the Tradition

The Squadron has fifteen Huns to its credit to date. Not bad going for a new Squadron. Fifteen to one is good arithmetic. I wish I could claim a little honour in this fine record.

May 7.—My poor old diary has been sadly neglected the past few days. Yet much has happened of interest in the squadron. No luck for me, though. I have yet to kill my first Hun.

I'm beginning to get a little depressed with my shooting. I have fired at sixteen Huns to date, and they are all still alive! I have always flattered myself on being a good shot too. In fact, I know I am.

I've had a long talk with Mick about it. He thinks I am allowing too much for deflection. That is, I'm aiming too much in front of the enemy. He has advised me to do a slight traverse; to sight about 5 yards in front of the engine, then to fire and, while firing, to bring the sight back as far as the pilot, and then to push it forward again. If I do this, he says, I can't help but hit the machine somewhere. I must say it sounds reasonable enough. This is what he says he did at first. With experience, he says, I'll get accustomed to making the correct allowance for the enemy's speed and direction instinctively.

This talk with Mick has bucked me up no end. Let's hope I will benefit by his advice. Skeddon was also listening to Mick's talk. Like me, he is a little weary of seeing bullets "appear" to be hitting their mark, but nothing happening. To-morrow, we are going to test Mick's instructions on the first Hun we see. The one who gets the first Hun in flames is to pay the other 100 francs. So here's hoping!

Since I wrote last, the Aussies have lost three pilots, two of whom collided in a dogfight. Against this loss, they have destroyed two. Poor arithmetic, I admit. Cobby got the two Albatrosses.

Our squadron has increased its total by four in the meantime. On the 3rd, Mick's flight bagged an L.V.G., while on the following day Mick again led his flight with such skill that three highly-camouflaged triplanes were sent spinning into the ground in the vicinity of Zillebecke Lake, near Ypres. This is good arithmetic!

The day before yesterday, all our "Bohunks" from "God's Country"—Skeddon, Clements, Richardson and Russell—went to see their tough-guy pals who are holding the Vimy Ridge with lead bullets and cold steel. They all came back with the same idea: "Thank God we're in the Air Force!" A true sentiment, O King! Our war is a picnic compared with the infantry. Really, air fighting is just a dangerous game, not war at all. At least, that is how I feel about it at the moment. Perhaps I'm speaking too soon. Skeddon agrees.

A replacement for Zulu has arrived. His name is Barton. He seems a nice fellow, if rather quiet. Zulu's crash has now been solved. He was wounded in the right buttock, from which a bullet has been extracted. No wonder that he fainted or that his right buttock was so painful. He has now left for the base, for transfer to England. Everyone is sorry he is gone, because he was so well liked. I hope to meet him one day in Pretoria. Fancy coming all that way to receive a shot in his bottom! South Africans have proved, equally with their brother Colonials, their loyalty to the Mother Country.

We have had air raids in the vicinity most nights. A few minutes ago—it is now 11.15 p.m.—a Gotha flew slap-bang over our huts at about 300 feet. We could see the observer leaning over the side. A little distance away from here there is a searchlight battery. The Hun made for it, and the observer shot into the beam, compelling the operator to shut up shop. It was very funny. I don't think he saw our aerodrome, as he passed directly overhead.

8

MAY 8.—The Squadron is in mourning, but our spirits have not dropped. Every squadron must expect setbacks. We are experiencing one to-day. There were four vacant chairs at dinner to-night, those of Skeddon, Bright, Stuart-Smith and Piggott. Although they were not with us as of old, we felt that they were there in spirit, and so we had a beano in their memory. I quite agree with Grid. It is the only thing to do to keep the morale of the squadron up. Besides, we have all agreed that it shall be so. We put their field boots and their caps in their places, and then drank to their future happiness.

The death of Skeddon is a terrible blow to me. I've been crying at intervals all day. But I've had my revenge. The whole tragic story can best be recorded if I start from the moment I got up this morning. At 6.30 a.m. Butler, our batman, called Skeddon and me. C Flight was to leave the ground an hour later. I was to lead my first patrol.

After having a cold sponge, we strolled across to the mess for a little breakfast. We have decided it is not good to fly on an empty stomach. We don't feel so fit without any food within. About seven o'clock we got into our flying kit, Skeddon not forgetting to wear the lucky charm which his lady friend in Toronto had given to him. We were off the ground at 7.15 a.m. B Flight had taken off ten minutes before. Both flights carried the quota of bombs which we had been ordered to drop on Menin. It was my intention to climb steadily as far as Ypres, which I had hoped to pass at an altitude of 15,000 feet, and then fly east, using the Menin road as my guide and dropping my eggs over the objective.

When I got to Ypres, I was still only a few feet above 11,000 feet, so I decided to climb to the requisite 15,000 before crossing. I continued climbing in the direction of Houlthulst Forest, all the time searching the sky eastwards for machines.

Suddenly I spotted two formations, one of six and the other of ten. The six I recognised as B Flight, and the ten as enemy triplanes. B Flight was at about 16,000 feet, halfway between

95

Ypres and Menin. The Huns were a couple of thousand feet higher, over Menin, making for Ypres.

"Young is for it," I said to myself. I wondered if he had seen the enemy. I felt he must have. Then my confidence wavered. A terrible feeling of helplessness came over me. How could I warn him? I was three miles away. Instinctively, I thought of shouting. Then I realised the childishness of the thought. I felt I must do something quickly. I fired as many red lights as I had. Giles, Skeddon and Birch did the same, but Young did not alter course. He was making straight for the enemy. It was a terrible sight. There was I, a helpless spectator of a cruel play which was about to be enacted, the killing of friends.

The Hun leader was very clever. He led his flight southwards, going away at right angles from Young. I think he was afraid Young had seen him and that he would rightly turn round, make for our lines, and get away. So he encouraged him to continue his eastern flight. I could almost sense the devil's thoughts. I ordered my flight to drop their bombs, and pointed the nose of my machine in the direction of Menin, climbing as steeply as I could.

When Young got over Menin, he dropped his eggs, then turned round and made for Ypres. As soon as he did this, the Hun leader also turned round. His flight came hell for leather towards Ypres to cut Young off. Young was now at 18,000 feet, the Huns at 19,000 feet, and my flight 3,000 lower. I decided to take my flight below the impending fight in order to help push off any stray Huns who might drop out of the battle above. It was a silly thing to do, really, but I thought there was every chance that a B Flight machine might come down below the fight with a Hun on its tail. We could have knocked him off.

The triplanes cut off the S.Es. over Gheluvelt, and the unequal contest started immediately, the Hun leader firing on Kiddie. Kiddie turned under him and avoided his bullets. The fight soon developed into the usual dogfight. It was a grim business we witnessed. There we were beneath the battle, just circling round and round, looking upwards at our pals fighting for their lives. We could do nothing to help. Nothing! Nothing but look on in a state of anger and helplessness. It was a terrible feeling. May I never have to endure it again. I would prefer a dozen Huns on my tail, any time of the day.

Within a minute of the start of the fight we saw an S.E. come hurtling down, smoking badly, before bursting into flames. It passed quite near me, but owing to the smoke I could not recognise the number on its nose. I know now it was poor old

SOME FAMOUS FLYERS

From Top Left: General Sir Pierre Van Ryneveld; Lt. A. P. F. Rhys-Davids; Air Marshal Sir Charles Longcroft; Capt. Albert Ball, V.C. (*centre*); F/Lt. S. M. Kinkead; Col. Keith Caldwell; Col. Louis Strange.

The S.E. 5—the Spitfire of World War I.

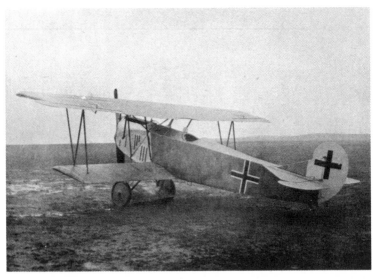

The Fokker DVII—the Messerschmitt of World War I.

Stuart-Smith. A little later on, another S.E. passed down, burning fiercely. It was Bright. By God, it was a grim sight! Then an S.E. came spinning through, with a tripe following.

"This is my chance," I said as I saw the enemy pass below us. I made a dive after him. So did the others. I had not dived for more than a few seconds when I felt my machine vibrating badly and the engine over-revving. I tried to pull my throttle back. It was jammed tight at full bore. I had to pull out gently, and as I did so, I saw Skeddon and Giles whizz past after the Hun, firing for all they were worth.

The Hun, hearing the machine guns behind him, left the S.E. 5 and dived away east. The S.E. came out of the spin at about 2,000 feet, then glided towards our lines. We saw him crash in the trenches. It was dear old Piggott. Whether his machine crashed on the enemy's lines or on ours we are not sure. But it was a real smasher. We have little hope of his being alive. As we have no news of him, he is no doubt a goner.

After we had crossed our lines we saw two S.Es. also crossing, but independently. They were in a hurry. One was Young, who was so badly shot about that he had to land at Marie Capelle, and the other Kiddie, who was the only member of B Flight to get back to our aerodrome. You should have seen his machine. I didn't know the Huns had so many bullets left.

God! What a grim business this war is.

And now to the death of my partner and pal.

When C Flight crossed the line, we re-formed. As my throttle was still frozen, I decided to fly up and down the lines until the patrol time was up. I made for home at last and we got back at 8.35 a.m.

When we reached the aerodrome, Skeddon cheerfully chucked his usual half-roll on top of a loop, but as he did so both his wings collapsed. His machine went spinning into the ground, making contact almost in the middle of our aerodrome. On touching ground it burst into flames. And that was the end of one of the whitest and bravest fellows I have met, a real pal and a gentleman to his finger tips. A true son of Canada. May his soul rest in peace, and may God give me power to avenge his death. I'll do my best, Skeddon, old lad! I've started already. To-night I destroyed my first enemy—thank God, in flames.

When I saw Skeddon's machine burning, I felt sick in my stomach. I knew that there was no hope. It was a terrible moment when I realised my pal was in there, burning. Who can blame me for feeling not only physically sick, but mentally cowardly? I decided I could not land on the aerodrome to taxi past the roasting corpse of my hut companion. So I flew on to Clamarais South.

In order to land there, I had to switch off. I could not pull my throttle back, and this worried me. I knew the cylinders were being flooded with petrol and that, should I need to switch on again, the engine might catch fire. Gliding in to land, I saw I was undershooting. I had no option but to switch on. As soon as I did so, there was a terrific bang. The noise so frightened me that it put the finishing touch to my already strained nerves. I completely lost my sense of judgment. A few minutes later, I was being helped out of my inverted aeroplane, the mechanics of No. 1 Squadron kindly lifting the fuselage to make it easier for me to crawl out. I was furious. Borrowing a car, I drove swiftly back to my squadron. Yes! Skeddon was dead. Kiddie and the others confirmed the death of Stuart-Smith, Bright and Piggott. The Huns had given us a hiding.

My blood boiled. My soul cried for revenge. In despair, I got permission to borrow Birch's machine. I immediately ordered Flight-Sergeant Hobbs to get it bombed up and ready for action.

Knowing this would take a quarter of an hour, I ate a little more breakfast. Then I proceeded to my hut, where I had a damned good cry. I took care that no one knew I was being so childish by locking the door. With every sob, my soul cried out for revenge and by the time I was finished, I felt I could murder every German without a qualm.

Once in the air I made a beeline, regardless of gaining height, for Bailleul—the nearest part of the enemy's line. Diving at the Hun trenches, I dropped my bombs. I hope I killed someone.

Coming back to our lines I climbed to 15,000 feet, crossing the line at Ypres, and made a tour via Menin, Tourcoing, Lille, Armentières, and back to Bailleul. But not a single Hun could I see. I was determined to kill or be killed. I was out to avenge Skeddon and my other comrades. But there was nothing doing, either way, and this angered me. I became desperate, and decided to go down low and do some ground-strafing. Near Kemmel I found a large number of Huns in trenches without dugouts, and some in shell-holes. I used up my ammunition on them, and I could see them wasting a little on me in return.

On my way back I thought of Skeddon, the hum of the engine encouraging my mind to ruminate. All the happy incidents in one another's company—and they were many—came back to me. I cried copiously.

Builders of the Tradition

After lunch, quiet and restrained, Grid gave us a cheerful little speech. He advised us to "liven up," and said our comrades who were gone would not wish us to mope, but to go and knock hell out of the sods, the Hunnerinoes. Most of us acted on his advice, and went up in the afternoon. We came across a few Albatross and Phalz. They were all in a yellow mood and would not fight, so we came back empty-handed. We poured our bullets into the trenches between Bailleul and Kemmel Hill on the way home, but everything seemed disheartening to me.

After landing, Giles and I started to pack Skeddon's effects. We had to read his correspondence (Skeddon and I had agreed to do this for each other in case of death). Both of us had tears in our eyes as we read the proud letters from the parents who were now bereaved of their only son.

The letters from Skeddon's mother will haunt me in my sleep to-night—proud letters encouraging him to do his duty, and ending: "God bless you and keep you." Similar letters are now on the way here, and no doubt she is writing such another at this moment—too late. Oh, dear! Too late.

The packing upset me so much that after tea, although very weary, I went up again. Thank God I did. At 6.25 p.m. I spotted a two-seater coming towards Bailleul from the direction of Armentières at about 4,000 feet. I was then at 3,000 feet, over Hazebrouck. The sun was behind me, nice and large. I climbed quickly to 8,000 feet towards Merville, then back towards Bailleul. Hun "Archie" warned the enemy of my approach by sending up a series of puffs. Apparently, he did not see it. It would not have mattered if he had done. I had made up my mind to get him, even if I had to ram the sod.

I got up to point-blank range before firing. Then I let him have it. Almost at once he commenced smoking. There was a faint glow. Then a lovely bonfire as he went earthwards. I followed him down to the ground, firing all my bullets at him. I then flew round him as he burned fiercely on the ground near Nieppe. I knew the enemy in the vicinity were firing hard at me. I did not care. My soul was satisfied. It was a grand sight to see that Hun burning. I had had my revenge.

Flying over our trenches, I could see our troops waving frantically. I waved back joyfully. They were not half as happy as I. I had destroyed my first Hun, in revenge for my pals, and it was a great feeling.

As I was late in returning, Cairns and most of the Flight were on the aerodrome, waiting for me. They said they thought I was a goner. Walking from the aerodrome to my hut, I passed the covered tender where Skeddon's body lay. I peeped in. All I could see was an army blanket, but it was enough for me. I went straight to bed and slept until dinner-time.

Now I am feeling quite refreshed. Writing alone in my hut, without interruption from Skeddon, I have an ache in my heart and a feeling of loneliness which is indescribable. For the first time in my life, something has passed out of my life, leaving a void too painful to describe.

I have often seen comrades killed and a great sadness has come over me, for I am very emotional; but never previously have I experienced this awful feeling of helplessness. It has brought the meaning of war nearer to me.

No. 1 Squadron lost two machines to-day and had one pilot wounded. So did the Aussies. The Huns have had a profitable day.

It is now 11.30 p.m. Some of the tough lads from both squadrons are still revelling in the mess. More power to their elbows. I'm positive it's the only way to keep one's morale.

May 9.—Piggott is safe. We had a phone message from Van Ryneveld early this morning to say he had been rescued by some Australian Tommies and was safe in their keeping. Damn fine show.

There can be no hope for Stuart-Smith and Bright unless a miracle happens. Yet many miracles have happened in this war. Even my war history to date is not exactly what one would call ordinary. Ten aeroplane crashes and twenty-one months of France without a scratch, if not exactly a miracle, is some near relation to it.

Skeddon was buried this afternoon at Ebblinghem Cemetery, not far from here. It was very difficult to realise that that small bundle wrapped in the brown blanket was the remains of my fighting partner and hut companion. I made a vow, as I looked down into his grave, that I would never rest contented until I had destroyed half a dozen Huns. May God give me strength to do so.

Giles has come into my hut in place of Skeddon. I am delighted, for I am very fond of him. He is so sound. I mean he is steady and reliable, not a half-wit (as is usually the case when people say so-and-so is "sound"). He has a very subtle sense of humour and loves a joke. Just the type of fellow I can get on with.

Did three patrols to-day. Couldn't get near any Huns. Neither could Mick nor anyone else. They appear to have the breeze-up for some reason, although they ought not to have after their victories yesterday. Perhaps 20 Squadron's wonderful show took the wind out of their sails. Van Ryneveld told us this morning that the Bristol fighters of this squadron had destroyed eight triplanes yesterday. No. 20 is a first-class squadron, commanded by Johnson, a South African from the Cape.

I don't know what we should do in this war without a gramophone. Ours is kept going at full pressure all the time. I love the music of "Danny Boy."

May 12.—Poor old Dolan is missing, probably dead. We have had our revenge. Six Huns out of a formation of eight will be very lucky if they eat any more sausages.

The weather up to four o'clock had been dud. At 5.30 p.m. an order came through for a squadron patrol. We were flying in three layers, about half a mile apart. Mick was leading A Flight, the lowest and foremost formation. At 6.15 he spotted a formation of eight Huns, Albatross and Pfalz. He stalked them for a quarter of an hour in his inimitable manner, gaining height until he got them manœuvred into a favourable position for attack. We were at 13,000 feet and the Huns at about 11,000 feet over Wulverghem, near Ploegstreet Wood, when he gave his signal to attack. Our flight was some distance away when I saw him start to dive. Without waiting for Cairns to give his signal, I pushed off with Giles to join in the fun.

When I got down to the level of the engagement I could see pieces of aeroplane floating about in the air. Yellow pieces, black pieces, red pieces and silver pieces. "Splendid!" I said to myself. "It's a Hun." Then I saw some brown pieces. I shuddered. I thought an S.E. had collided with a Hun. I was relieved to hear later that this was not the case. Mick had cracked a Hun, who had side-slipped into a companion. It was a grim fight.

The whole of the squadron was in the battle in a flash and I first picked out Mick tickling a Pfalz's tail. He went spinning down immediately and crashed. Then I saw an Albatross on Roxburgh's tail, pumping lead at him for all he was worth. I sneaked behind him and opened fire at about 25 yards' range. My tracer bullets appeared to splash around his cockpit. Immediately, the machine was pulled up almost vertically. I was not prepared for this manœuvre and nearly collided with him. For a moment I was frightened. The Hun was seen to get on its back, leaving the field of battle spinning in an inverted position. I did not see him again.

While I was looking for him, I suddenly saw Dolan go spinning past to crash near Wulverghem. Simultaneously, a yellow Albatross gave me a packet to get on with. With the arrival of his bullets I was smothered in liquid. "My God!" I thought. "He's got my petrol tank. I shall be on fire at any moment now." I felt for my revolver, which I always carry for such an emergency. No roasting alive for me, boys, if I can help it. Nevertheless, I really think it is the ideal way for an airman to die, if he must die. It can't be so painful as it looks. I bet you're asphyxiated before you know where you are. Let's hope so, anyway!

As soon as I thought of the petrol I dived westwards, at the same time turning off the taps and switching off the engine. After a few minutes my propeller stopped. "My God! I'm in for it this time," I said aloud, thinking the Hun was still behind me. Luckily, he wasn't. Cairns had pushed him off.

I landed eventually at Proven Aerodrome, where there was a French squadron of Breguets. There was a bullet in my radiator and my engine had seized. The French were very charming, but as no one could speak English and I couldn't speak their lingo, we had to show our mutual respect and love for each other by smiling, gesticulating, laughing loudly and drinking citron and red wine; by clinking glasses, and shouting: "*L'Entente Cordiale! Vive la France et l'Angleterre!*" Toasts always go down well with our Froggy friends. One fellow, in very broken English, said: "God save the King!"

I phoned Grid and told him where I was. He promised to send his car to fetch me at once.

I got back to Clamarais about midnight, feeling very hungry. Our Squadron was revelling with No. 1 at their mess. My appearance brought forth much whooping and halloing. I was carried shoulder high round the mess to the strains of "Men of Harlech" on the gramophone. Rox then thumped the piano, while the rest of the company sang themselves hoarse. Wine was flowing freely. C. C. Clarke, Owen and Clayson were very full-out, while our lads showed no trace of morbidness.

The loss of Dolan is a severe blow to us. He was a very full-out guy, and very popular. Only yesterday he shot down his sixth Hun, which is good going for a beginner. I'm afraid he is killed. He looked dead enough to me by the way his machine was going down. The spin was very fast. Damned bad luck. He was a bosom pal of Grid and Mick, so I expect to see some Hun feathers flying about to-morrow, if they can find any.

This fight was the most successful the Squadron has had so far. Mick bagged three; Young, Giles and Roxburgh one each.

This is Giles's first victory. He is very bucked about it. When we were getting ready for the patrol, he told me that he was feeling a little bloodthirsty and wanted to avenge Skeddon. There is no doubt that the spirit of revenge should be cultivated during a war. It helps the fighter to put a little more ginger into his fighting. "Kill or be killed" is a good motto. I hate half-measures. Nothing annoys me more than to watch pilots going half-hearted at their enemies. If a man considers the moment is not propitious, he should wait until it is. Then, having decided on the moment, he should go all out for his objective. To-night, I watched one S.E.—the same pilot who got a telling-off from Mick the other day for leaving his formation—firing at a distance of between 200 and 300 yards. Hopeless!

Roxburgh's fight was a thrilling little affair. As I was not engaged at the time, I watched most of it. Rox had singled out a brownish-looking Pfalz. He was going down on it at a flattish angle when Young with his flight dashed past and engaged the Hun first. Young put paid to its account with a short burst, not opening fire until he was right on the poor old Hun's tail. I could see he was determined to wipe out a little of his account with them. Although he is not a cunning patrol leader like Mick, Young is full of guts. As an individual fighter, he is most determined. I cannot make out why he doesn't put a little more cunning into his leadership, though. Perhaps he doesn't see the Huns soon enough. This is also a weakness of Cairns.

Well, to come back to Rox. After Young had whizzed past him, he made a left-hand climbing turn. Two Pfalz were approaching him, head on. He saw them just in time, pushed his nose down and went underneath. Their wheels just missed his top planes. God, it was a near shave.

No sooner was he clear of them than he made a vertical zoom to gain height, turned round and gave chase. Continuing to climb he was soon above them in an attacking position. The Huns did not appear to see him. I think they were watching other S.Es. ahead of them. Old Rox made full use of their carelessness. He approached to within 70 yards before opening fire at the nearest to him. His bullets must have sped unpleasantly near, for the Pfalz immediately spun down a few hundred feet before flattening out. Rox then concentrated on his other pal, getting within 50 yards before firing. No sooner had his tracers flashed from his guns than the Hun pulled up vertically and went down out of control.

Rox tells me he followed the Hun down for some distance.

Tiger Squadron

He went so close to him at times that he could see the pilot collapsed in his cockpit. No doubt he was dead, for he was seen to crash.

This fight was indeed the goods. I hope we'll have such another soon. The more dead Huns, the sooner the Peace—and the sooner the nights in dear old Piccadilly. Poor old Dolan! Another pal to avenge.

The fighting was at about 120 m.p.h. When diving it went up to 180 m.p.h.

May 13.—This part of France is a little more undulating than the area we mostly fly over. The town of Cassel nearby is situated on the top of a quite decent-sized hill. General Plumer's staff can actually see a bit of the Great War from there with the aid of binoculars. It must be thrilling for the A.D.Cs.! Plumer is the most popular general in France with the troops, who have tremendous confidence in him. His admirers claim he has never lost a battle. General Harrington, Plumer's chief of staff, is reputed to have more than the ordinary allotment of grey matter.

Our brigade comes under Plumer's Second Army. Whenever anyone gets a decoration, Plumer sends him a vellum parchment, congratulating him.

I cannot get the idea out of my head that decorations, like Naval prize-money, are quite wrong in principle. To accept that a Britisher at war requires an incentive in the form of hard cash or decorations to do his duty passes my understanding. The necessity for such prizes is as fallacious and wrong as the system which ties a man to a gate or a gun wheel. Neither achieves the object which is intended. Both do much harm. The Oriental barbarity of No. 1 field punishment breeds hatred and hardens the soul. The award of decorations breeds that cankerous, villifying germ, jealousy.

Whenever I think of decorations, I cannot help thinking of Ginger Mitchell, our C.O., and the dear old Sergeant-Major. This case will always remain a classic to me. They both received the Military Cross in the same *Gazette* notice. Major W. S. Mitchell had a great war flying record. The Sergeant-Major had none!

Three new lads have joined the Squadron: Battell, Sifton and Nixon. They are all under nineteen years of age. Battell ("Bats") is replacing Skeddon, so Giles and I have decided to have him in our hut. He is a very charming little fellow who looks about fifteen. A Canadian by birth, he hails from Moose Jaw, wherever that is. He has informed us already that he has a sweetheart in

Builders of the Tradition

Saskatchewan. We have warned him he won't get much time to think about her when he gets a Hun on his tail! Nixon ("Nicky") is also posted to our flight. A very likeable boy.

Mick and his flight had an amusing five minutes this morning. They were over Merville at 5,000 feet, with not a Hun in sight. Suddenly, a two-seater popped out of the clouds, plumb in front of them. They were so amazed by its unexpected appearance that before anyone had thought of firing, the old Hun had popped back into the clouds again.

Mick noticed the direction, however, and so flew along underneath. In a minute or two, out popped the Hun. This time all the lads, who had their top gun down ready, poured lead into him. Signal rockets must have been set alight, for a peculiar coloured smoke volumed out from the rear cockpit. Soon the observer was seen throwing various coloured lights overboard. Mick and his hounds thought the lad was on fire. When they realised that he wasn't, they were too late to catch him. He had wasted no time in diving hell for leather towards his Fatherland.

Later they trapped two Albatrosses and used up all their ammunition on them, failing to kill either. Mick was furious with himself. Clem and Howe (Swazi) haven't stopped laughing yet.

Clem has bet Giles and me 5 francs each that he will get a Hun before Saturday. To-day is Monday, but I wouldn't have known it unless Clem had told me. We lose all count of days or dates out here. One day is like another. Sleep, food, fly and fight is the order of the day. Occasionally we vary the routine by a nocturnal visit to St. Omer, to enjoy a little of the night life of this gay city. It is not at all a bad war. What more does a boy of twenty want? This is indeed Life, with a capital "L."

May 17.—Another eventful day in the life of the squadron. This morning Nixon was shot down in flames on his first flight over the lines. This afternoon Barton was killed by "Archie." The devils got a direct hit on him at 7,000 feet. His machine dropped to earth in pieces. And this evening Russell crashed badly on the aerodrome. He has gone to hospital.

Some time to-day, one of the new members, who has been with the squadron only three days, turned yellow. He has been sent back to England. Why the hell he wasn't sent to the trenches or shot, I don't know. He went sobbing to Grid that he couldn't do the job. That he had nerves. And he has not even been over the lines! He'll now become an instructor or a staff officer and get promoted, I suppose.

Tiger Squadron

Grid and Mick were speechless. Mick had the fellow's wings torn from his tunic.

As I look out through the door of my hut at the dusky sky, it seems to be in keeping with my feelings. It is nine-tenths covered by big, jet-black, angry-looking clouds; the remainder being a streak of lightish blue, with a slight tinge of gold. Although depressed and annoyed, I can still see there is a silver lining.

In spite of our losses, our balance sheet shows a little credit, thank God, on the day's working. Mick destroyed an Albatross two-seater and a single-seater in flames, while I bagged my second Hun—a silver Hanover two-seater—also in flames.

Nixon's end was a sad affair. Terribly keen to do his first show, he implored me to ask Cairns if he could come up with C Flight on our 8.30 show. Cairns agreed, and asked me to look after him. I lent him my machine, which had a fine engine and a black cat as a mascot (why, I don't know, for I am not in the least superstitious). I borrowed Swazi's machine.

Before leaving the ground, I told young Nixon several times to keep with me if we got into a scrap. On no account must he dive away from a Hun if he found one on his tail, but put his machine into a vertical bank and keep circling. I promised to try to get the Hun away from him. He nervously promised to obey my instructions, but like so many other new pilots he forgot all about his instructions as soon as he heard the staccato bark of the Spandau guns behind him.

At 9.30 we were over Merville at 8,000 feet. A silly old greenish-black Albatross two-seater came meandering around. While the others were rubbing their eyes, I got under his tail and gave him a lively tickling up. He was last seen making vertical dives alternated by monstrous zooms—either completely out of control or a grand bluffer. Birch followed him down to 4,000 feet. He said he was still doing his stuff when he last saw him, near the ground.

As soon as Cairns saw the Hun go down, he gave the signal to re-form by firing a red light and waggling his wings. Having re-formed, we flew back towards our lines, climbing steeply. This was a good idea. Archie was busily plastering us, particularly Birch, who was a few thousand feet below and all alone. Also, there was a suspicious-looking formation a few miles to the south.

Having crossed our lines, Cairns climbed to 10,000 feet, then made off in the direction of the formation, which was now about a mile away, flying up from the direction of Bethune. Since they were not being "Archied," I concluded they were Huns and was

106

glad to notice they were a few hundred feet below us. Below and a little in front of the formation were two two-seaters, obviously Hanovers. "Aha!" I said. "Decoys!" I quickly and earnestly prayed Cairns would not buy the pup. My prayer was answered, sinner that I am.

At 9.15 Cairns gave the signal to attack. I went up alongside Nixon, who was just in front of me, waggled my wings and waved to him. He waggled his wings and waved back. I then got in front of him and led him into the fray.

The enemies were Pfalz scouts, well-flown and most aggressive. Quite a change to find Huns who will fight, I thought. I picked out a light-green fellow, who was sneaking away from the battle and climbing—an old trick of the experienced fighter to get above his opponents unseen and attack them with surprise and tactical advantage. Since he was well on his own, I thought this would be a good opportunity to give Nicky a chance to draw his first blood. I fired a few shots at him, then zoomed up to watch Nicky have a go.

What the devil actually happened, I don't know; but when I had finished my zoom and had steadied myself to look for Nicky on the Hun's tail, I saw to my horror quite the reverse picture. The Hun was pumping lead into Nicky, who was diving in a straight line away from him. Before I could help, my dear old machine with my mascot and poor old Nicky was enveloped in flames. Why have we no parachutes, for God's sake?

A fine fellow had gone west through forgetting the golden rule of air fighting: "Never dive away if a Hun is on your tail. Turn, old boy. Turn!"

It is amazing how beginners fail to carry out these very simple instructions. When new pilots arrive, we always give them about a week to a fortnight's practice on our side of the lines, in order to get them used to the country. Every day and almost all day, we drum into them that old maxim about never diving from the Hun. Yet they still do it. It is very sad.

I chased the fellow who got Nicky, but he dived away below the fight, so I pulled out when I got to the level, zoomed up and joined in the maul. First, a green-and-black gentleman and I had a little fiery argument. Next, I disputed with a yellow-and-black gent. Finally, I tangled with a silver Hanover which had foolishly come to join in the fun. This poor hoot was easy money, and I made no mistake about him. I think I must have conked the pilot, for he went into a vertical dive immediately after my first burst, which was from under his tail at a range of about 50 yards. A little later, smoke started coming out of the fuselage, and, within a few seconds his doom was sealed. To see even an enemy machine in flames is a horrible sight; though, at the time, it gave me great satisfaction, since I felt it was but a tooth for a tooth.

Mick, who gets most of his Huns in flames, is getting very peculiar over the business. Whenever he sends one down in flames he comes dancing into the mess, whooping and halloing: "Flamerinoes, boys! Sizzle, sizzle, wonk!" Then, at great length, he tries to describe the feelings of the poor old Hun by going into the minutest details. Having finished in a frenzy of fiendish glee, he will turn to one of us and say, laughing: "That's what will happen to you on the next patrol, my lad." And we all roar with laughter. Grid usually gets in the last word by telling him that, last night, he dreamt he saw him hanging to the tail skid of his machine while it floated gently earthwards, burning fiercely, and that circling him was a circle of jeering Huns.

Some time later you will see Mick in a gloomy mood, sitting with his elbows resting on his knees and his clenched hands supporting his chin. Ask him what he is thinking about, and he will usually answer: "That damned Hun in flames." I think he is getting obsessed with this form of death. It is getting on his nerves. Occasionally he will say: "Why the hell haven't we got parachutes?"

Yesterday, Mick got a silver-and-black Pfalz, which broke up in the air. Swazi says the fuselage went down minus wings. Gee! What a death! There is no doubt that this flying game has introduced a few new types of grim passings out of this life. Cold sweat comes out on my forehead when I think of some of them. I am prepared to believe in the Biblical challenge, "O, grave, where is thy victory?" but not "O death, where is thy sting?" Licking flames have a nasty sting, I'm prepared to believe. Even going earthwards without wings cannot be so cheerful.

Van Ryneveld told us to-day that a captured German had stated he knew we were at Clamarais with 4 Australian Squadron, and that we had S.Es. with certain markings. He also thought we were a circus commanded by McCudden (evidently referring to Mick). This speaks well for our squadron and its successes in air fighting. That's the stuff to give 'em.

Giles and I have been doing extra patrols every day, trying to catch high-flying machines. No luck, though.

Huns do a lot of night bombing around here. They may be looking for us.

Builders of the Tradition

New pilots, Stewart and Batstone, arrived during the past few days. Both went to A Flight. Mick has been testing their offensive spirit by relating gruesome stories of Huns going down in flames, and so on. If they laugh heartily, or appear to get a kick out of the story, he decides they are all right. If they assume a slightly sickly appearance when they smile, he's suspicious. One of these fellows nearly vomited.

Had a long letter from my mother, chiefly about what Lloyd George had said. Also, that they had specially mentioned my name during the weekly prayer meeting at Capel Mair. Why this distinction, I cannot think, unless they realise my soul can do with a little support, for I am well able to look after myself physically. I'm sure not all the prayers in the world would keep Udet—the crack German airman who is now reported to be working on our front—off my tail once I let him get on it.

I'm told it is a big mistake to keep a diary. Personally, I like writing. It amuses me.

9

MAY 18.—Mick shot down his fortieth Hun yesterday. I don't think anyone will ever nail him. He's cunning and more wily than a hungry Welsh fox, and knows more tricks than a menagerie of monkeys. As for guts—salute!

Grid never worries about tactics or orders. Where the enemy is, there goes Grid. Without any disrespect to all the wonderful fellows I have met so far in this war, I feel I must hand the palm to Grid for individual valour. It is prodigious, and impossible adequately to describe. All our squadron patrols which he leads are nightmares. He frightens us as much as we frighten the Huns. The Hun, by the way, has been very gutless of late. Day after day, we patrol far over his lines. The further over we go, the further east his fighters go. Can't make them fight at any price. I often wonder if they are trying to make us run out of petrol.

It is very annoying to spot the devils and not be able to make them scrap. They've obviously got the wind-up about something. The result of this listlessness on their part is to encourage us to shoot down the two-seaters who are co-operating with Fritz on the ground. These are the very people they are supposed to protect! I feel sorry for those fat old Huns on the line. They are to be found, usually at about 5,000 feet, above territory where a battery shoot is taking place and blissfully ignorant of the presence of a formation of S.Es. up there at 18,000 feet and keeping an eagle eye on them until the moment when they will come tumbling down in a series of side-slips and dives in a mad race to be the first to get their tracer bullets into the bellies of the Huns. Poor devils! Fated to be killed because their "protectors" are shirking their duty.

Mick is a wizard at that game. We often practise that dropping game after patrols.

We return to our aerodrome at 18,000 feet. Then the flight commander gives the signal to drop. In a second, all the machines are tumbling earthwards and the first machine to fly low over the sheds wins. It is a grand sight to see the squadron coming down in this fashion. The mechanics love it. As a matter of fact, we really do it as much for their benefit as for our practice. They are such damn fine fellows, and they don't get much kick out of the war. It is just a war of hard work to them, but they are mighty good about it.

There is no doubt that as a squadron, we are a terribly happy family. It's a unit of hundred per cent. effort. Everyone does his damnedest to pull his full weight. One can do no more. The fact that one pilot is more successful than another doesn't matter. It is the honour of 74 Squadron that looms largest in our minds. Grid sets the example. We follow. Giles and I have been suspicious for some time that Grid and Mick occasionally shoot down a Hun and then give the credit to a junior member of the patrol, to encourage him to greater efforts. Our suspicions are founded on observation. One cannot but feel proud to fight under such fellows. To die while following them would be an honour; that is the spirit of 74 Squadron. We've been nicknamed the Tiger Squadron!

Mick came back in a furious mood from a patrol this morning. He had taken Howe out on a private war to see if he could help him get a Hun. At 11.20 a.m. he spotted half a dozen Albatrosses flying in formation towards Bailleul from Armentières. At the same time he noticed a flight of Camels nearby, so he flew up to the leader and waggled his wings at him. This is a recognised signal that the machine wants you to follow.

The Camels followed up to the Huns. Then Mick dipped and pulled up the nose of his machine alternately in the signal to attack. Mick went down on the enemy, and a rare old dog-fight started; but when he had time to look round, he and Swazi were alone. Some distance away were the Camels—flying away!

The Camel flight belonged to the squadron commander who was so rude to me when I made my forced landing on Estree Blanche Aerodrome. Mick and Swazi were lucky to get away with whole skins, for some Huns came down on them from above during the fight. As soon as he landed, Mick got Grid to report the affair to Van Ryneveld.

That the Camel pilots saw Mick attack is not disputed. They confirmed him shooting one down in flames. Everyone in the squadron is very indignant and probably the less I write about it, the better. It is so hard to prove cowardice because the isolation of a pilot in flight is so complete that what he says is difficult to disprove. Certain pilots have a happy knack of getting symptoms of engine trouble whenever there are Huns in sight, and so leave the formation for home. Others get engine trouble when they get to the lines.

A favourite chestnut is: "Boiling radiator, Flight Sergeant. The temperature went up to a hundred." Tested on the ground, however, the engine is found O.K., and when the flight commander flies the machine he finds nothing wrong. But is one justified in calling the suspect a liar and a coward? No one can disprove his story. Besides, it stands on the word of "an officer and a gentleman." I suppose it is only natural that the Air Force has its quota of cowards, but why on earth are they not punished instead of being promoted? That's what I want to know. I am astonished to hear that some of the senior officers have never fired a shot in anger, let alone killed an enemy, while they have not piloted a machine since 1914—if at all.

I got a Hun and a half for lunch to-day. The half was a grim affair. I feel certain I shall dream of the scrap to-night. I generally re-fight my battles that way, and the extraordinary thing is that I am always the one who is shot down, sometimes in flames. Ugh! Well, back to the Hun and a half.

At midday, Cairns took us on our second patrol. While we were passing over Ploegstreet Wood I spotted bursts of our own anti-aircraft fire over Poperinghe, and just in front I could see a little black speck, the size of a swallow, moving swiftly along in our direction.

I dashed up to Cairns, drew his attention to the bursts, and made off for the black speck. We made contact east of Dickebusch Lake at 9,000 feet. The enemy was an Albatross two-seater, almost as highly camouflaged as a merchant ship. As he was moving east and I was coming up from the south, my first burst at him was at right angles—the most difficult of deflecting shots, as the pilot has to allow for distance and the speed of the enemy. Such calculations are most difficult to make correctly in an air fight, due to the rapidity of approach and the excitement one feels in an action of this kind. I knew, however, that his approximate speed was 150 m.p.h. He had his nose well down and was travelling at the rate of 70 yards per second. Further, I knew that the bullet's velocity was $813\frac{1}{3}$ yards per second.

I opened fire at about 200 yards' range, aiming about 30 yards in front of him, and then bringing my sights into his propeller. Nothing happened. He continued to dive. I followed him from beneath, so that, because of the rush of wind, his observer could not operate his guns. Though he gained a little on me as I turned to get under him, I soon caught up again.

My S.E. was diving full out, doing about 180 m.p.h. Once I got to within a hundred yards, I throttled back my engine and adjusted the speed of my machine to his. Then I took deliberate aim, just in front of his nose, and straddled him. I continued firing on a long burst until I got right up to him by slightly opening my throttle. Soon the ominous streak of smoke appeared, and next the small flames. Finally, a sort of explosion took place and the whole machine disintegrated in a flaming mass. I felt quite sick at the horrible sight. "Archie" did not help to soothe my nerves on my way back to Bailleul at 3,000 feet.

No sooner had I crossed the line than I spotted our "Archie" bursts at 4,000 feet over Hazebrouck, a short distance away. A machine was going round in circles in the middle of the bursts. This seemed too good to be true, yet there it was. I made a bee-line for the machine. Soon I could see the black crosses.

I immediately tried to attack, but the "Archie" batteries would not stop firing. I kept between the machine and the line, knowing that sooner or later the pilot would have to make a dive for it and eventually, he came right through the bursting shells. It was a wonder to me he was not blown to pieces. As soon as he got in front of the bursts, I fired white lights as a signal to the batteries that I was going to attack and wanted them to cease fire. They kindly obliged, so I got on with my job.

As the Hun came in my direction I attacked him, head on, at his own level. It was a weird feeling as we approached one another, but I got him in the centre of my sights and opened fire at about 400 yards, keeping the guns going until I got to about 100 yards from him. Then I pushed the nose of my machine down in order to get below him, and quickly turned completely round. When I had completed this manœuvre, I found the Hun was about 100 yards in front of me. Opening my throttle wide, I gradually crept to within 30 yards, pulled down my top gun and let him have it.

Suddenly, I noticed that bullets were splashing my machine. Where were they coming from? We were still over our lines and I knew there could not be a Hun on my tail. Such happenings were now only fairy tales and relics of the past. So I concentrated on my enemy.

I closed up beneath the Hun until he was about 30 yards above me, and it was then that I noticed a machine gun peeping through a hole in the enemy's fuselage. I had not met a machine like this before and quickly got out of the way, zoomed up

H

above the Hun, and then dived, using my Vickers gun. In a second the observer appeared in his cockpit and started firing upwards. So I quickly popped below him again. I did this two or three times. It was great fun. Eventually I decided to remain below him, just moving from side to side, for I noticed that the lower gun had stopped firing.

The observer continued firing at me by pointing his top gun down over the side of the fuselage while the pilot banked the machine to give him a better aim but after a few seconds, I noticed that the pilot was becoming rattled. He was tilting his machine very quickly and roughly from side to side, trying to prevent me getting in an easy shot. He was a good pilot. I kept firing short bursts to tantalise him, often only taking pot-shots without proper aim.

Very suddenly he tilted his machine very steeply, and it seemed as if a black object had been deliberately thrown at me. I thought at first it was the observer's gun, so I slithered quickly to the other side and as I did so, looked for the object. To my amazement, I saw the body of the observer, falling with arms outstretched and legs wide apart, and going down in a series of tumbling circles. It was a horrifying sight. He fell in the trenches near Meteren.

I was so fascinated by this fearful mishap that I forgot everything, and by the time I recalled that I still had an enemy to shoot down, my bird was a long way in front. I chased him as far as Armentières, where I fired my last shots at long range. The Hun was then diving steeply near the ground. I returned to our lines, escorted by all the projectiles that Fritz on the ground could spare. I was not hit.

When I got back to Meteren I circled our trenches at about 50 feet, opposite from where the Hun observer had fallen. Our infantry were waving and cheering, so I climbed to 55 feet and chucked a couple of tight loops to show them that I also was bucked. Then I came home. Who said that air fighting wasn't sport?

Late this evening, I spoke to Captain Cartwright, who was in charge of the "Archie" battery. He said he had thought at first that it was I who had fallen out. God forbid! I'm meeting him at George Robey's Café, St. Omer, to-morrow evening for dinner.

May 19.—Kiddie and I were congratulated by Van Ryneveld to-day for our balloon show this afternoon.

The Colonel phoned through at lunch-time. He said the

Brigade Commander, Webb-Bowen, wanted us to shoot down a balloon, because the French had shot a couple down yesterday. Grid called for volunteers. Everybody volunteered, so Grid drew lots. I won, with Kiddie drawing second favourite. The plan was for me to go for a balloon. If I failed to get it alight, Kiddie was to come down and have a go at another one.

I decided to attack a "sausage" from a position near Nieppe village, and Cairns and I worked out a scheme whereby I might effect a surprise attack. C Flight would escort me at 15,000 feet over to Armentières, where we hoped to get well "Archied." When a burst came near me I was to pretend to be hit and go tumbling down, out of control, towards the balloon. When I was half a mile away, I was to pull out of my nonsense and have a go at the surprised occupants and their paraphernalia.

The scheme worked like clockwork. At 4.55 p.m. C Flight was over the spot, being well peppered by "Archie," and when a burst came near me, down I went in a series of dives, zooms, side-slips and what-nots, trying to imitate the dead Huns I had seen out of control. I was allowed to get to my "sausage" without any interference, but I must say that I was rather fearful of Huns whom I might not have spotted coming after me. Anyway, before the enemy realised the bluff, my drum of Buckingham incendiary flat-nose bullets was revolving in my Lewis gun at a furious rate.

I had opened fire at about 200 yards' range, and kept at it until I got to within 40 yards. Two men jumped out of the balloon and to avoid colliding with it, I turned sharply to the right and then came back to it again. Then, for the first time in my life, I saw at close quarters a couple of men going down in parachutes. I immediately attacked them, one after the other. I could see no point in setting the cumbersome-looking "sausage" on fire if the observers were allowed to get away with their information and their lives. I think I hit them. I hope I did. But I could not pay too much attention to them. A flaming-onion battery got going from the ground, and I was soon in a maze of hate. The balloon was going down in flames and a huge volume of smoke rose to signify the importance of the occasion. I came back to our lines on the carpet, and felt happy when I looked down on Hazebrouck once more.

Safely back, I turned round towards the lines to join my flight, and in the direction of Comines I saw another balloon on fire, and a little machine coming helter-skelter towards our lines, smothered in corruption.

I went to meet it and made contact over Kemmel. It was old Kiddie, the rascal!

This show of his was typical of the spirit of the squadron. There was no need for him to come down; but as he said afterwards, "What the hell was the use of bringing my flat-nose Buckingham back to the armoury? Grid would have —— himself."

Balloon-strafing is no fun; in fact, it's a hell of a game. The balloons are usually two or three miles back and as we have to go in low—to-day, I was down to 2,000 feet—there is little hope of getting back safely if the engine gets hit or goes phut. The chance of being wounded or killed is great. Hell is usually let loose as we go zigzagging—terrified—back to our lines. Every Fritz, even staff officers, I believe, has a go at us with some missile or other. The relief one feels on reaching our lines is worth it, though. You feel you've achieved something. You've shown the Huns that you don't give a damn for them.

I want to crack another balloon at dawn to-morrow, but Grid won't let me. Perhaps it's just as well. I'm probably slightly intoxicated with my success and Van Ryneveld's congratulations. To my mind, personal congratulations from a worthy senior are more encouragement to a fighter than a decoration. To gain the esteem of a better man than oneself is to me the greatest of honours.

Roxburgh got a two-seater in flames over Dickebusch Lake this morning. Otherwise, we can claim no more killings to-day. Old "Dad" is proving himself a rare old sticker. Often, married men show a tendency to support the motto, "Safety First." But not "Dad." That the strain of combat affects his nerves is obvious from a cursory study of his actions and speech after landing. Although he laughs and is apparently full of the elation of the fight, it is obvious that inwardly he is suffering acutely from reaction. A married man with a family who fights without flinching, although afraid, is to me the bravest of the brave. "Dad" is such a one.

Hun bombers have started their bit of fun over here again to-night, but it's now ten o'clock and I'm damn tired. I'm going to bye-bye, Huns or no Huns, bombs or no bombs. They might put me to my final sleep, but it is certain they will not waken me. Giles is already asleep, but very restless. He is muttering something about "Get away!" He is no doubt requesting Udet to get off his tail. Udet has taken Richthofen's place as the Hun ace of aces.

The night before last, the enemy got a direct hit on the ammunition dump at Arques, near here. The explosions could be heard miles away, while the flare of the fire lit up the sky around. The old Hun must have been delighted with his work. Another Iron Cross! One bomb fell in the middle of our aerodrome last night, but did not explode. As a result, we have distributed our machines in the hedges round the aerodrome to-night, with their noses well hidden in the hedges. They remind me of ostriches sticking their heads in the sand, thinking their enemies cannot see them.

Our mechanics, and also a number of officers, have been pushed off to billets about three miles away for the night, in order to give them rest. Seven of us have stayed behind. We could not bother to go. I presume we are fatalists. Anyway, here's to happy dreams.

May 20.—No bombs fell near us last night, after all.

Major R. W. McClaughry,[1] who had previously done night flying, went up after a Hun after I had gone to bed, but he failed to get him. As he went up without lights or flares, it was a stout show. I take my hat off to him.

Received a long letter from "Dingbat" Saunders which is full of the doings of his squadron, No. 84. He is full-out, as usual, and doing his stuff. He speaks very highly of his C.O., Sholto Douglas. Major Douglas was Giles's C.O. when he was an observer in 43 Squadron. Giles also lauds his praises loud and long. There is no doubt that if a squadron is going full out, the origin of its success can be traced to its C.O.

"Dingbat" was going to ask Douglas if he would apply for Giles, Skeddon and me if 74 had not been formed.

"Ruggles" Thompson is also doing his stuff. He has already shot down his No. 1 Hun, while "Dingbat" has cracked at least half a dozen. But 84's star turn is little Beauchamp-Proctor,[2] a South African. Lately, he has been making a speciality of balloon-strafing. He will soon be rivalling the Belgian balloon expert, Willy Coppens. However, he does not confine his activities to balloons. He is very aggressive in his air fighting. "Dingbat" says that a few days ago he took off at 3.30 a.m. to intercept some Huns who were bombing Amiens. He decided the best way of making sure of them was to fly over to their aerodrome, which he would spot by the flares on the ground. Eventually a Hun, a

[1] Later Air Vice-Marshal. Killed on a night flight in World War II. In the same aircraft was Lady Tedder, who was then serving on R.A.F. welfare work. She was also killed.

[2] Later awarded the Victoria Cross. Killed in a flying accident, 1921.

twin-engined bird, returned. "Proccy" had a go at him and fought him down to 2,000 feet, when his guns jammed. The Hun then fired a red light, and "Proccy" had to put up with a severe dose of flaming onions and machine-gun fire from the ground. He was lucky to get away with a whole skin. That's the stuff to give 'em.

"Proccy," who hails from Kimberley, is only 5 foot tall—much smaller than I am. I shall never forget the first time I met him. It was in the South African Officers' Club. I was shaving in the bathroom, which was a communal affair. Suddenly, I heard a whistle. I looked round, but could see no one. A little later I heard the whistle somewhat louder. I turned round again. Nobody was in sight. The bath was full of water, but no one was in it. I carried on shaving. Then the whistle came again. It was obvious someone was pulling my leg, so I made a thorough inspection of the room. Looking into the bath, I saw a tiny figure under the water, holding his nose. It looked almost like a doll, but it was Captain A. W. Beauchamp-Proctor, M.C. and bar—without his decorations!

Captain H. P. Smith, "Dingbat's" flight commander, put up a rasping show on the 17th. He was leading his flight, escorting some D.H. 4s on a show, and got mixed up in a rare old dog-fight, as is usually the case on these missions. He followed a Hun down to 6,000 feet and eventually crashed him. But having got below the fight, a few Huns naturally availed themselves of the invitation to crack him. A triplane got on his tail as he was making for our lines, and he soon felt a bullet in his right ankle. Shortly afterwards, his petrol tank was hit and his engine ceased to function.

Smith now dived hard to get away, kicking his rudder from side to side, so that the "tripe" could not get a straight shot. He finally crashed in "no-man's-land," near Villiers-Bretonneux. The Hun gave him a parting shot, which hit him in the other ankle, and then the Fritz on the ground opened up with his machine guns, and poor old Smith was cracked in the arm, breaking it, while clambering into a shell-hole. In the end, he was rescued by some gallant Aussies. They got him into their trenches, but not before one of them had been badly wounded. Great stuff, this spirit of the Royal Flying Corps.

I landed at Droglands Aerodrome to-night to see 10 Squadron. Everyone was very excited over a show that "Sammy" Hughes and Peacock had put up. Sammy was flying his old "Ack-W" at 7,000 feet on a photography job near Zillebecke, when he was attacked by three triplanes. He wisely and pluckily accepted the challenge, and flew his machine with such skill—arching most of the time—that his observer was able to destroy one Hun, send another down out of control, and scare the third away. Sammy's machine was well peppered. A great effort. If anyone deserves a decoration, well, old Sammy does. Major Murray was delighted. He was pushing out a good boat in honour of the occasion.

By Jove! I take my hat off to these Corps squadrons. They do all the dirty work, getting very little praise. You see them daily, flying about over the trenches in the middle of shell bursts and corruption, ambling about, waiting to be hit. Doing their exacting duties with precision and ease, regardless of the possibility of being shot down.

We on fighting patrols get all the fun, and—as far as I can see —most of the decorations. It should be the other way round. This is another objection I have to the award of gongs.

May 21.—Mick cracked four Huns to-day! It sends a thrill through me as I write it. It has taken me seven weeks to do this!

What is the secret? Undoubtedly, the gift of accurate shooting, combined with the determination to get to close quarters. Being cunning is the measure of life in air fighting, since we have neither wireless to guide us nor parachutes to save us.

It is amazing, though. For there is no pilot in France who goes nearer to every Hun he can approach than Grid, yet he can't get them down. Over and over again, I've seen Grid sit tight on a Hun's tail, and watched his tracer bullets apparently perforating the pilot's body. And nothing happened, except that the Hun flew on, unconcerned. On the other hand, I've watched Mick approach a Hun at right angles, heard the fierce crackle of his guns for a couple of seconds—and the next thing I knew, the Hun was in flames. Amazing! And this with a dud left eye, too. He must have treble use in the other.

In his first fight, which commenced at 12,000 feet, there were six Pfalz scouts flying east from the direction of Kemmel Hill. He shot one to pieces after firing a long burst from directly behind and above; another, he crashed. It spun into the ground after it had been hit by a deflection shot. Then Mick had a fine set-to with a silver bird while his patrol looked on. It was a wonderful sight. First, they waltzed round, with Mick tight on the bright lad's tail. Then the Pfalz half-rolled, falling a few hundred feet beneath him. Mick did the same, firing as soon as he got his enemy in line. The Hun looped. Mick looped, too, coming out behind and above the other, firing short bursts. The

Pfalz spun. Mick spun also, firing as he did so. This shooting seemed to me a waste of ammunition. The Hun finally pulled out. Mick, who was now down to 4,000 feet, did the same. The Hun started twisting and turning, a sure sign of "wind-up," and Mick administered the *coup de grâce* with a burst from directly behind at about 25 yards' range. The Hun went down, obviously out of control, and crashed.

This really was a remarkable exhibition of cruel, calculated Hun-strafing. I felt sorry for the Hun. He put up as fine a show of defensive fighting as I've ever seen. It reminded me of my little effort on April 12. The only difference—a vital one—between him and me was that I had a machine which could show my enemies a clean pair of heels, and he had not.

I asked Mick after we had landed why he fired during the spin. He replied: "To intensify his 'wind-up'." And a very good answer, too!

This is the first time I have seen a machine loop during a fight. It was obvious to all of us that to loop gives no advantage. Mick, by following him, kept on his tail the whole time. As the Hun came out of the loop, he obviously lost his bearings relative to Mick, for he flew aimlessly for a few seconds, obviously trying to discover Mick's whereabouts. Mick told me he only looped after him for a bit of fun. He felt the Hun was cold meat. However, he swears he kept him in sight during the manœuvre. I doubt it. Anyway, he says that what he should have done instead of looping was merely to have made a zooming, climbing turn as the Hun looped, then half-rolled and come back on his tail. Thus, he would have kept the Hun in sight all the time, while retaining perfect control of his own machine.

Grid and Young also collared a couple of Pfalz during the fight.

Mick's other Hun was a Hanoverraner two-seater, which he shot down after a burst at right angles. The old boy crashed into a tree at La Couronne, south of Vieux Berquin.

A pilot from 24 Squadron landed on our aerodrome about dusk. He had lost his formation and his way. Apparently, he did not see Clamarais South Aerodrome, which is flat and three times as large as ours. He told us of a thrilling fight to-day between Captain C. N. Lowe, the famous English Rugby wing three-quarter, a Lieutenant Mark and some Huns.

Mark's top plane started wobbling, breaking up after he had dived on an enemy. Another Hun got on his tail, so he started back to our lines. While doing so, he saw a Hun on C. N. Lowe's tail, forcing him down. Without hesitation, he went to Lowe's assistance, although he was still being fired at and his wobble was getting worse. He pushed the Hun off Lowe's tail, probably saving his life. The Hun then turned on Mark. Lowe, seeing this, attacked the Hun and shot him down. Then both machines made for our lines. Having noticed Mark's predicament, Lowe escorted him back to our lines. Mark crashed on landing, and his machine ended a glorious innings by bursting into flames. Mark is O.K. The spirit of the Royal Flying Corps, boys!

Clements has crashed in the trenches, but is O.K., I believe. We had a message from a major of the Buffs to say he was being looked after, but that, owing to the shelling, it would not be safe for him to return until nightfall. I bet he pinched a few buttons!

All pilots have to go to "Brighton," our dispersal quarters, to-night, by order of Van Ryneveld.

May 22.—No bombing last night after all. Grid, who remained alone in the Squadron, pulled all our legs unmercifully to-day. He alleged that he had never had a more solid and delightful sleep. Mick, as usual, was going down in flames, hanging on to his tail skid!

I'm feeling very tired to-night, having done four shows. I can hardly keep my eyes open. My legs, especially my calves, are feeling all groggy. So there it is not going to be much doing to-night.

The sky has been full of game all day, particularly scouts. I've had seven scraps—not fleeting affairs, but real wizards. It was great fun. I went out with Mick on early patrol, and we had a wild time. In all, we must have come across fifty or sixty Huns. Mick, with great skill, kept us above the lot. We attacked various groups from time to time, using dive-and-zoom tactics. That is, we would dive at the Huns until we got to within about 50 yards of them, then pull out of the dive and climb up again, repeating the dose as circumstances permitted. Mick and Howe got one each. This was Swazi's first Hun, and he is very bucked about it. Two out of sixty does not sound very clever, but shooting down aeroplanes is not as easy as knocking down coconuts in a fair. We did not lose any.

With Cairns leading, at lunch-time C Flight attacked a bunch of Pfalz at 13,000 feet over Quesnoy. I cracked one, which went into flames.

In the afternoon, Birch and I went up on a lone patrol against high-seater reconnaissance machines. We caught a Rumpler over St. Omer, but he was too speedy at 20,000 feet for us. He just put his fingers to his nose and simply ballooned away from us. We were furious.

This evening, leading C Flight, I caught four Pfalz over Fromelles. I got between them and the setting sun, which was lovely and large, ideal for a surprise attack, and managed to send one down out of control, smoking badly. A grand sight.

Clements is back in the Squadron. He has had a first-class "wind-up" experience.

He was diving at a Hun two-seater over Armentières when his engine conked, so he had to get back to our lines the best he could. I can imagine his feelings as he was trying to make our lines. I've had some. He aptly described both our feelings when he said: "I was trembling like a jelly. My bones were not rattling like all bones rattle, but a hundred times louder." Eventually he deposited his S.E. 5 with great skill in a shell-hole, carefully placing the engine under water, so that Fritz could not see it. With greater skill, he managed to avoid further damage to his good looks than a dented nose and a black eye.

By the time he had disentangled himself from the wreckage, a couple of Tommies with a stretcher had arrived on the scene. Clem hurriedly informed them that he did not want a stretcher, but a cigarette, which amused the Tommies very much. He was taken to a dugout belonging to the 1st Buffs and treated right royally. Fritz made sure of the complete destruction of his S.E. by dropping a few trench mortar shells on it.

Clem is naturally a little shaken. So would I be.

10

MAY 24.—To-day has been a lazy day. No flying, owing
to dud weather. I spent the morning in sleeping and writing
letters. I find I want a lot of sleep these days. I don't know
whether it is because of the high flying.

This afternoon, the great General Plumer paid us a surprise
visit. It must have been a surprise to him, too. He is a funny little
man to look at, but very nice to speak to. He is about 5 feet 8
inches tall, inclined to be rotund, has a podgy, red face, white
hair and moustache, a twinkle in his eye, wears a monocle, and
stands like the grand soldier he is—very stiff and erect. Though he
flattered us on our fighting efforts, I have a suspicion that he did
not approve of either the cleanliness or the mode of our dress.
Mick, in particular, "shone" in this direction. With no hat or
collar, no Sam Browne, long hair, and muffled, he looked a
typical bushranger.

When we had all rolled up (there is no other word), Plumer said
to Grid: "Which is Mannock?" Our D'Artagnan was duly
pointed out to him. I really thought Plumer was going to pass
right out. However, with a masterly effort he pulled himself
together and staggered up to Mick with arm outstretched. Mick's
dirty paw clutched his gloved hand and squeezed it in his usual
hearty manner. Plumer's face twitched; for a second, I thought
he was going to give a yell.

"Mannock," he said, "let me congratulate you on your D.S.O.
and on your first day's work."

Mick replied: "We expected that, sir."

Plumer's face wore a puzzled look; then he smiled faintly. I
have an idea he went away wondering what sort of fellow this
Mannock could be. I don't blame him.

When Plumer had gone, Grid phoned Van Ryneveld and told
him what the "old man" had said about a D.S.O. Yes; it was
quite true. Van Ryneveld had been asked to keep it quiet until
the General had done his stuff.

We are all delighted in the squadron; no one more than I.

If decorations must be given, well, Mick deserves his quota. When I add, "And what about Grid?" it is only because I think he also deserves recognition.

To-night, even while I write, the Squadron is celebrating Mick's D.S.O. in no half-hearted manner. Assistance is being rendered by Cobby, King and Watson, of the Aussies; Clayson, Owen and Johnkrie, of No. 1; Nigger Horn, Longton, McGregor, Springs, Callaghan, Grider and Artie Daniels,[1] of 85; Venter, Ross and Morrison of 29. The mess is chock-a-block with celebrating pilots in various stages of exuberation and intoxication. Our cocktail king, Richardson, has put one over the boys with a concoction christened by Grid the "74 Viper." I had a sip to see what it tasted like—it burned my throat and stopped my breathing. That was only the result of a sip. What a mouthful must be like, God only knows.

It has surely been a grand night, but—what about to-morrow morning?

May 25.—Poor little O'Hara crashed this morning and was burnt to death on the aerodrome. Stalled. Horrible sight. Thank God, his death must have been instantaneous. He dived in from about 100 feet.

Did a couple of line patrols, but no Huns knocking around. Clem and I dropped some cigarettes and tobacco on the Buffs' trenches; also a few Cooper bombs and bullets on the Hun trenches.

May 26.—Had six scraps to-day, but no Huns. In fact, I was lucky not to buy a packet during my last scrap this evening. Mick shot the gentleman off my tail, just when he was getting the upper hand of me. My friend was an Albatross with a black tail and green fuselage. I'm very thankful to Mick. My Vickers gun had a stoppage which I could not clear, while my Lewis drum was empty and I was too harassed to change it. So I was properly in the soup.

The last fight of the day was a beauty. There were about thirty S.Es. and Bristols of 20 Squadron and about forty Huns. Machines, friend and foe, were whistling past one another, missing each other by hair breadths. It was really a most gripping affair.

You suddenly would see one of your own machines coming straight at you and, turning sharply to avoid it, you would find yourself confronted with a creeping, camouflaged Hun. Turning again quickly, it would be only to experience tracer bullets

---

[1] Now General Daniels, Chief of the South African Air Force.

whistling past and to hear the muffled cackle of Spandau guns behind you. Next, a Hun would come hurtling past, with a Bristol fighter, firing hard, tight on his tail. On the Bristol's tail Would be a couple of Huns. And on your tail . . . Oh! What a nightmare it all was. It lasted ten minutes.

Mick got one and Roxburgh got one, while the Bristols claim five. We lost no machines. Good arithmetic. But what a game!

A Bristol and I engaged a Pfalz simultaneously. It was seen by other members of the patrol to crash near a railway, about a mile east of Ploegstreet Wood. I have not claimed it. It was impossible to say whose bullets did the trick. The main thing is that the Hun crashed. Whether he is dead depends on his luck.

A new pilot joined to-day. He has a wooden leg, an M.C. and a D.C.M. His name is Sidney Carlin and he is a Yorkshireman. Before the war, he was a farmer near Hull. He must be a stout lad. Spiers knew him at the C.F.S. and Jack Scott and Zulu Lloyd (C.O. and Flight Commander at the C.F.S.) highly recommended him. He has been christened "Timber-toes." He has a release gadget on his leg when he flies, so that he can detach it if he crashes. As Spiers says he lands no better than I do, I am looking forward eagerly to seeing a one-legged pilot hobbling away from a ruined S.E. It will be a grand sight.

May 27.—Lovely day. Just a few low clouds.

Giles (Twist) and I went out at 10.30 a.m. to intercept two-seaters working between Voormezelle and Ypres. As I was leading, I decided to cross the lines high over Bailleul, pass on to Armentières, and then come back towards Ypres, thus hoping to take the enemy by surprise. When we got over the lines, we could see Huns all over the place. I was in a quandary. Which should I go for first? I could see this patrol was going to be a question of the survival of the fittest, especially mentally, so I decided to pick out my birds.

There were four scouts climbing towards us from the direction of their aerodrome, north-east of Armentières. When they reached 10,000 feet, we were at 13,000 feet. I gave the signal to attack. The Huns saw us coming, turned round and ran away. We chased them down to 5,000 feet, then pulled out. Giles got well on the tail of one of his enemies. We saw him go down, obviously in trouble, but he landed apparently intact in a field near Courtrai. I wonder if the pilot was hit. Perhaps, like Simpson of 10 Squadron, he was mortally wounded. Giles did not put in a combat report for this scrap because the Hun did not crash, so it is not credited as a victory.

This business of crediting pilots with a certain number of victories is to me as much tripe as the awarding of decorations. It is a fighting pilot's duty to shoot down Huns, so why make a song about it? If a two-seater pilot on artillery co-operation shoots down a couple of Huns—grand show! He has done something to deserve a decoration, for shooting down Huns is not his job. No doubt, our generals would say it was "in self-preservation" and deserved no decoration, as they did in the case of Sammy Hughes of 10 Squadron.

I suppose senior officers must find some excuse to give their juniors medals, which they deserve, as an excuse for plastering their own breasts with gaudy decorations. I have noticed that the more senior the officer, the more childish he appears to become regarding honours. Strong rumour has it that one Air Force brigadier-general is dreaming about a D.S.O. As he has not done a real job of work since he joined the R.F.C., I doubt if he'll get it. Perhaps a knighthood will come his way one day to show a nation's gratitude.

Giles and I came back towards Ypres, but all the two-seaters had gone down on the carpet as they saw us coming, "Archie" giving them the tip. We worked down south again. At 11 a.m. I spotted a couple of two-seaters working over Merville. At 2,000 feet above them were twelve scouts. Studying the situation, I decided the thing to do was for Giles to go and attack the scouts from above, while I slipped in and had a crack at the two-seaters. By a prearranged signal, Giles went off, climbing east, while I hung around over Bailleul.

Giles soon got well into the fangs of "Archie." The Hun scouts (although below), attracted by the bursts, went after him, leaving the two-seaters to look after themselves. Here was my chance. Making a long, steep dive from over Bailleul to Neuf Berquim, I got beneath a silver Albatross two-seater's tail before he realised I was about. As soon as I was within 75 yards' range, I opened fire with both guns. The Hun immediately put his nose down and dived. This was splendid. He now gave me a straight shot. I followed him down to 500 feet, firing at intervals. He ended up entangled among the shell-torn branches of some trees. I gave him a burst in this position, then scampered for our lines as hard as I could go.

Looking up, I could see Giles and the dozen Huns having a party. I did not feel uneasy. I knew it would take more than a dozen Huns to shoot Giles down if he started the fight with the advantage of height on his side. There ain't no flies on W. B. Giles.[1]

Safely back over our lines, I started to climb to join him. I saw him coming towards Bailleul. We joined forces again and started looking for more trouble. We had not long to wait. At 11.30 we spotted a mottled Halberstadt two-seater flying at 8,000 feet towards Bailleul. Climbing north-east, we got above and on the east of it. When I decided it wasn't looking, I dived to the attack, approaching from behind and underneath, while Twist dived down on top of it. Between the two of us, we made it go down over the vertical, but we had to leave it at 4,000 feet. Some scouts were making a bee-line for us. What happened to it, I don't know or care. What is most important is that we got back safely. There are plenty more Huns—we can have them to-morrow. I fear I'm fast becoming a disciple of Mick, not Grid. Mick's theory is more logical to me. No one minds dying, but why throw one's life away?

Had a letter from "Dingbat." He has been awarded a Military Cross, and "Proccy" a bar to his M.C. Jolly good show.

Crashed on landing to-night. Somersault.

May 28.—No machine. Very fed up. It has been such a lovely day. Ideal for fighting. There have been lots of Huns around. Most of the boys have had a party.

The C.O. saved Giles's skin to-night. Giles very carelessly allowed a black Albatross to pounce on him while he was concentrating on the destruction of a silver-grey two-seater. Giles has had his leg pulled unmercifully. We declare he was decoyed. Pilots hate admitting they have been taken for suckers.

Clem tells me that Mick saved his life to-night, too. Appears to have been a lot of life-saving going on. But this is a part of the air-fighting game.

Mick and Clem went up for a bit of fun after tea. They got all they wanted. First, they dived on a couple of scouts, east of Kemmel. They had to scurry away when they heard the kak-kak-kak of enemy guns behind them and saw two Pfalz diving on them. Back to our lines and climbing again, they soon went after another couple, this time over Ploegstreet Wood. On the way to cut them off, Clem spotted a large formation of Huns, obviously making a bee-line for them.

Clem put on full throttle and put his nose down to catch up with Mick, who, as usual, was wasting no time in getting at his

[1] Now Manager of Alliance Assurance, Corn Street, Bristol.

enemy. Mick had seen the Hun formation all the time. He was just going to have a snap-shot at the isolated Huns. Seeing that he could not manage it without being properly trapped, he turned west quickly and dived. The Huns followed, firing. Mick saved Clem by losing height directly beneath them, drawing them on to him while Clem got clear. Clem says it was a rotten sight to see one S.E. being attacked by such a bunch. Had it been anyone else but Mick, he would have been anxious about his safety. But we all believe no Hun will ever shoot Mick down.

One Pfalz was following very closely. Suddenly, Mick went down, apparently out of control. He was on his back, spinning, doing everything imaginable, from 8,000 feet to 4,000 feet. At 5,000 feet the Hun, completely fooled, flattened out to watch the crash. Then Mick decided he had had enough. He, too, flattened out and made for the lines, diving hard. The Pfalz dived after him, but in doing so got below Clem, who was waiting for Mick over Dickebusch Lake. Clem joined in the fun and cracked the Hun, who now left Mick and turned round to fight Clem. A stout Hun, this—a breed we don't often meet. The other Huns now came down on Clem, so he and Mick decided to clear off towards Ypres, accompanied by the whizzing of bullets. The Huns must have decided they were hopeless cases. They left, returning to their lines surrounded by haloes of "Archie" bursts.

Having got clear, Mick and Clem climbed to 10,000 feet, to be joined by the C.O., who was also on a joy flight. Going over the lines together, they attacked the first Huns they saw—a couple of Albatross Scouts. No sooner had they done so than a phalanx of Huns showered down on them from nowhere. They fought their way back again, getting clear by sheer speed of the S.E. The wires were screeching with fear, the engines roaring with bursting energy. The pilots' nerves were taut. The speedometers registered nearly 200 m.p.h. Oh, boys! What a game!

The Squadron moved to "Brighton" again to-night. The Huns have re-started their bombing activities. Giles and I decided to remain here, as it was not compulsory to go. It was compulsory for the other ranks.

May 29.—Cloudy most of the day, but cleared up towards evening.

Did two shows: one after lunch, when there was nothing doing, and one late this evening, when we had lots of fun.

Mick took Clem and me up at 7 p.m. After climbing with great patience for a long time, we came across a dark, camouflaged Albatross two-seater, flying east from Kemmel. Mick pointed it

[Air Ministry photograph

Two famous air fighters, N. ("Fanny") Orton and "Cobber" Kain, of whom the Author writes in this book.

NO. 4 COURSE, 53 O.T.U., R.A.F., HESTON, MAY 28TH, 1941

Back Row: Sgt. Collinson; Sgt. Batchelor; Sgt. Barbour; Sgt. Baz; Sgt. Clayton; Sgt. Evans; Sgt. Campbell; Sgt. Bremner; Sgt. Phillips; Sgt. McDonald; Sgt. Cameron; Sgt. McIvor; Sgt. Rouleau; Sgt. Dean.

Middle Row: Sgt. Fish; Sgt. Carpenter; Sgt. Ford; Sgt. Spenge; Sgt. Preece; Sgt. Ames; Sgt. McCloud; Sgt. Hood; Sgt. Rae; Sgt. Gordeau; Sgt. MacAdam; Sgt. Crist; Sgt. Rickman.

Front Row: P/O Busbridge; P/O Crakanthorp; 2nd/Lt. Mitchell; 2nd/Lt. Booth; F/Lt. Jaffrey; W/Cdr. Kent, D.F.C., A.F.C.; Gr. Capt. Jones, D.S.O., M.C., D.F.C., M.M.; Sqd/Ldr. Llewellin; 2nd/Lt. Montgomery; 2nd/Lt. Gross; P/O Baker; F/O Cookson.

out to us when we were over Armentières at 19,000 feet. The Hun was a couple of thousand feet below. It looked to me as if it were gaining height before crossing our lines on a late reconnaissance. Anyway, Mick did not take long to put paid to its account.

Manœuvring to the south-east of it, he gradually approached before making his attack. The Albatross saw the S.Es. coming and hastily dived north-east, but it was too late. We did not take long to catch it. Mick's S.E. was soon tight on its tail and his incendiary bullets penetrating its fuselage. A few minutes later, all that remained of it was charred wreckage, beyond recognition.

We re-formed at 10,000 feet and proceeded to climb again, looking for more trouble. We soon got it.

After a while, we came across a formation of six S.Es. Mick went up close to them, and we realised by their markings that they were 85 Squadron, newly arrived from England.

Their leader turned out to be Nigger Horn, not Bishop, their C.O., who specialises in fighting alone, not in formation. Nigger recognised our squadron markings, for he and Grid have been bosom pals since the good old 60 Squadron days. Mick waggled his wings, dipping them alternately, as an invitation for Nigger and his flight to follow us. This they did, like lambs being led to the slaughter. And here begins my big fight story.

Just after 8 p.m., Mick spotted about a dozen Huns coming from the direction of Roubaix. We were now over Lille. As we had not too much time for a fight, having already been up for more than an hour, he decided to go straight at them. We had a slight advantage in height. The Huns—Albatross Scouts—were of the stout variety. At least, their leader was. He accepted the head-on challenge.

Both Mick and the Hun leader opened fire on each other from about 300 yards' range, but nothing happened. This was the signal for as fine, as glorious and as frightening a dog fight as I've ever been in. Friend and foe fired at and whistled past each other at tornado pace. It was a real stunner. I have never been so frightened in my life.

Of late, I have been able to keep very cool during actual fighting. To-night, I became so flustered that occasionally I fired at my own pals in the effort not to miss a chance. Thank God, my shooting was erratic. How terrible it would have been if I had shot Mick down. The thought gives me the creeps. I'm afraid I completely lost my head. It was an experience worth having. Now, having come through it O.K., I must try to benefit by

I

Tiger Squadron

it. I got so worked up during this fight that I have not yet fully recovered. I must make a supreme effort to keep cool next time.

Mick sent down two slate-blue chequered Albatrosses, apparently out of control. Clem bagged his first crashed Hun. He is tickled to death about it. It is wonderful how bucked a pilot becomes when he shoots down his first Hun. His morale increases by 100 per cent. That is why Grid and Mick occasionally give Huns away, endeavouring to encourage beginners. 85 Squadron claims an "out of control," too. The main thing is that we did not have a casualty.

No. 1 Squadron had a good scrap to-night, too. Clayson bagged two, while E. E. Owen and C. B. Henderson sent a couple down out of control. No. 1 is commanded by an Australian named Adams, who is very popular.

The balloons on our front have been having a thin time of late. The old Hun sneaks over at all sorts of odd times and manages to bag one here and there. To-day, he collared a couple belonging to 25 and 39 Companies, in flames. I hear one observer was killed. When I write this, it goes against the grain. Killing an observer sounds unsporting, yet it is quite correct in principle. War is war. Really, a balloon observer must expect to be killed, like any other combatant. After all, he is responsible for many enemy casualties. I shall always try to kill the observer, if I can—distasteful as the job may be. "Kill or be killed" should be the airman's motto.

May 30.—Destroyed my sixth and seventh Huns to-day. Skeddon is avenged. I now feel happier.

The first Hun I got was an L.V.G., camouflaged to the eyebrows. I was leading C Flight on an afternoon show when I came across it, about three o'clock, a few miles east of Kemmel at 8,000 feet. It was working on some show, probably artillery co-operation, between Kemmel and Bailleul. I watched the Hun operating for a little while and decided to attack him from the east. Mick had taught me that the best way to get at a Hun on artillery co-operation is to attack it from its own lines. The big idea is to watch the Hun flying on a certain line, diving to the attack so that you meet him just as he turns on the point closest to our lines. In this case, I got to the Hun just as he had completely turned around. I opened fire with both guns at about 100 yards' range. He went down, partly enveloped in flames and smoke. Following until he crashed, Birch and I gave him a parting burst of machine-gun fire.

In the evening, towards dusk, I caught a Halberstadt two-seater at 4,000 feet over Nieppe Forest. He was being engaged by our anti-aircraft guns. I got to the east of him quickly and attacked. After much manœuvring and firing, I got under his tail and fired a long burst from both guns. He fell in flames on the Bois de Biez, where he settled down to roast to death in a tree.

It is very funny, but I never realise that there are men in these machines.

This evening, at 6 p.m., instead of a squadron show there was a series of comic mishaps. To begin with, Mick failed to become airborne and then Grid, who was leading, fell out. Young, the deputy leader had to retire and so had I, the deputy-deputy-leader. A few of the boys carried on, and nobody seemed to know *who* was leading. Clem, who carried on, told me his story.

He continued to climb north and west of Ypres. Not far away he could see a formation of Pfalz, so he climbed to 15,000 feet before crossing Zillebecke to drop his Cooper bombs. And then he came over our lines to gain more height. The remainder of the Squadron, led by Giles, had gone south, followed by the Huns. Clem got above the Huns, climbing east to 18,000 feet.

Over Armentières he found a formation of Albatrosses at 1,000 feet below him. He decided to attack the rear right-hand member. Having first got a good bead on him, he pressed the triggers. Nothing happened! Furious, he zoomed to keep his height. When he had rectified the gun-jam and returned to the attack, all the Huns had pushed off.

Seeing what appeared to be Huns over Nieppe, he tried out his guns, then dived to the attack. The machines were French!

A little later, he saw three Huns coming towards Bailleul from Armentières. From over Merris he watched them crossing the line above Bailleul. Then, just as he had decided to attack, an S.E. appeared from nowhere and whistled past him. It was Birch. In a few seconds, a yellow-and-brown Albatross was spinning to earth. Good old Birch!

Clem carried on after Birch. He got into a good position on a Hun's tail. His sight was good. He pressed the trigger. And again his gun failed. A Hun has probably survived yet another life, while Clem returned in an angry mood. It is only the genial and smiling-faced little "Gibspring" who saves him from suicide!

It is very rarely that our machine guns fail, especially the Lewis. I have not had a jammed Lewis gun since I have been out here.

Jolly old Mick was awarded a bar to the D.S.O. to-day. We

heard about it too late to celebrate to-night. To-morrow night, yes!

We are just off to "Brighton" for the night. The Huns are still being troublesome. Blast them!

May 31.—Great fun all day. It has been glorious fighting weather. Delightfully warm at high altitudes, and not a cloud in the sky.

Started off at breakfast-time, with Cairns leading an offensive patrol. We toured behind the enemy's lines at 18,000 feet over Menin, Lille, La Bassée and Bethune; the result being two footling scraps with one formation of six Pfalz and another of four Albatrosses. In each case, the enemy ran away. I must admit that Cairns attacked them with the tactical advantage on our side, so perhaps they were wise in their decision. All the same, they were well over their own territory and might at least have put up some sort of a show for their Kaiser and the Fatherland, which we hear so much about.

Giles saw a two-seater off between Armentières and Lille. The old boy was going down, smoking healthily, when I saw it last. It was leaving a trail of curling black smoke. If the Huns are still alive, they are lucky. Good luck to them.

At 3 p.m. Cairns led us on another offensive patrol. Giles had engine trouble and returned. We toured the same region as this morning. At 3.50 p.m., we came across twelve Hun scouts, all silver-coloured. We had height on them, so Cairns led us to the attack at once. A grand schemozzle followed for about five minutes. The Huns were trying to get us down to their level, but we refused to be drawn. We fired all our ammunition without bowling any of them over. I thought Birch had got one once, but he was only bluffing. We were chased back to our lines by bullets flying from about half a dozen of them. As we were faster than they were, we did not worry unduly. Fast as our machines are, it is well to remember that bullets are even faster. Not a pleasant thought.

Giles was annoyed about his engine trouble, so after tea we decided to go up and look for some Huns on our own, since there were no more flight shows on. I'm glad we went up. We had a grand time. Here is the story, as I put it briefly in my combat report:

"At 7.10 p.m., I observed 12 E.A. Scouts flying west from Menin at 10,000 feet. Lieutenant Giles and I climbed to the north and east, eventually getting between them and Menin. We attacked them over Ploegstreet Wood. I fired a good burst at the rear machine, which half-rolled and dived away. I then engaged the leader at 75 yards' range from above and behind. This E.A. got on its back and went down vertically from about 5,000 feet, when his wings collapsed and he crashed at V26A, Sheet 28. The remainder dived east. Termination of engagement, 7,000 feet.

"On returning from this engagement I observed another formation of 10 E.As. coming from Armentières at about 8,000 feet. We again climbed north and got east of them, attacking at 7.35 p.m. After a short engagement these E.As. dived east without any decisive result being obtained.

"At 7.45 p.m. I observed three Pfalz Scouts just below, apparently trying to climb up to me. I half-rolled and fired a good burst from both guns at the nearest E.A., which got into a spin with full engine on. This E.A. was still spinning at about 2,000-3,000 feet. I was unable to observe whether he crashed, owing to my being engaged with the other two, who eventually spun away and dived east.

"The 7.45 p.m. combat took place over Comines."

This report may not read very excitingly, but as far as I am concerned, I got as many thrills as I want in an hour and a half, and I am sure Giles did. The reason why I failed to crack a Hun during the second fight was that within a few seconds of the start of the fight I saw poor old Giles going down with a black-and-white chequered Pfalz on his tail. I had to leave my bird and go after him. Opening fire at long range, I managed to push him off. While I was doing this a Hun got on my tail, but after zooming up in a climbing turn I found myself above him. Apparently thinking this was not fair, he dived eastward and joined his brave companions.

I later found that Giles's engine had choked during the dive and cut out. Giles says he was very frightened. So would I be. This is an experience I have yet to relish.

When I landed, another S.E. followed me. It taxied up to where I had come to rest. Out got Grid, with a beaming face. "Well done, Taffy," he said. "I've been watching you for the past hour. Who was with you?"

I told him it was Giles. He gave us both verbal pats on the back before all the mechanics. This was indeed a reward we did not expect. I felt very proud as I walked into the hangar to tell Cairns of my luck. To-night's success made my score eight destroyed and four out of control. Not bad for a small boy.

A few minutes before we sat down to a dinner in celebration

of Mick's bar to the D.S.O., a message came through from Van Ryneveld to say I had been awarded the Military Cross. No doubt my mother will be very pleased and proud when she hears.

The dinner, as usual, was very boisterous. Richardson's "74 Viper" made sure no stone would be left unturned in order to make the party cheery. It has been a great evening.

Cairns made a very witty speech. I did not know he could be so funny, but I suppose every Irishman has Mark Twain's baton hidden somewhere upon his person.

Clem shot a Hun off "Timber-toes" Carlin's tail this morning, and probably saved his life. Carlin's engine went dud. He crashed on our side of the lines. He is O.K., though.

June 1.—Poor old Cairns was shot down this afternoon. No doubt he is dead. One of his wings came off.

To-day has been a hell of a day for fighting.

I led a dawn patrol, leaving the ground at 4.30 a.m. It was beautiful, grey and cloudless, with a crisp bite in the air. I got up at 3.45 a.m., had my cold sponge-over to help me wake, and then went into the mess to have the usual cup of tea and biscuit. Giles, Birch, Battell and our cocktail king were the others. As we were a bit early, Birch and Richardson continued their slumbers. They were suffering from slight headaches.

I thought this new sleep was bad for them, so I put on the record of Violet Lorraine singing "College Days." This woke them up immediately. Books and magazines were soon flying about my head. That was just what I wanted. There is nothing better than sudden violent exercise to wake a man up.

Putting on our flying suits in the mess before going over to the aerodrome, we could hear the distant explosions of our "Archie." This told us that the first Hun two-seater or balloon-strafer had arrived over our trenches. We hurried off to our machines. When we got to the aerodrome, they and those of B Flight's were ticking over, all heated up and ready to take off. The mechanics looked very weary and fed-up. They had been sleeping out at "Brighton," and had to get up at about 2.30 a.m. Ugh!

We took off punctually to time, climbing towards Ypres at about 80 m.p.h. (the best climbing speed for the S.E.). Turning east just north of Ypres, I crossed the line at 15,000 feet. We flew over to Menin, accompanied by "Archie" bursts, and dropped our six Cooper bombs. Where they fell, God knows. Let's hope He is on our side.

At 5.15 a.m., I spotted three Albatross Scouts over Armentières, so I led my flight to the east and above them before attacking. They were completely surprised, but through bad shooting we failed to bag one. Personally, I lost my opportunity because I forgot to load my guns during my initial dive. We only engaged these fellows for about half a minute before they scooted away towards Berlin.

Leaving the fight, we re-formed quickly. I made for Dicke-busch Lake, a favourite landmark of mine, where I could see some of our "Archie" bursts trailing a black speck. It was a dark, camouflaged Pfalz Scout returning at 3,000 feet from a balloon-strafe. I had to take a right-angle shot at it. This time, having made sure my guns were loaded, I was more successful. I did Mick's trick of traversing. Almost at once we had the joy of seeing him go down, spinning fast, to crash one and a half miles south-east of the lake. We foolishly followed him down to the ground. Birch and I fired a parting shot into the wreckage to make sure of our enemy. Mick has always warned me against doing that, but although I know he is right I find it irresistible. I get so excited, once I find I have really got my opponent, that I become bewitched, and cannot resist following him down if there are no other Huns about.

On the way back to our lines, many bullets perforated our machines. Young Battell had a forced landing near Cassal, with engine trouble.

Reforming after this fight, we flew south, climbing near Haze-brouck. We came across B Flight, so I joined them and we went home together. On landing, everyone in B Flight rushed up to Young's machine. He was so slow in getting out of his machine that I thought he must be hit or something. But when I saw him being slapped on the back and heard the loud laughter, I knew he had been up to some dirty work. He had shot down two two-seaters in flames, one of them in our lines. Great show.

Three Huns for breakfast is not bad. Everyone was very bucked.

As I am going home on leave to-night, Grid suggested that I did not do another patrol, but when Mick started chipping me about getting shot down if I went up with him in the afternoon, I took a bet of 100 francs that I would survive. Since he was leading, I knew this was a safe wager and that we would not be surprised. For the rest, it was up to me. My scrap with the black triplane has given me infinite confidence in my ability to get away from any Hun.

The flight with Mick in the afternoon turned out to be the

hottest dog-fight I've been in for a few days. Mick led A and C
Flights on to seven Pfalz Scouts, camouflaged dark, with white
tails. It was cloudless where we fought—over Estaires, between
4.25 and 4.35 p.m., at 13,000 feet.

For ten minutes the ten S.Es. engaged the seven Pfalz; and
when the battle ended one enemy had gone down in flames, one
had crashed, and one had gone out of control—all to Mick's guns
—while we had lost our flight commander. A determined Pfalz
got to within 25 yards of him and gave him the gun. His right
wing was suddenly seen to break up, the nose of his S.E. dipped
viciously, then downwards he spun at a terrific rate.

I watched him for a short while, sickness overcoming me. It is a
terrible thing to see a pal going to his death. Then I saw red, and
went for everything in sight, but my aim was bad. I got nothing in
revenge.

Never mind. Wait till I return from leave.

Cairns was a great gentleman, and we are all very cut up. As I
write this, just before packing to go home, there are tears in my
eyes. Somehow, I feel I ought not to go. I ought to remain
and help my flight to avenge the death of our leader—a gallant
gentleman. I cannot imagine why we have no parachutes.

I I

JUNE 16.—Back from leave. Giles and I went to a church service and Communion in No. 1 Hangar this morning. Padre Bankes, of No. 1 Squadron, took it. He shot a good line, as I expected him to. He is one of the better type of padres. No humbug about him.

While I was in church, Mick was killing Huns over Zillebecke Lake—a couple of black Pfalz. There were eighteen of them against six of ours. Mick tells me he took them completely by surprise, attacking them from above and from the direction of the morning sun. His flight adopted the dive-and-zoom tactics, while the Huns tried to counter by pulling up the noses of their machines and firing almost in the stall. These tactics of the Hun are quite wrong in my opinion. When the machine is almost in the stall, it is practically stationary, and therefore an easy target. It is strange, though, how only Mick managed to get any Huns. Good shooting, I suppose. There is no doubt that once a pilot gets into the knack of deflection shooting, the rest is easy.

There were bags of Huns about to-day. I started leading C Flight on a noon patrol, but after flying for about twenty minutes I signalled to Giles to take over. I had a feeling I was lacking in confidence, both in leading and in flying my machine.

Giles has led C Flight most of the time since Cairns was killed, although he is not the flight commander. A most reliable fellow is Giles. You can always depend on him to join in a fight, and also to get out of any mess he has got into. This ability of his is evenly distributed throughout the flight. It is a great source of solace to the patrol leaders.

I had a go at three Pfalz to-day, but the game ended in a draw. I was really fighting with an inferiority complex, as I have not yet recovered my balance, so to speak. When I opened fire the first time I even jumped with fright at the noise!

June 17.—Bags of Huns again. Ideal for fighting. Just a few billowy clouds at 10,000 feet—at the right height for surprise attacks on Huns below.

After breakfast, I went up with Mick's patrol. I felt I could do with a little inspiration from him. I was quite frank with him about why I was going up. He laughed and said: "Taffy, old lad, I've often felt like you. Come up with me, and I'll send one down, sizzle, sizzle, wonk. It will just put you right. You can fly on my left. You'll get a better view from there."

At 9.30 I spotted our "Archie" bursting over Berques. I went up to Mick's level, waggling my wings to attract his attention. I was only 10 yards away. When he saw me, he just laughed and pointed to the "Archie." Marvellous what eyesight he's got, despite his dud eye.

We commenced to climb eastwards at once, as the Hun was at 18,000 feet, and we were only at 15,000 feet.

The first thing Mick always does, if he can, on spotting a Hun is to get on the east of him. He does this for two reasons. One: the Hun must pass him to get home. Two: there is a better chance of surprise attack.

I should hate to be a Hun. He never knows from what angle he is going to be attacked over his own territory. For our part, when we are on our side of the line, we just dream of home and think of some sweet fairy. We never think of a Hun. To us, the war does not commence until we are a few miles over the enemy's lines.

Well, to continue our patrol. At 9.45 we were getting close to the Hun. Mick decided on a head-on attack. About half a mile away, Clem, who was on Mick's right, was suddenly seen to drop out and dive for home. Mick and I saw him go simultaneously. We stared at each other and looked behind. We both thought there might have been Huns diving at us and that Clem was giving us the tip. Later, we found that his engine had conked.

This little episode put Mick off his target slightly, but he continued on his deadly track. When the Hun, a lovely silver Halberstadt, was 200 yards away, he opened fire with a short burst. Almost simultaneously, he dived steeply below the Hun, turned and came up under his tail. The formation did likewise. Our friend was not hit, but was diving steeply away—a foolish thing to do. Mick had now only to dive at the same angle directly behind him and he was sure to be hit. He was in a direct line with the flight of the bullets.

It was a grand sight to watch. There was Mick, just in front of me, doing 180 miles an hour, with the bullets pouring out to the accompaniment of the vicious barking of the two machine guns.

At 8,000 feet it was plain that the enemy had bought it. He was going down at a steeper and steeper angle. I pulled out to watch the end. It came in a cloud of dust.

My blood lust had been re-awakened. My confidence was returning. Good old Mick!

Later in the day, A and C Flights did a combined stunt which ended in Roxburgh sending a Fokker biplane to the eternal home. An extraordinary affair, it happened at 15,000 feet, just east of Dickebusch Lake.

When we first saw the Fokker, it was at 19,000 feet. Mick and Roxburgh left the formation and flew underneath it, nearly at full throttle. The remainder of us flew on in front as decoys, trying to make it dive down on us. The Fokker was not having any. Mick got sufficiently close to it to attract its attention. He flew in front of it, tempting it to come down to his own level. The Hun made a half-hearted attack. It was laughable to watch Mick's machine swinging from side to side (he was kicking his rudder), as he pulled the Hun's leg. Occasionally, he would pump-handle his controls and the machine would bounce about like a bucking bronco. Very funny, it was. I could imagine Mick roaring with laughter.

While the timid Hun was watching Mick's ridiculous antics, Roxburgh was getting nearer and nearer. I was getting as excited as he must have been, and kept on asking myself: "Why doesn't he open fire? The Hun will see him in a second. For God's sake, give him the gun, Rox!" At last I saw the tracer bullets leave his guns. A second later, the Hun was tumbling down.

I turned back and dived for him, in case he was bluffing. I saw him reeling over on his back, halting there for a few seconds, then suddenly flicking out of that position and making a steep vertical dive. He came out of the dive after dropping a few thousand feet to continue with a sweeping, gigantic zoom which ended with him on his back again. I knew then that Rox had done his work well. The Hun pilot was either dead or unconscious.

Alexander Roberts, one of the Americans who trained with me at London Colney, has come to join us. Like most of the other Yanks, he is a fine fellow who should be an acquisition to the Squadron. He is from Havana, Cuba. He goes to C Flight.

Mick reckons that the Hun he destroyed to-day is his fiftieth. He is a wonderful fellow, and so modest.

June 18.—I crashed my first Hun in revenge for Dick Watson to-day. Leading a patrol at noon, I spotted two D.F.Ws. working at 8,000 feet below some clouds over Kemmel. Getting to the east of them, I led my flight down as they passed underneath a cloud and caught them on the hop as they reappeared in the open. One was camouflaged. The other was all silver. I attacked the latter, coming up under his tail. After I had fired a long burst, the right-hand top plane started buckling and he went into a spin. We all followed him down to 3,000 feet. Young Battell thoroughly enjoyed himself shooting him up. Why, I don't know. The Hun ended in the trenches, about a mile north-east of Bailleul.

The camouflaged bird got away. I was very annoyed that the other lads had not concentrated on him instead of unnecessarily beating up mine. The latter's day of reckoning was already booked when his wing collapsed.

Later in the day, Roxburgh sent a D.F.W. hurriedly earth-wards, apparently out of control, near the same spot.

Mick went off on a spot of well-deserved leave this afternoon. It is very noticeable to me, after an absence of ten days from his company, that his nerves are very much on edge. It is easy to spot when a pilot is getting nervy. He becomes very talkative and restless. When I arrived in the mess this morning, Mick's greeting was: "Are you ready to die for your country, Taffy? Will you have it in flames or in pieces?"

June 19.—Colonel Van Ryneveld came round this morning to tell Grid that Mick was to go and command 85 Squadron on his return from leave, in place of Bishop. Bishop was returning to England at the request of the Canadian Government. They did not want their hero to be killed. This is a precedent in war.

Everyone is fed up to the teeth, although we realise it means promotion for Mick. To me, it's amazing that it has not happened months ago.

Grid has wired to tell Mick of his promotion, so I expect the R.F.C. Club in Bruton Street will be bubbling over with champagne and Irish humour to-night.

I did two shows to-day, both of which have an interest.

It was the turn of C and A Flights to do a patrol this morning. Since it was drizzling steadily, with rain and clouds down to 800 feet, Grid washed out the patrols, but sent Giles, Gordon and myself up to do a line patrol. Leaving the ground at 9 a.m., we patrolled from Ypres to Forest Nieppe on our side of the lines. After about an hour, we gave it up as hopeless and returned. Imagine our surprise when, an hour later, Nigger Horn phoned Grid and told him of Bishop's wonderful feat, before going home to-day, of shooting down four Huns on our front and at the same time as we were up.

We went over to St. Omer and read his report.

Apparently he went through the clouds and found a formation of five scouts at 1,500 feet. He attacked them. Two immediately collided. One he shot down. Going down through the clouds, he found another Hun, which he destroyed on his way back from over the enemy's line. He says he finished up his ammunition by shooting up troops he saw near Kemmel.

What we can't understand is, first, what a formation of Huns were doing above the clouds—a thick layer, with no breaks in it—since they could not see the ground. Secondly, why didn't we see the Huns below the clouds? Luck of the game, I suppose.

The Colonel asked to see me about the show when he visited us this morning. As the general weather conditions were "overcast" and "rain" all along the Ypres Salient front, he exonerated us from our failure to assist Bishop in his heroic achievement.

This is the sad story of a Hun balloon-strafer. At 5.30 p.m., approaching Hazebrouck, I noticed Grid, who was leading, waggle his wings and then put his nose down to dive like hell towards the ruined town. It did not take me long to spot some "Archie" bursts and a balloon going down, smoking badly. Also, a couple of Huns circling round it. Not satisfied with this triumph, one Hun went towards another balloon.

"The cheeky devil," I said to myself. "You are asking for trouble, my lad."

And he got it. It was really a sad sight, for as far as I could see he was spotted by all the pilots in the area simultaneously. Everybody was going down in a headlong rush, straight for the sportsman. His pal saw our approach. He wisely scampered homewards as fast as he could go. But "Little Willie" was blind, either optically or alcoholically. He made no effort to leave for home until he heard Grid's guns barking behind him and his bullets tickling but—as usual—not hurting his ears. It was then too late.

Cobby, who was leading the Aussies, had got into a position east of him. When "Little Willie" saw this, he commenced turning and firing wildly everywhere. Then the greatest fun I have seen in this war began. There was this poor blighter in the middle of us, being potted at by all and sundry, while we in our eagerness to bag him we were missing each other by inches. Friendly bullets whistled at hair's-breadth distances past our ears. It was screamingly funny, yet terrifying.

After a few seconds I gave up trying to get at him. I decided it was too damned dangerous when a couple of Camels zoomed up within a few feet of my port and starboard wings simultaneously, and an S.E., in its haste, flashed downwards past the top of my propeller. It was better to conserve my energies for a death duel with some future foe than to die by the hands of a friend to-night. I climbed clear of the area and sat aloft, watching the grim fun in safety.

It was great to watch those S.Es. and Camels zooming, diving, turning steeply and quickly, spitting fire at every possible opportunity at the erratic little flying wasp in the centre of the fray, who obviously had not a hope in Hell. It was only a question of time, I knew. Really, I felt sorry for this Hun as I watched his vain but heroic efforts to get back to his own lines and his agonising movements when he found every avenue of escape blocked. It reminded me of the day when the black triplane sat on my tail.

At last a Camel—it turned out to be my pal, Cobby—poured a torrent of bullets into the machine from about 30 yards' range. The Hun zoomed for the last time, turned on its back and spun down invertedly on to the trees of the Nieppe Forest, where is got jammed in the branches.

Then followed a sort of target practice. Machine after machine dived and gave a burst at it before zooming steeply upwards. Cobby has been rightly credited with the "kill", although a pilot from 29 Squadron also claimed it.

The body of the Hun pilot was placed in one of our hangars for the night. He must have been "blotto." He was dressed in pyjamas and a dinner jacket!

I have been promoted Captain.

June 21.—Yesterday was overcast, with low clouds all day, so to celebrate my taking over A Flight, we all went down to Boulogne in the C.O.'s car.

To-day, I led my first A Flight patrol. I got a great kick out of it. It's a grand feeling to realise that you are in complete charge of a number of pilots and aeroplanes. When leading odd C Flight patrols it had never struck me what a responsible position the leader holds. I looked on my temporary job merely as one which somebody had to do. As the flight commander was absent, I had been ordered to lead the patrol as a stop-gap. I led it more as an individual than as a leader.

When I took off at the head of my flight this evening, I had a feeling of great responsibility. Was I not donning the mantle of

Mannock, the greatest patrol leader and fighter that the war had produced? That mantle, I felt, belonged to a *man*. And I was only a boy. However, I flatter myself that by taking care of myself and using my brains, I may fit the mantle better in time.

So—onward and upward, crossing the enemy's lines over Bailleul—temporary Captain J. I. T. Jones, M.C., M.M., led his first command in search of enemy formations. For an hour, with Clem and Swazi, Gauld and Roxburgh, I searched the skies. Not a formation could we find, though we scoured the sky from Roules to Bethune. Only one solitary Hun did we espy, a fat old L.V.G., flying low in the vicinity of Ploegstreet Wood. In the end I had to decide to lead my flight down on to him.

If we could only bag him, I thought, it would be a triumph for A Flight and myself. He would be the squadron's hundredth Hun destroyed and out of control. The climax to a wonderful squadron record. More than an average of one Hun per day. We had been on fighting patrols exactly seventy days.

We were up at 18,000 feet, roaming around in a cloudless sky. My Hun friend was down as low as 3,000 feet, moving about beneath a layer of large, billowy clouds.

When I gave the signal to attack, none of my flight had the remotest idea where our prey was. I was losing height in the approved Mannockian fashion—side-slipping stalls. The Ploegstreet Wood "Archie" gave us hell on the way down. It is a fair terror, this battery; about the best on our front. Unfortunately, the L.V.G. saw us coming down, so he wisely dived lower. This defensive move did not deter me from having a go at him, however. I was determined to show my flight that they did not have a yellow flight commander.

As I was the first to approach the Hun, I threw discretion and tactics into the winds and dived bull-headed on to his back guns. It was a most unwise thing to do, but I wanted to secure him, myself, if I could. To get the squadron's hundredth Hun on my first patrol as a real live flight commander was an opportunity not to be missed.

The enemy observer showed his nervousness by commencing to fire when I was about 500 yards away. That was his undoing. His guns stopped firing when I was about 100 yards from him. I guessed he had a stoppage. It was my chance. I let him have it, good and hearty, with both guns. At first I could see I was missing him. I was too excited and was aiming too much in front. He then dived steeply for the carpet, making the shooting easy for me, giving me almost a straight shot. He never came out of his dive. He went straight through to Australia, leaving a volcanic-looking hole which belched ominous black smoke as a sign of defeat.

It was thus that the squadron obtained its hundredth Hun, and A Flight and its new flight commander achieved the honour of the victory. No other British squadron can claim such a distinction. The closest is the famous 56 Squadron, which destroyed and sent down 100 Huns in just under three months. I feel a very proud man to-night, and shall be able to sleep well.

Much champagne flowed at dinner, but I did not have any.

Our trip back along the carpet was accompanied by every type of missile the Germans could throw at us. It became so intense that I had to keep on changing direction to avoid running into the perfect barrage which they put up in front of me.

I don't know whether it was because of my streamers (which identified me as the leader and the assassin), whether it was coincidence or imagination, but it struck me that all the muck was being directed at me. At one moment things looked so black that I had to turn back and fly east for a few seconds, in order to ease off the pressure. In fact, there was one awful moment when my engine coughed, and I said aloud: "My God! It's hit. Where shall I land?" I looked anxiously below. All I could see was shell-holes and Huns potting at me with rifles, as if I were a pheasant coming over. That definitely decided me to make a bee-line for our lines, and to hell with the Kaiser. My tactics may have been reckless and ill-advised. The main thing is that I got back in spite of the Huns and myself.

As I crossed over Dickebusch Lake, I trembled like a jelly. My bones rattled like a battalion of ghosts taking horizontal exercises on a corrugated iron roof.

My theory of life has now developed into this: It must be judged not by the number of years, but by the number of thrills.

That being so, I shall soon make Methuselah look like a babe in arms.

From Top Left: Gr. Capt. H. Broadhurst, D.S.O. (and bar), D.F.C., A.F.C.; F/Lt. A. C. Deere, D.F.C.; Sqd/Ldr. J. A. Kent, D.F.C., A.F.C., V.M.; Sqd/Ldr. Whitney Straight, M.C.; W/Cdr. T. G. Pike, D.F.C.; Sqd/Ldr. W. M. Churchill, D.S.O., D.F.C.; F/Lt. E. N. Ryder, D.F.C.; F/Lt. N. Orton, D.F.C.; F/Lt. John Dundas, D.F.C.

Above: Major "Mick" Mannock, V.C.

At Right: The "Flying Father" of the R.A.F.: Air Marshal Sir John Salmond.

12

JUNE 25.—Had a great scrap to-day, and lots of luck.

Just after eleven I decided to go up and wage a private war. Battell, Roberts and Swazi volunteered to come with me, so I took them. Placing Roberts nearest to me on my right, as he was a new hand, Battell on my left, with Swazi behind Roberts, we left the ground in formation, climbing steadily at 65 m.p.h., heading for Ypres.

After a while, Roberts's engine gave trouble. He fired a green light, the signal that he was returning home. I was really relieved. I could see several birds in the distance that looked very much like Hun species to me, and this was going to be his first offensive patrol. Since Nixon's death, I have been rather nervous of pilots on their first flights across the lines. One never knows what they are going to do. The excitement of the first flight seems to be too much of a test in self-control. They *will* dive away from their opponents instead of fighting them.

About noon I was patrolling over Merville at 18,000 feet, being "Archied" by some dud battery. There were many Huns about in spite of the lunch hour (the Hun usually packs up for lunch, and must be fond of his food). As I had height on them and their "Archie" was pointing us out to them, they would not come near. At last, a high-flying Rumpler passed nearby, flying homewards. Birch, in his enthusiasm, left me to go after it. It was very silly of him. The Hun was higher, quite as fast, and also going east. I could not help laughing as I watched him vainly chasing his bird to Berlin. The Hun must have laughed, too. He did not even return Birch's long-range fire (quite a mile!).

At 12.10, Battell and I were rewarded for our patience. We observed three machines at 10,000 feet, between Steerswerck and Armentières, apparently fighting.

I could see by their size that one was a two-seater and the others single-seaters. It looked like Huns attacking a Bristol fighter. After a hasty glance round, I decided to join in the fun.

K

145

I call it fun because I know a Bristol fighter, well flown, can see off a couple of Richthofens whenever he likes.

Giving Battell the signal to attack, and pointing in the direction of my objective, as he is not too happy over the lines as yet, I throttled back and dived straight and steep for the fray. When I got close, I was amazed to find that the machines were three Huns, monkeying around a cloud: a dark, camouflaged Halberstadt two-seater and two Fokker biplanes, one with a red nose and black body, the other with chequered squares. This unexpected sight rather took me aback. I pulled out of the dive for a few seconds to have a good look round. This business looked too much like a trap to me. However, I could see no wolves in the offing, so on to the Huns I went, closely followed by young Battell.

On our approach, the scouts dived through the clouds. Whether they did so because they saw us coming or whether it was coincidence, a part of their light-hearted game, I cannot say. Anyway, the pilot of the Halberstadt did not see us dive on him. The observer did. He was waving both his arms and had no gun, as far as I could see. Wasting no time, I opened fire at 200 yards' range, maintaining a steady burst with both guns up to 25 yards. My tracer bullets were smoking the Halberstadt's occupants and engine, and soon it burst into flames, falling earthwards. A terrible sight.

I had no time to burst into tears or hold a funeral service, because the two Fokkers suddenly reappeared, coming towards me from the east at my own level. I could see Battell nowhere, and became worried. Was he underneath me? If so, the Fokkers might bag him, and I would never forgive myself. To lose a pilot in my care as a leader always haunts me.

I quickly decided that as he might be below, and as the wind was strong and westerly, I had better attract the Huns, tempting them to follow me to our lines before having a crack at them. I had sufficient confidence in my S.E. and myself to get above them when I wanted to and see them off. And so it was to be.

They followed me at a distance of about half a mile, which I took jolly good care was not reduced to a shorter range, since they were potting at me spasmodically. I kept on slithering my machine from side to side as usual, to make the shooting more difficult. We were doing about 150 m.p.h., making for the Nieppe Forest. I don't know why, but whenever I see the forest near at hand I seem instinctively to make a bee-line for it. Ever since my experience with the black triplane, it seems to receive me comfortingly, with open arms, and attracts me like a magnet.

Near Merville I throttled back. Slithering from side to side, I let the Fokkers get nearer. When they were about 200 yards behind me, on my own level, I turned on them, doing a half-roll on top of a loop. It was a stunt I had never previously done in a fight and one I shall never do again. For a few seconds I lost touch completely with the enemy—like Beatty at the Battle of Jutland. Thank God, I found them again, much quicker than they did me.

The Huns must have been completely surprised by my manœuvre. When I spotted them again, they were spinning round in circles, a few hundred feet below, like bluebottles in a sealed jam-pot. Nearest to me was the red-nosed gent, so, first making sure my guns were cocked, I got on his tail. Luckily for me, his pal was a few hundred feet below us, for I had to manœuvre for quite a while before I got into a respectable position for a reliable shot. In the end, I got a good burst at him from a right-angle position. His left wings collapsed and came clean away. The remainder made for Australia in a fast, whirling nose-dive, hitting Mother Earth on the western outskirts of Estaires, among some trenches. The other Fokker, seeing this, hastily departed for his lunch, and I returned to mine. I knew who would enjoy it the most.

Colonel Van Ryneveld was in the aerodrome when I landed, and congratulated me. The reaction was so great that I could hardly tell him the story for stammering. It seemed to amuse Grid and the Colonel, but it was most embarrassing to me. Thank God, the story eventually unfolded itself. There were bursts of hilarious laughter as I tried vainly to get out a certain word. I only managed to say it in the end by prefixing it with an expletive.

Battell had not returned, and I was worried for a while, fearing he had been hit by "Archie" and had to force-land in Hun territory. He turned up later, however, full of smiles. He had followed the blazing Hun down, then gone for a balloon, which he failed to fire. I advised him not to do it again, pointing out that he needed to keep himself for shooting down Huns, not balloons.

"If I can't shoot down Huns, I must shoot down something," he replied. A grand spirit. The spirit of 74.

Met the great Maxwell in St. Omer this evening, at George Robey's. He says his squadron has been buying a lot of packets lately.

Clayson and Cobby have been awarded the M.C. and D.F.C.,

respectively. They deserve all they get. They are both great scrappers.

June 30.—Since I wrote last, half the squadron has been laid up with 'flu. This epidemic appears to have spread to most of the squadrons around. Grid, Spiers, Birch, Richardson and Roxburgh have had it worse than the others. I don't expect they will be fit to fly for at least a fortnight. The result is that the remainder of the squadron has had to work overtime. Fortunately, we like it, but three or four shows a day over the lines, being "Archied" like stink all the time, is a little trying. It is not so bad if we can break the monotony with a fight, but often we can't get near a Hun. They are not very brave, on the whole, considering they are fighting on their own side of the lines. They have everything in their favour except height, and I take damned good care they don't get that.

I managed to bag three Huns, though; a Hanoverraner, a D.F.W. and a Fokker biplane. Clem brought a Rumpler down in flames on our side to-day. It was on photographic duty. Clem was up, alone, trying to catch such a bird. He spotted it coming from the direction of Boulogne and managed to sneak up under its tail at 19,000 feet while over Cassel. His first burst penetrated the Rumpler's petrol tank. That was the beginning of the end. It fell 400 yards north of Fletre.

In the afternoon, Clem and I went out to salve it. We had much difficulty in finding it. It had fallen among the reserve trenches. We had an idea where it was. When we got near the spot, as we thought, we came across a field-gun battery and some gunners.

We asked them excitedly, with a touch of bravado: "Where did the Hun fall, do you know?"

"Wot 'Un?" asked one of the gunners. "Ain't seen no 'Un fall. Plenty of ours, though."

The icy reply was too much for us. We moved forward speechlessly, each wondering whether it *was* a Hun Clem had shot down, and not a Belgian or a Froggy. Eventually, we found the charred wreckage being gazed upon by a few Tommies, who had confiscated all the instruments as souvenirs. There was still a small black cross on the tail, so Clem hastily cut it out. The bodies had fallen out. They could not be found. I wonder whether they will be buried, or whether they have fallen into some disused trench or shell-hole, where they will be dealt with by Nature—another ideal passing for a war airman.

July 10.—The great McCudden is dead. What a blow! He was on his way out to take over 60 Squadron. They say he did a climbing turn off the ground, stalled and crashed. I can't believe it. Not McCudden, surely! He was one of the finest pilots in the Corps. Does this mean that even the best and most careful pilot will occasionally tempt Fate? Only to find himself the loser? What a pity. The Huns will be delighted. I can imagine their rejoicings. Damn and blast them! Anyway, Mac has the laugh on them. Fifty to one is not bad odds.

July 15.—Grid celebrated his return by leading a typical "Caldwell" squadron patrol at breakfast hour. As usual, he totally disregarded tactics. Crossing the line at Ypres at 12,000 feet, he made straight for Roulers Aerodrome. Here he circled around until a large formation of Huns arrived from above to accept his challenge. Then an unholy dog fight started. About forty machines dived and fired like madmen at one another; zoomed, turned, twisted, dived, and fired again and again. Machine guns spat their venom quicker than a gossiping old duchess. I saw an S.E. go spinning down with a cloud of Fokkers on his tail. It was poor old Grey.

"What murder!" I thought, spinning round on my axis to get on the tail of an all-black Fokker. He saw me coming. Round and round, faster and faster we went, neither able to get a shot at the other. Another Hun got on my tail, Roberts joined on to his, and another Hun swung in behind him. And so it went on, until the whole affair developed into a mad merry-go-round, with death the price of faltering.

Grid closed to within a few yards of a Hun's tail, pouring lead at him. Even a Fokker could not stand that. He got windy, got out of his turn, and dived away. It was fatal. Soon everyone was flying all out to miss the floating pieces and one another. If the others felt like me, they gasped and felt sick as the bare fuselage, now turned coffin, dived vertically to destruction. Grey was avenged—but what a death! What a war! What a game!

As so often happens in these fights, as soon as some catastrophe happens which is obvious to all the remainder of the party breaks away. The fight fizzles out with a couple of toughs having a final go at each other in a private war. Hunt and Roberts are our latest recruits for these private battles.

When we got back to the aerodrome, we discovered that Swazi had not returned. No one saw him go down. Later we were relieved to hear that, although wounded and crashed, he was in a field hospital near Hazebrouck. He had tried to get back to the aerodrome, bless him. Owing to loss of blood, he had packed up on the way. He will now be whisked off to Blighty, so his connection with 74 comes to an end. Funny business, this war.

July 19.—The past four days have not been good weather. Storms or gales have persisted. Until to-day, nothing of interest has happened.

B and C Flights did a breakfast offensive patrol, their orders being to escort and co-operate with some Bristol fighters carrying out a bombing raid in Courtrai. Glynn was leading, but he had engine trouble, so Roxburgh, as deputy, led the patrol.

The Bristols and the S.Es. had no trouble reaching their objective and dropping their eggs. But as soon as they turned back, they found a large formation of Fokker biplanes and triplanes and Pfalz Scouts ready to attack.

Roberts was seen to pounce on a Fokker biplane, shoot it up good and hearty, then follow it down beneath the general engagement. Fatal. He was pounced upon by a biplane and a triplane. When last seen, he was still fighting for dear life. I hope he's not killed. He deserves a better fate. But it's no use being impetuous if you want to survive a dog-fight. Dogs of the air have no mercy; they know this is a game of kill or be killed. There is no room for any of this chivalry of the air we hear so much about. Once you've got your man on your side of the lines, perhaps—but not in the air. No one really *wants* to die for his King and Country. That he is willing to do so is another matter. Airmen who are afraid to die must have a thin time in the war, unless they can sneak away and hide in some ground funk-hole.

Roxburgh had a rollicking time in the fight and returned looking a wreck. He'd spent all his time avoiding collisions and helping to save our cocktail king's life. During the general mix-up, when he had a Pfalz well set on his tail, he suddenly spotted an S.E. going hard for our lines, zigzagging for dear life, with a couple of Fokkers tight on his tail. The S.E. pilot was obviously in distress. So, loyal to the creed of the squadron, Roxburgh lost his Pfalz and dived after the Fokkers. Opening fire at long range, he miraculously bowled one of them over. It was seen to go down out of control and crash by some of the Bristol pilots who were on their way back.

The other Fokker kept on after the S.E., firing as opportunity offered. Rox managed to get him off Richardson's tail, and then the Fokker turned on him. At once there was a devil of a row as round and round they buzzed. Neither could gain the advantage and hold it long enough for effective fire. The Hun broke off the fight by spinning away. This is a favourite stunt of theirs. Since they always fight over their own territory, I suppose it is the right thing to do when they decide they are beaten. They run away to live to fight another day.

Richardson landed safely in a cornfield. He was wounded in the arm, and his S.E. was shot up pretty badly.

Roxburgh went to see him in hospital this afternoon. He says the cocktail king was as cheerful as ever. No wonder he was cheerful. He is off to Blighty to-night.

Carlin got a balloon in flames later in the morning.

Mick phoned me to say he had got another Hun in flames—a two-seater.

F. E. Luff, a Yank from Cleveland, Ohio, arrived to-day. We now have four Yanks in the Squadron. They are all good value except one, the biggest of the lot. As is often the case with big men, his heart is not in proportion to his stature. He decidedly has no intention of dying for the Stars and Stripes, and openly declares that he intends to see the night lights of Broadway again. No "Death, where is thy sting?" for him. There is usually one dud in a crowd, however good his nation is.

July 20.—Carlin bagged another balloon in flames to-day. He is never satisfied unless he has a go at a balloon, if there are no Huns about. His aggressiveness often results in no decisive success. Unless flames are seen coming out of the gas-bag, the attack is not officially considered a success. All the consolation the unlucky pilot has is that he has returned safely and had an attack of jim-jams on the way back. To bring a balloon down is worth three Huns.

Mick got a couple again to-day. He is avenging McCudden all right. He was pulling my leg on the phone because I haven't got one since Mac's death. Funny, I've had a bang at one or two, but no luck. Actually, I've not been feeling too fit. I've developed a sniffy nose and a slightly tight chest.

Met Artie Daniels this afternoon in St. Omer. He introduced me to another South African, Kinkead, who is over at Marie Capelle with 201 Squadron. I took a great liking to him. He has a grand smile. His brother was with me at Winchester. Artie says he has shot down several Huns.

July 24.—At last! Crashed two D.F.Ws. to-night, one in flames. The first was over Merville at 2,000 feet. I got a good position, close up under his tail. After a short burst, he went down in flames. Gauld said this was the first machine he had seen in flames.

"Gee! Taffy," he said. "It's a hell of a sight. Ugh! It gave me the creeps. I shall dream of that poor guy to-night."

The second one I collared was almost over the same spot, and it crashed. I forced a third down but it's difficult to say whether it crashed or not. We've tried to get on to the A.A. battery in the vicinity of Kemmel for confirmation. No luck yet.

I phoned Mick to pull his leg. He retaliated to my banter by asking me to have lunch and tea with him to-morrow to explain my methods. Silly ass!

He told me he had shot a tripe's tail off a couple of days ago over Lille. Some lad is our Mick. I often wonder whether he will live to get his century. Personally, I can't visualise a Hun getting him down, unless by accident, although it does look as if death cometh sooner or later to all the star air fighters. Mine will come like the rest, I suppose. Well, I shall be quite ready. My only regret will be leaving my dear old mother behind me to mourn me. Mothers have a tough time in wars.

F. J. Hunt, who hails from Whitchurch, Hants, arrived a couple of days ago. Looks good. Christened "Mike."

July 25.—Just returned from 85. Had lunch, tea and dinner with Mick. I can't quite make out whether he has got nerves or not. One minute, he's full-out. The next, he gives the impression of being morbid, and keeps bringing up his pet subject of being shot down in flames. I told him I had got a two-seater in flames on patrol this morning before breakfast. "Could you hear the sod scream?" he asked with a sour smile. "One day, they'll get you like that, my lad. You are getting careless. Don't forget to blow your brains out." Everyone roared with laughter.

The squadron is very full-out. Everyone says they much prefer Mick to Bishop as a C.O. Mick leads all squadron patrols and produces the Hun on a plate. Bishop rarely did this. He was an individualist, and most of his victories were on lone patrols.

We took a lot of photographs. Almost everyone has a camera, although officially they are forbidden.

Mick took me to his room after lunch. He spoke to me like a Dutch uncle. I was informed that I was passing through a dangerous stage—one which he had passed through. I was apt to get over-confident. I was to stick to his tactics: "Always above. Seldom on the same level. Never underneath." And never follow a machine down to the ground. Further, I was doing too many patrols and might get nervy.

He is surely right. I have been a little reckless on occasions, but not when leading a patrol. No doubt, someone has told Mick this. He is a grand fellow. I love him. As we parted, he put his bony hands on my shoulders. Looking at me with a quizzical smile, he said: "Don't forget, Taffy. When that S.E. of yours goes sizzling earthward, it will kindle a flame which will act as a torch to others."

Everyone sang "Rule, Britannia!" with gusto, and danced the hornpipe.

It has been a great day. Mick told me that yesterday, Watson of the Aussies was shooting up an observer in a parachute as he dropped from his balloon. He severed the wire, or cord, or whatever holds the man to the parachute. The man dropped like a stone, and the parachute gaily floated around. The Hun must have been surprised. Mick was trying to calculate how much he must have bounced.

13

J ULY 26.—Mick is dead. Everyone is stunned. No one can believe it.

I can write no more to-day. It is too terrible. Just off with Grid to 85 to try to cheer the lads up.

July 27.—I can now realise how the Hun air force felt when they heard that Boelcke or Richthofen was killed. Mick's death is a terrible blow. We in 74 knew him better than anyone. I have a deep aching void in my breast. I keep on repeating to myself: "It can't be true. Mick cannot be dead." Yet dead I know he is.

I flew over the charred remains of his machine yesterday morning. It lay between Estaires and Colonne. I got its position from Captain G. B. A. Baker, now in charge of 85. Here is the sad story of his heroic death.

Mick had promised Inglis, a New Zealander from Canterbury, to get him his first Hun as soon as possible. So out they went in the morning, at the crack of dawn. At 5.30 a.m., at 5,000 feet over Merville, they spotted a two-seater. Mick, after pointing it out to Inglis, led the attack, diving under its tail and then zooming up and firing. Soon the Hun was spinning down in flames.

Contrary to his known aversion to the practice, Mick started to follow it down, still firing, as if he were afraid the enemy was bluffing. Eventually, he and Inglis were shooting up the burning Hun on the ground, two miles behind the enemy's front line.

Satisfied that the Hun was *kaput*, back they came, zigzagging at about 200 feet, Mick leading. Every Fritz on the ground was having a go at them. Suddenly, near Colonne, Inglis saw the nose of Mick's S.E. go down, and then, gently his left wing dropped away. Gradually, the machine developed a spin and Inglis could see a small flame and smoke emitting from the right side of the S.E. Round and round it went in its death-spin until it hit the ground among some trenches. On impact, it burst properly into flames. And in those flames, the greatest air fighter of all time was enveloped—Mick Mannock, the ruthless.

154

Builders of the Tradition

Inglis flew round and round the burning wreckage, as if hypnotised by the fire. But there was no sign of the great-hearted Mick crawling from the furnace. Death, the avenger, was taking his toll. How he must laugh during this beastly war. Just think how, in this case, he vanquished the victor, for within a mile of one another lie the charred remains of conquered and conqueror. Those who believe in Fate must glory in such instances.

Realising that the fire from the ground was increasing in intensity, Inglis hastened back to our lines. He only just made them. On the way, his engine was hit. There was a sudden cloud of smoke and a spray of petrol in his face, and the engine stopped. Inglis glided straight ahead until his machine cart-wheeled in no-man's-land. Thanks to Welsh troops, he was guided safely into our trenches on all fours. Once in the trench, he commenced to weep.

"The sods have killed my Major," he said. His nerves were shattered. He was terribly depressed.

So it was that the greatest airman of the war died, as he often feared he would, in the same dreadful manner in which he had sent dozens of his opponents to their deaths—in flames—the airman's greatest dread.

Last night, in Valhalla, there must have been great rejoicings. Full-out guest night. Blast the bloody Huns!

The apex of my desire for revenge has now been reached. To avenge Mick will be sweet. I shall never rest content now. "Kill or be killed" only can be my motto.

Mick has lit a torch for courageous Tiger pilots to carry high.

July 30.—To-day has been quite eventful.

McHaig, a new arrival, killed himself on his first practice flight. Carlin pushed a Fokker's face in. Shoemaker,[1] aided by George Gauld and myself, destroyed his first Hun.

It was a great show, and I'm glad he got the sod, because he nearly put paid to my account. There is no doubt I'm not intended to die just yet. My machine was written off. This is the sad story.

At noon, I took Shoemaker and Gauld up to look for high-flying reconnaissance machines. They usually sneak over at lunch-time. Their stunt is to cross our lines at about 20,000 feet and do a tour of our back areas—Abbeville, Calais, Boulogne. McCudden made a study of these birds' habits and shot down nearly thirty of them. I picked one up between Calais and Cassel when he was returning to his lines.

---

[1] American pilot; later killed.

155

At first, I was not sure whether the bird was a Hun, a Belge or a Froggy. He was highly camouflaged, and from a long way off I could not make out his markings. He was not being "Archied," although he was as low as 15,000 feet. However, he looked like a stranger to me, so I decided to investigate. Waggling my wings, I pointed him out to my companions. When they signalled that they could see him, I made a bee-line in his direction. And this is where I begin to explain how easy it is to get killed in war.

I was at 18,000 feet. As we approached one another, he saw us coming. He naturally turned, but did not dive away, and I overhauled him speedily. When he was about a quarter of a mile away, I began to have doubts about his nationality. Thoughts of a possible court-martial occurred to me. Deciding I must make sure of his credentials before taking hostile action, I nosed quietly up to him. I was now only a couple of hundred feet higher. I could distinctly see the observer standing up in his seat, manning his gun. But as he did not fire, I said, aloud: "Blast it! It's a Froggy. Why the hell do they camouflage, wasting all this time?"

I had not finished the sentence or completed my sigh of disgust before I realised that something unusual was happening.

Spurts of flame appeared around my machine. I could hear a peculiar, pinging noise. All at once I saw a big hole appear in my rear outer bay strut. I had a very definite hump on my backside.

Awaking out of my stupor—for stupor it must have been—I dived under the stranger's tail to get out of his fire and to attack. When I opened fire, he commenced a steep dive. Afraid that my wing would come off, I let Shoemaker and Gauld carry on with the good work, which they did with good results. I just quietly followed the battle.

Gee! That Rumpler pilot must have had the wind up. He dived almost vertically. I was very proud of my protégés, both of them full of guts.

When they had finished their job, I fired a couple of red lights and they re-formed on me. Since my wing gave no sign of packing up, although I was not feeling too happy about the strut, I decided to complete my patrol time. A firm believer in the sage saying, "Nothing attempted, nothing done," I went in search of more enemies. My luck was in. At 3,000 feet over Estaires I spotted an L.V.G., obviously carrying out an artillery shoot.

I watched him for a little while. Then, satisfied that my wing was still O.K., I got to the south of him and approached, unseen, from above and behind. I could see the observer manning his gun. A quick dive straight at him, a quick burst from both guns, and he was soon lying in fragments not very far from the remains of dear old Mick's S.E. This is my twentieth Hun.

George and Shoey were amazed when they saw my machine. It collapsed on landing. Two of the struts were shot about very badly. The cushion I sit on had nine bullet holes in it. Grid said I was a fool to carry on when I could see the hole in the strut. I can see him coming back in similar circumstances. Not likely!

I've got to the stage now where I don't care a damn what happens. We only die once, and what is good enough for my pals is good enough for me. One must expect to get killed in a war. After all, I suppose there is something very satisfactory in dying for your King and in the defence of your country.

Sorry I have lost my bus. It was presented by the Zanzibar Government, and I have shot down twelve Huns with it. A pilot gets very fond of his machine, like a dog. I'm really quite sad about it.

Feeling very weary. Flying four times a day since Mick went west, and sleeping very badly. Got out of bed seven times last night. Always being shot down in flames. Very trying.

Borrowed Shoemaker's machine and did a show after tea. Nearly bought a packet again. I met a Rumpler at 18,000 feet, crossing our lines over Meteren. He saw me approaching, turned back and dived east. I chased him as far as a mile on the other side of Armentières. He was too fast for me. These Rumplers are good value. Very strong.

Down to 14,000 feet, about to break off combat, I found myself being pounced on by eight black Fokkers. I had no alternative but to get into the middle of the picnic and fight for my life. It was some party. Every Hun was having a go as opportunity offered. They were so eager to fire that, at times, it looked to me as if they were shooting at one another. I got only one good shot. That was at a gent who came right across my nose. I had no time to sight. I just fired instinctively, as one does at a snipe. He stuck his nose down and started spinning fast. I couldn't watch him for more than a few seconds, owing to the general engagement.

I got another good burst on a bird with a red ring round his fuselage. I got on his tail for a second at 25 yards' range. It was a snap burst, but he looked to me as if he were hit. He rolled on his side and started to go down, all wobbly-like. I couldn't watch him, for while we were spinning around in tighter and tighter circles, I noticed a formation of ten diving towards us. "Thank God," I said. "Here come the boys."

Tiger Squadron

They were the boys, all right. Unfortunately, they all wore black crosses. I had not lost any height in the encounter, so I decided to bolt for home. Like a scared rabbit among bracken, I made the shooting as difficult as I could by zigzagging and diving flat out.

I crossed our trenches low over Bailleul, but well ahead of any opponents. Perhaps a little frightened, but not sufficiently so to create a violent reaction. It's a hell of a game, though. A little trying.

August 1.—The past couple of days have been lovely, but hazy. The haze goes up to 10,000 feet, and it is difficult to spot any machines a mile away. If you look towards the sun, you can't spot a machine half a mile away. From above, you can see through the haze easily. So the tactics I adopt are to go up above. If I see any Huns, I go down and attack them from the direction of the sun. Complete surprise is usually attained.

Nos. 10 and 53 Squadrons have been having a lot of casualties lately. A pilot of 53 crashed in taking off this afternoon. As usual, the old Harry Tate burst into flames. Both the pilot and the observer could be heard screaming. Ugh! That's one good thing about the S.E. She rarely turns nasty on crashing.

Stidolph, a New Zealander from Wellington, is a new arrival.

Our squadron is known as the "Coloured Troops Squadron." Mostly Colonials. And the goods.

August 3.—Lots of fun yesterday. The squadron was on wireless interruption duty. The game is played as follows. A Hun leaves his aerodrome to co-operate by wireless with his artillery on a shoot. He calls up the battery concerned. One of the many Air Force wireless operators working with our artillery picks up his signals and reports the presence of the enemy to our Wing Headquarters. The Wing phones up the squadron on duty for the job, and two pilots standing by jump into their machines. Then off they go in search of their game, who must be driven off if they cannot be shot down.

Jack Hunt and I had a job before breakfast. We only managed to drive our bird away. After breakfast, George Gauld[1] and Freddie Gordon[2] went up and bagged a new type of L.V.G. Got him down on our side, in the Belgian Army Zone, north of Poperinghe.

It's quite a funny story. They first spotted him at 9.25 a.m.

[1] George Gauld was from Mimico, Ontario, Canada.
[2] Freddie Gordon was from Hillsboro, Auckland, N.Z. His sister was Major Caldwell's wife.

at 4,000 feet over our side of the lines near Kemmel, and to find a Hun at this height on our side is something new, so they got quickly to the east of him before attacking. He got away by diving low over his trenches. The ground fire became so violent that George and Freddie scampered back, after following their bird for over a mile without any luck. Once safely back, they joined up again and patrolled up towards Ypres, but on looking across the lines, they could see their bird still flying around. After five minutes, they saw him come back towards our lines—this time over Dickebusch Lake. They let him cross, then got to the east of him again. This time they made no mistake, pressing their attack home with determination. The Hun gradually moved further westward until suddenly it crashed near a Belgian battery. After the crash, one of the occupants started running away, and George shot him up, wounding him in the shoulder. Finally, Belgian troops appeared and captured both men. George and Freddie returned triumphant. It was a great show.

As is the custom when a machine is brought down in our lines, we at once sent out a lorry to bring the trophy back to the squadron. George, Freddie and I accompanied the lorry. When we got to the crash, we found that the Belgians had already packed the machine up to take away. I asked them to let us have it, as we had shot it down, but they refused. Then there commenced a little private war, in which, after offensive action (mostly vocal), there was a decisive British victory—Canada and New Zealand playing the most prominent physical part.

Having transferred the trophy to our lorry, we proceeded to a nearby hospital, where the prisoners had been taken. It is run by Belgians, who seemed to be very hostile towards us because we wanted to fraternise with the Boches (as they called the prisoners). At last they allowed us to see them. They were in different wards.

We went to speak with the pilot first. He is a nice lad of eighteen, with very fair hair and complexion, and is the son of a professor in a Berlin university. This was his first flight.

We asked him why he had crossed our lines. He replied that his friends had told him they always did it! When we told him that he was the first German we had seen so low over our lines on an artillery shoot, his face was a study.

He told us that he had been wounded in the arm over Kemmel. His observer had tied his arm with a handkerchief to stop the bleeding, and then they had carried on again. The second time they were attacked, his controls were affected. He could not turn his machine towards his own lines, so he had to land. Splendid fellow. I really feel sorry he has to stay in that hospital. Of course, the Belgians have suffered terribly at the hands of the Germans.

Before we left him, he gave me his name. I am going to drop a lot of notes over the lines, to-morrow, in the vicinity of the trenches, to say that he and his pal are alive. This is really not permitted, but I think it's a nice thing to do. If the position were reversed, I'd like my opponents to do the same for me. I can imagine their mothers' sorrow and anxiety.

We gave the pilot several packets of cigarettes and some money before leaving, but we gave the observer nothing. He was a nasty piece of work. A typical Boche: big, square head; short-cropped, stiff hair; and a sour expression. Knowing he could speak some English, I approached to ask him if I could do anything for him. His reply was to spit in my face. As he was wounded, I could not retaliate in any way. We left him in agony. Apparently, he was annoyed because George had fired at him on the ground.

In the mess, later, George said to me: "I wish I had killed the sod."

I replied: "If he could have shot as well with his guns as with his mouth, you and Freddie wouldn't be here."

As the joke was on me, all the Mess roared.

Timber-toes blew a balloon up this afternoon. He is full of guts, in spite of his wooden leg, and an example to many Britishers with two good legs.

August 4.—This bloody war has now been on for four years. I wonder if it will ever finish?

Personally, I don't care much, now. Having lost so many of my pals, life somehow has lost its lustre. I almost feel a coward, living; yet it's Kismet, I suppose.

Shot down two two-seaters the past couple of days. One yesterday and one to-day. This evening's bird is a story worth telling.

Most of the Squadron was sitting outside our mess after tea, talking shop or reading. Suddenly, we heard "Archie" in the distance. Scanning the sky in the direction of the Forêt de Nieppe, we spotted a Hun flying unconcernedly among the puffs of smoke. For a joke, I said: "I'll bet 100 francs I'll get to that Hun before he gets away."

"Taken!" was the quick chorus.

"Come on, Mike," I said to Hunt. We both dashed off to our machines, and in ten minutes we were on our way. The Hun was still being "Archied." I flew low down to the south of it, then got to the east of it. We met, end-on, at 500 feet. I opened fire from 400 yards away and kept it up until we almost collided.

The Hun dropped his nose. I zoomed over him, then half-rolled back on to him again. He was flaming nicely and hit the ground half a mile west of Estaires. Hunt and I flew around him for a few seconds, firing at the Hun troops running around.

When we got back, Mike had a bullet hole which came up through the cockpit between his legs, yet missed him completely. I had a few holes in my wings and elevator. The fellows who had been watching the show through binoculars from the mess were tickled to death. So were Mike and I. We shared the 100 francs. I doubt if the old Hun saw the joke, though.

Young was promoted Major yesterday. He has gone to command No. 1 Squadron at Clamarais South, in place of Adams. Rox has been promoted Captain and has taken over B Flight. Good show.

Was awarded a bar to the D.F.C. to-day. Bit silly, when Grid's got nothing. Feel very awkward about it, and told Grid so. He just laughed and told me not to be so damned wet. "It's the honour of the squadron that matters, my lad," he said. "I'm going on leave to-day. Look after yourself. And keep on cracking the sods."

August 5.—Had a terrible nightmare last night. Jumped out of bed eleven times even though I tried to stop myself by tying my pyjama strings to the bed. Each time I jumped out, there was a devil of a row. Poor old Giles got fed up to the teeth, as I kept waking him up. It was the usual old business, chiefly, of being shot down in flames and jumping out of my plane. One of the nightmares took a new line. I was forced down and crashed on top of a wood. As I wasn't hurt, I slid down a tree and ran to hide in a bush; but the Hun kept on chasing me and shooting me up, wounding me every time. At last, he landed in a clearing and chased me with a revolver until he caught and killed me. Lovely dream! This must have been the result of George's effort with his Hun.

Feel very weary to-day. Did two shows. The clouds have been low, and some rain. No luck.

No. 1 Squadron has left Clamarais for the south.

To-morrow, at 9 a.m., Roxburgh, Carlin, Glynn and I have to be at Wing Headquarters. The King is going to be there to inspect pilots from the Second Brigade. Pity Grid is away and Mannock dead. The King will miss seeing two of his finest officers.

14

AUGUST 6.—The greatest day of my life. I've shaken hands with my King.

I was very nervous. The King noticed this and did his best to put me at my ease. He is the personification of charm, and amazingly natural. I expected to meet quite a different kind of person. His manner is the antithesis of pomp or arrogance, which are the principal characteristics of his cousin, Kaiser Bill. He has a much more natural manner than most generals I've met. Sign of greatness.

My day has been full of interest. At dawn, since I couldn't sleep and it was such a lovely morning, I decided to get up and go on a lone patrol. An hour later, I was crossing the lines over Ypres at 15,000 feet. There were no Huns around, or any of our machines, as far as I could see. Even "Archie" was silent, much to my relief.

I climbed steadily in the direction of Roulers. Played around over the place for a while. Still no "Archie." I started getting nervous. The sun was rising in a blaze of glory. I wondered if any Huns were approaching me from its direction. I couldn't see, because of the glare. Even when I put my fingers up against the sun, to lessen the glare, I couldn't see much better. Anyway, as I was at better than 18,000 feet, I did not get unduly worried.

At about 7.30 a.m., I spotted a V-formation of nine scouts at 10,000 feet, climbing south-west from the direction of an aerodrome east of Armentières. I got around behind them unseen. Then, having made sure no other Huns were about, I very excitedly pulled back my throttle and dived on the last machine. When I was 100 yards off, I pressed my triggers. Nothing happened! I'd forgotten to pull up the charging handle of my Constantinesco.

Quickly I pulled my stick back, pushed my throttle open wide and zoomed, at the same time pulling up the handle. It was a terrifying moment. When I looked over the side of the cockpit, I expected to find myself above a hornet's nest. Not a bit of it!

The Huns were just ahead, still in the same peaceful formation.

I was in a quandary. Should I immediately dive and scrap the lot, probably getting shot down for my trouble, or should I follow them until they got closer to our own lines before having a go at them? I decided the latter tactics would give me the better chance of getting away with it. Besides, I wanted to meet my King. That was something I did not want to miss. Every loyal citizen longs for that honour, and I might not get another opportunity. In the circumstances, I felt justified in not emulating Ball or Grid. And as luck would have it, my hesitation in attack did not end in the failure it deserved.

I followed behind the formation, about 500 feet above and dead behind the last man on the right. They flew over towards Bethune, then made an old man's turn back towards Bailleul. They were Fokkers. Most of them had black fuselages, with different-coloured tails. The fellow directly below me had a white tail. They all looked half-asleep. Not even the leader had a single look behind him. I don't know whether it was because he was leaving the protection of his tail to the others.

I was terribly excited as I followed. My heart was fairly thumping. I had an awful feeling that I was being led into a trap; that other Huns were coming at me from the sun. Though I kept looking behind, I could see nothing. That made me more confident that the Fokkers could not see me, even if they looked behind.

Suddenly, in front and below, I spotted Hun "Archie" firing at an R.E. 8 only a few thousand feet below over Merville. I thought to myself: "What a sportsman. You're asking for trouble, my lad." And sure enough, he was. Two of the "sleeping" birds dived simultaneously in his direction.

Now was my time for action, and quick, too, if I were going to save the R.E. 8. I dived full-throttle after them. My heart was thumping in my mouth, my whole body in a state of tremendous tension.

Fortunately, the R.E. pilot saw the Fokkers coming at him. He nose-dived for our lines. This gave me a little more time to get nearer to my birds, who were flying very close together. I fired from about 200 yards. It was a straight shot. At the sound of my machine guns, the two Fokkers quickly turned and collided. Then, firmly interlocked, they started going down in a sort of slow spin. I could see one of the fellows struggling as I dived and fired on them until they were well alight. It was the best fire-works display I have ever seen. Horrible!

The remainder of the flight came down on me, but after about a minute they all left me except one. I easily got away from him. Crossing the lines at Meteren, I joined the R.E. We waved frantically to each other. The old R.E. wagged his tail with joy. It was a machine of 4 Squadron. I hastened back, as it was past eight o'clock. On the way, I had a terrible reaction. I crashed on landing, turning head over heels.

From the crash, I dashed to my hut to get ready for parade. All the others were ready. It was decided that we should wear the old R.F.C. uniform. As I had none, I borrowed Giles's breeches, boots and tunic, and Clem's cap and Sam Browne. A handkerchief was my only possession. Thus, dressed in borrowed plumes and very nervous, I appeared before my King.

The officers were all lined up, ready for His Majesty's arrival. I can't imagine what he must have thought of our uniforms. There were about half a dozen different sorts. He shook hands with all, and when he came to me, he stopped and chatted for about five minutes. He was very interested in my opinion of the Hun machines and pilots. When I said that one Britisher was worth three Huns, he laughed loudly. I was quite taken aback by his geniality. What a lovely laugh he's got. Plumer and Horn, who accompanied him, also laughed, but Webb-Bowen had a face like a sour apple.

When the King left me, he said: "I wish you the best of luck, and a safe return." This kind remark has touched me very much. I shall now fight like hell.

My stammering was very bad while I was speaking to His Majesty, but he didn't seem to mind. Old Plumer appeared to be tickled with it and had a twinkle in his eye all the time.

One amusing incident happened while the King was looking at my medals. Pointing to the silver rose in my D.F.C., he asked: "What's that?"

I replied: "Bar to my D.F.C., sir."

"So!" said His Majesty, looking somewhat surprised. "You've got an M.C., D.F.C. and bar. How many enemies have you brought down?"

"Thirty-five, including out of control, sir," I replied.

Turning to Webb-Bowen, he said: "Make a note of that."

After the parade, Van Ryneveld held a conference on the subject of raiding Hun aerodromes with the Wing—a stunt I have advocated for months. Why not go over and smash up their happy homes for them, instead of wasting time trying to get them to fight in the air? To me, it's the obvious thing to do. The arrangements were made. All we want now is Webb-Bowen's permission.

We are going over at lunch-time in order to catch our birds on the ground. What fun it will be!

Poor old Giles crashed this afternoon north-west of Poperinghe. He has gone to hospital at Bergues with a strained back. I hope it is not serious, and I'm glad it wasn't worse. He's a great lad, is Giles. If anyone deserves a decoration, it is he. To think of his active service: dispatch rider, trenches observer, pilot, and twenty months of facing death. Yet he gets nothing for it. No decorations. No promotion. And some yellow-bellied men have surreptitiously secured both. It makes my blood boil.

August 7.—Moved to Clamarais South, and took over the quarters of No. 1 Squadron. No. 53 is sharing the aerodrome. Two great pals of mine are in that squadron: Davies, from Pretoria, and Lewis, from Cardiff. Scott, who is observer to Davies, is a jolly good lad, too, and very stout.

Destroyed my twenty-fifth and twenty-sixth Huns to-day. Crashed my first, a silver L.V.G., with the patrol at noon, near Estaires. I appeared to take him completely by surprise. Got up under his tail before he knew where he was.

The second was also a two-seater, but of a type I've not seen before. He was flying around Thorout at 10,000 feet when I first saw him. As I had the patrol, I flew south, away from him, in case he had seen us. All the while, I watched him over my shoulder. There were no other Huns around. I changed my direction east, and after a time, to north. I was now well on the east of him at 15,000 feet.

My bird, as I expected, flew towards Houlthulst Forest. When he commenced coming back, I gave the signal to attack. We were being heavily "Archied." Hunt got ahead of me at first, but I soon made up lost ground by stalled side-steps. By the time we had got to the level of the Hun, my guns were the first to spit fire. It was a difficult end-on shot, but I opened fire a long way off in order to get in as many bullets as possible. We followed him down to 5,000 feet. From there, we watched him go into a shell-hole full of water, and as he hit his "better 'ole" there was a mountainous splash of water. When it subsided, only the fuselage protruded from the shell-hole. My machine had several bullet holes in it. Crashed on landing.

Morrison crashed and hurt himself on the aerodrome. He's gone to hospital.

Sleeping very badly. Found myself out of bed four times. Can't understand it happening every night. Damn' silly.

15

I will quote no more from my diary. The extracts already given should enable the reader to form some impression of the day-to-day life in a fighter squadron. For what happened in 74 was duplicated in all the other squadrons. I hope it will not have been without interest for the youngsters of to-day to learn something of the fighting methods and the intimate thoughts of the pilots who fought—without parachutes—in World War I.

Shortly after the inspection of the Second Brigade by King George V, described in the previous chapter, there was one innovation for which I think I may justly claim some credit. This was the massed attack by 11 Wing, to which we were attached, on the Hun aerodromes.

The attacks were made by four layers of squadrons, three units of S.E. single-seaters and one Bristol Fighter unit. The Bristols flew on top, so that their observers could keep special guard. The four squadrons met at a prearranged spot before crossing the lines, while the enemy anti-aircraft batteries were being distracted by minor bombing raids and shelling.

Linselles Aerodrome, believed to house about thirty Hun aircraft, was the target for the first mass attack in which 74 Squadron took part. Each machine of the S.E. 5 squadrons dived in turn upon the aerodrome, released its 25-lb. Cooper bombs, then zoomed clear of the target. The Bristols, who had been keeping guard, then swept down to add to the destruction with their heavier, 112-lb. bombs. There followed a grand machine-gun "strafe" by all hands on ground personnel, administrative buildings and the officers' mess. Only the observers of the Bristol Fighters were forbidden to join the party. They had to reserve their ammunition for protective duties on the return trip.

Many similar raids, involving hundreds of aircraft, followed. As far as 11 Wing was concerned, I cannot recall any casualties. But we certainly did plenty of damage.

One or two incidents of individual combat remain in my memory from this period.

Builders of the Tradition

There was the day in September when "Grid" Caldwell and Carlin collided while going for the same Hun. Carlin made a successful landing, but "Grid" had a miraculous escape. He jumped off the wing of his plane as it was crashing in our reserve trenches.

He had to get out of the cockpit during the time the machine was starting its spin towards the ground. By balancing with one foot pressed hard on the rudder and the other on the wing, with one hand pulling the joystick sideways and the other gripping a centre-section strut—a heroic feat, which Brigadier Webb-Bowen afterwards called "self-preservation"—he was able partially to stabilise the machine and stop its tendency to spin.

"Grid" amazed the troops in the trenches who rushed to his aid by his cheerfulness and complete composure. To him, it was just one more job. The fact that it was so sticky only amused him.

In October, an American pilot who had joined the R.A.F. was posted to 74 Squadron. He was Lieutenant J. Ferrand, who said he came from 332 Newbury Street, Boston, Massachusetts, but also gave the address of 504 East 8th Street, Chattanooga, Tennessee. According to custom, he was groomed for the fray on our side of the lines for a few days. Like most of the American pilots I met, he was a good type, and anxious (perhaps a little too anxious) to get at "them guys." He made history on his first offensive patrol, shooting down three Fokkers and winning the Distinguished Flying Cross. The latter was an immediate award on the field. A great honour.

The citation in the *London Gazette* read: "On October 26, this officer took part in an engagement with a large hostile formation. Singling out a Fokker, he attacked it at close range, driving it down to crash. Being isolated from his companions, he turned to regain our lines, but was at once attacked by seven Fokkers, who kept up a running fight for many miles.

"He maintained a stout defence against these long odds, crashing two of the enemy machines, and eventually reaching our lines with all his ammunition exhausted."

Of this epic fight, all he had to say to me was: "Taffy, when I joined the fighting Seventy-Fourth, I realised I had to uphold the famous squadron tradition by fighting like a tiger."

Ferrand was a typical Tiger Squadron pilot. But then, I have always had a lot of time for American pilots. They share our outlook.

I got home on leave in October, and went to stay with Sir F. H. Hamilton and Lady Hamilton at Margery Hall, near

Reigate. There, one day, I received a letter from Caldwell, telling me that I had been awarded the Distinguished Service Order as an immediate award in the field.

I can honestly say that it was the tone of "Grid's" letter, more than his news, which delighted me. I knew that if he did not rate a D.S.O., I most certainly did not. But I had never dreamed he held me in such high esteem. He was not given to flattery, and his standard of personal bravery was so high that I had never ventured to hope my own efforts could rouse him to any enthusiasm.

A few days later a telegram arrived, requiring me to attend at Buckingham Palace on Thursday, October 24, at 10 a.m. At the South African Officers' Club, on the morning of the Investiture, I was too excited to eat my breakfast. Nervousness had exaggerated my stammer almost to the point of speechlessness. "Cheer up, Captain Taffy," said the sympathetic waitress. "You look just as if you were going to be thrown to the lions."

"I'm j-j-just off to B-Buckingham Palace," I explained.

"That's all right, dear," she replied, cheerily. "King George won't eat you."

A few minutes before ten o'clock my taxi crossed the quadrangle leading to one of the entrances to the Palace. Feeling like a small boy starting his first term at school and about to be introduced to the headmaster, I was relieved of my cap and stick and ushered into a long chamber adjoining the Investiture Room.

As I stood in line, waiting to be presented to His Majesty, I got into conversation with an R.A.F. major who was waiting a couple of paces behind me. He was the famous Kennedy Cochrane-Patrick, late commanding officer of the crack 60 Squadron, and a man of whom I had heard "Grid" speak exceedingly highly. He was to receive the D.S.O. and bar and the Military Cross. I can't imagine why he had been placed behind me in the line, unless it was because I was to receive four "gongs" against his three. But if I had the edge numerically, he certainly outclassed me in quality.

When I told him that I was in "Grid's" squadron, he became very friendly. Soon we had forgotten our surroundings, and were back in France, fighting like the devil. It was only the playing of the National Anthem that recalled us to the job in hand.

In due course, my name was called. Almost overcome with stage-fright, I managed to navigate the strip of carpet which led me into the correct position before His Majesty. The medals were pinned on my breast, one by one.

When the King had finished, he said: "Didn't I meet you in France the other day?"

All I could get out was a strangled "Y-Y——"

He understood my difficulty, and carried on: "Near St. Omer. How long have you been home?"

I told him. And then, ignoring my stammer, he chatted with me for several minutes.

"Are you going back to France?" he asked at last.

"Yes, sir," I replied. "As soon as I can."

"Then God-speed," he said, smilingly graciously.

I bowed and walked away as if in a trance.

The Investiture over, Cochrane-Patrick and I lunched together at the Piccadilly Grill. And be sure we toasted well the health of the greatest democratic Monarch of all time. A King worth fighting and dying for.

It was a good leave and an exciting one, but I was glad to get back to France and to my comrades of 74 Squadron. With so many "chairborne" warriors ruling the roost, a little of Blighty went a long way with an ordinary fighting airman.

I got back just in time to share with the squadron a bitter taste of our own medicine—the mass air raid. It happened a week or so before the Armistice.

Moving forward with the victorious Army, the squadron found itself occupying Marcke Aerodrome, near Courtrai, a spot which we had previously bombed. One night, just after dusk, a couple of Hun night raiders returned the compliment by dropping a dozen bombs on us. They obviously knew the aerodrome well. Probably it had been their own temporary quarters. At any rate, their accuracy was uncanny. Two bombs fell on the hangars, completely destroying more than a dozen aircraft. Another landed on the transport section and wiped it out. A fourth dropped on some huts in which passing troops of the Middlesex Regiment were sheltering. There were about fifteen victims, most of them killed. The aerodrome itself was scored with craters.

Fortunately, not a bomb fell on the château where the pilots were quartered; otherwise, the Tigers who had created so much havoc among the Huns would have been wiped out.

During the first days of November, the last days of the war, we devoted ourselves to ground-strafing the retiring Hun army, now almost broken and fighting a desperate rearguard action. We could all see that the end was very near.

On the morning of November 11 we took off as usual. We had

orders not to cross the front line on any pretext whatever. Still, we hoped that if there were any Huns in the air they might be tempted to put up a final show by attacking us on our side of the line. But it was not to be. There was not an enemy in sight. We learned later that the German Air Force, that historic morning, was too busy destroying its machines or flying homewards to risk conclusions with us.

As the clock hands neared 11 a.m., we flew closer to the retreating armies. As the hour passed, we flew right over them. They took no notice. For the last time, 74 Squadron turned back towards its own lines.

As each aircraft reached the aerodrome, its pilot stunted wildly, diving, looping, zooming, rolling, spinning at minimum safety height before landing from his last patrol.

And so ended duty well done.

Tiger Squadron ended the war leading the field in 1918, with the imposing score of 225 Huns destroyed for fifteen pilots of 74 Squadron killed or taken prisoner.

My own flight, while I was leading it, was never "jumped." And because my team carried out my orders always to keep above the Huns, I am proud to say that I never lost a pilot.

These were the lessons we learned in combat:

Keep fit, and keep mentally alert.

Train your eyes to spot the enemy. This gives you the initiative.

Practice air to ground firing.

Keep cool when the fight begins.

Get close, never further than 100 yards, before opening fire. See the whites of their eyes!

Fire in short bursts to conserve your ammunition.

Allow for deflection.

Be determined to get your man.

Develop the offensive spirit.

Those were the traditions we passed on to the men who were to follow in our footsteps. And how well, how gallantly, they maintained them. The fighting and the psychological outlook of the pilots in World War II were no different in principle from those in World War I. Should World War III come—which God forbid!—they will still hold good. The attacked and the attacker will still have to outmanoeuvre one another in order to gain the initiative. The only significance change will be the speed of the battles.

In June, 1941, accompanying (quite unofficially!) an offensive sweep over northern France led by that ferocious Canadian ace fighter, Wing Commander John Kent,[1] I got mixed up in a dog-fight with a pack of yellow-nosed Huns. Incredibly, joyously, I found myself waltzing round the sky at 300-400 m.p.h. in my beloved Spitfire with the "74" painted boldly on the fuselage. What a change from the leisurely fighting of World War I. And what a thrill for the old-timer! I seemed to be spending most of the time dodging my pals.

Then, suddenly, I realised I was somewhere over the English Channel—alone. Oh, boy! Was I unhappy? It was noon, so I kept the sun on my left wing-tip and prayed hard.

When I hit the English coast I did not know where I was. I began calling Flight Lieutenant Billy Drake[2] over the R/T, and eventually found him orbiting Manston Aerodrome at 10,000 feet. We kept contact, and he gave me my direction. He sounded amused.

Coming in Dover way, I saw a machine in the distance. It looked no bigger than a sparrow. I called over the blower: "If that's you in the distance, Billy, waggle your wings."

To my relief, I saw the little machine begin to tilt. I opened the throttle and went after it. Eventually, I tucked myself under Billy's wing, and he led me back to Heston Aerodrome. I have loved sparrows ever since that day.

Kent claims that shortly after landing, I came up to him with a beaming face and stammered: "W-w-wasn't it b-b-bloody fast f-f-fighting, John?"

I'll say it was!

---

[1] Now Group Captain.   [2] Now Wing Commander Drake.

Interlude

1918–1939

16

AFTER THE ARMISTICE on November 11, 1918, "Grid" Caldwell was posted to command 65 Wing and I was given command of Tiger Squadron. Thus early in 1919 I took the cadre back from France to Lopscombe Common Aerodrome, near Salisbury, where I handed over to the Station Commander all the squadron documents and the trophies of Huns shot down. A month or so later, I volunteered for the private war still being pursued on the Murmansk and Archangel fronts in North Russia.

I've got to admit that when I volunteered to fight the Bolsheviks I did not really believe the panic reports in the papers concerning the urgent necessity for a "Relief Force." The fact that Britain was at war with the Soviets interested me little. The only thing that mattered to me was that I could get in some more battle flying.

Actually, the show turned out to be very disappointing. I never met a Russian fighter in the air. Bombing gunboats, though novel, was dull work. However, the ground-strafing, especially when it was carried out many miles behind the Bolshevik lines was exciting enough. Towards the middle of September, 1919, after some three months of a muddled campaign, I boarded H.M. Troopship *Ulua* at Archangel to return to England.

Just before leaving I saw the first complete list of officers who had been granted permanent and short-service commissions in the R.A.F.'s peacetime establishment. It was a real puzzler. How the Powers that Be had decided on those selected I cannot imagine.

First-class men with distinguished fighting careers in France had been left out of the list, while youngsters with little or no active service had been included. Officers who had been captains during the war were now to be senior to others who had been majors, and lieutenants were to be senior to wartime captains. One name on the list made me shudder. It was that of one of the greatest cowards I had known.

I was one of the lucky ones. I had been given a permanent commission, and I was naturally delighted. On returning to England, I was posted for flying duties to Fort Grange Aerodrome, Gosport, Hampshire, where I remained for two years, acquiring, among other things, some experience of the art of landing on an aircraft-carrier.

I do not propose to recapitulate here the subsequent details of my Service career. They have little bearing on what is, first and foremost, the history of 74 Squadron. Those interested will find them in an earlier book of mine.[1] There are, however, one or two incidents which are *à propos*.

It was in 1932, while holding a staff appointment at Auxiliary Group Headquarters (then called No. 1 Air Defence Group), that I became responsible for the V.C. Gallery at the R.A.F. College, Cranwell. Visiting the College one day, I noticed that the walls were bare of portraits of great fighters of the past. I took the matter up with Air Chief Marshal Sir Arthur Longmore, who was the popular Commandant at the time. He eagerly accepted my offer to start a "Tradition Gallery" of portraits.

I began with a painting of Flight Lieutenant S. M. Kinkead, a South African with a brilliant air fighting record. Later a Schneider Trophy pilot, Kinkead was killed in the Solent off Calshot in March, 1928, while attempting to be the first man to fly at 300 m.p.h.

The next portrait to be hung was that of Flight Lieutenant Richard Waghorn, who won the Schneider Trophy (I was in charge of his machine on the water before the race) in 1929. He was killed a few years later while acting as test pilot at Farnborough.

Following Waghorn's portrait came that of Air Vice-Marshal Sir Sefton Brancker, first Director of Civil Aviation and a most gallant veteran airman. Brancker was determined that civil aviation should be a success, and it is undoubtedly due to his pioneer efforts that Britain's passenger- and freight-carrying services hold such an honoured reputation to-day. It was my privilege to be Sir Sefton's personal pilot for a couple of years of happy flying.

Finally, I commenced the V.C. Gallery. It took time to complete, as I had to have good photographs of all the holders of the Victoria Cross, and many of them were from the Colonies and Dominions. However, it was a real labour of love. When the

[1] See *An Air Fighter's Scrap Book*, by Ira Jones.

From Top Left: W/Cdr. R. A. Holmwood; F/Lt. G. Allard, D.F.C., D.F.M.; Sqd/Ldr. M. H. Brown, D.F.C.; F/Lt. J. W. C. Simpson, D.F.C.; F/Lt. J. C. Mungo-Park, D.F.C.; F/Lt. P. S. Turner, D.F.C.; F/Lt. J. I. Kilmartin, D.F.C.; W/Cdr. R. R. S. Tuck, D.S.O., D.F.C. (two bars); W/Cdr. M. Robinson, D.S.O., D.F.C.

INSTRUCTORS, NO. 53 O.T.U., AND "HUSH-HUSH" AMERICAN PILOTS,
R.A.F., HESTON, JUNE 12TH, 1941

Back Row: Lt. Clapham; Sgt. Chiolé; Sgt. Jones; F/Lt. Newton; F/O Taylor; P/O Hookway; F/O Read; F/O Glaser; F/O Mugridge; F/Lt. Dawson; Sgt. King; Sgt. Crozier; Lt. Greenfield.

Middle Row: Lt. Mitchell; Lt. McGovern; Lt. Hubbard; Lt. Kelly; Lt. Wilson; Lt. Gross; Lt. Montgomery; Lt. Greasley; Lt. Green; Lt. Viar; Lt. Faurot; Lt. Merriam; Lt. Booth.

Front Row: F/O Sulman; F/O Stephenson; F/Lt. Wright; F/Lt. Gibson, D.F.C.; F/Lt. Clowes, D.F.C., D.F.M.; F/Lt. Ritcher; W/Cdr. Farqhar, D.F.C.; Gr. Capt. Jones, D.S.O, M.C., D.F.C., M.M.; Col. Cummings; F/Lt. Innes; F/Lt. Bell-Salter; F/Lt. Yule; F/Lt. Sherrington; F/O Fokes, D.F.M.

job was completed, the officers and cadets of the College very kindly presented me with a delightful gift as "a small mark of appreciation."

It is a curious coincidence that 74 Squadron was reformed on September 3, 1935—four years, to the day, before the outbreak of World War II. In view of its illustrious record in World War I, I can only conjecture that it had not been reformed earlier because none of the Air Staff could proudly claim to be "one of the Tiger boys." It has been more than a puzzle to me to fathom why, when deciding on the squadrons which were to form the peacetime Air Force, they did not include *one* of the three —Nos. 40, 74 and 85—in which Major "Mick" Mannock, V.C., the greatest British air fighter, had served.

Indeed, it was not until I stirred up a little hornets' nest in the 'thirties that 40 Squadron was formed at Abingdon. So much for the Air Staff's idea of R.A.F. tradition. Now that senior Air Staff positions are held by ex-Cranwell cadets, their long experience no doubt will encourage tradition as the Royal Navy does. Nelson still lives—as every naval cadet who enters Dartmouth College soon learns.

I was in charge of the Direct Entry Officers' Courses at Uxbridge when a youngster named Malan came into the Service in June, 1936. I was immediately attracted by his sincere manner, quiet disposition, resolute speech and very strong face, which characterised determination and leadership.

I used to lecture on air fighting at these courses. Malan was the keenest of the newly fledged officers to ask questions afterwards. He would even come to my office, thirsting for further information. It was obvious to me that here was a young man who was a born air-fighter. I liked his steely, blueish-grey eyes; they held that "something" which few men possess.

Adolph Gysbert Malan was born at Wellington, South Africa, in 1910. Educated at the Wellington Public School, he decided on a sea career and joined the South African training-ship *General Botha*. At the age of fifteen and a half years he joined the Union Castle Line as a cadet. Before changing his mind and joining the R.A.F. in 1936, he had qualified for his second mate's certificate and served several years at sea. I once asked him what had made him choose the R.A.F. He replied: "Captain Beauchamp-Proctor, V.C., is a South African. He has always been my hero, and I've decided to emulate him."

There is little to choose between the glorious records of "Sailor" Malan and Beauchamp-Proctor, either as leader or air fighter. On the counts of courage and efficiency in the air, Malan also deserved a Victoria Cross. Undoubtedly, he was the outstanding fighter pilot of World War II. He was the top scorer of Fighter Command, with twenty-nine victories by June 30, 1941.

He held the record for three years, until he was "grounded." By the end of the war he had risen to the rank of Group Captain. He was the first air fighter of World War II to win the D.S.O. and bar and D.F.C. and bar. As a squadron leader and wing commander (flying), he was a hard taskmaster, but a brilliant leader. His pilots idolised him as much as the Luftwaffe feared him.

The country owes to the Mannocks and the Malans a debt it can never repay.

Before the war, Hornchurch Aerodrome was the home station of the Fighting 74. I frequently visited my old squadron and gave the pilots talks on my experiences with the original·Tigers, as well as on *esprit de corps* and morale. They were all as keen as mustard.

I was glad to see Flying Officer A. G. Malan, Flying Officer W. P. F. Treacy and Flying Officer Paddy Byrne in the squadron, since I had singled them out as "good types" when they were under me at Uxbridge. Indeed, I had asked a friend with authority in Air Ministry personnel postings to have them sent to Tiger Squadron. My judgment was good, for they all turned out to be great air fighters and men of steel. One of my most cherished possessions, to-day, is a card which was written and signed by Malan and Wing Commander A. C. Deere. It reads: "Taffy, you trained so many of the so FEW."

On June 26, 1936, I left the Royal Air Force after twenty-one years' service. But I was not done with flying. I was invited to take on an interesting job with the famous firm of Reid and Sigrist, whose most reliable flying instruments were fitted in all service aircraft.

The firm was now branching out into a new kind of work— the flying training of Royal Air Force Volunteer Reserve pilots. My job was to interview the ex-R.A.F. short-service pilots applying for posts as instructors. The Managing Director of the firm, Squadron Leader George Reid, D.F.C., had been one of the early R.N.A.S. war pilots. He was the principal actor in one of the most thrilling dramas of the 1914–18 air war. Here's the story, as he told it to me:

"At daybreak on March 24, 1916, flying a Short seaplane, I was one of five pilots who set off from H.M.A/C. *Vindex* to bomb an airship base believed to be located at Tondern on the Schleswig coast. On our way to the objective we had to fly through a snowstorm which became thicker and thicker as time went on. Only two of the five machines returned to the *Vindex*. While I was groping my way back, my observer, Chief Petty Officer Mullins, spotted a Sopwith seaplane on the water near the shore off Hoyer. The pilot was waving frantically. I throttled back and landed alongside. I found the Sopwith had engine trouble, so I tried to put it right.

"I had hardly started on the job when some German civilians appeared on the beach and shouted encouragement, obviously under the impression that we were Germans. Then some German soldiers were seen to be approaching, so I decided to strap the pilot of the Sopwith, Flight Lieutenant Hay, to a strut and take to the air again. The German civilians waved goodbye and good luck to us as we took off.

"The old Short, with its additional burden, staggered heroically through the snowstorm, and I was in high spirits. Then, suddenly, my heart almost stopped beating. One of the magnetos had packed up. There was nothing for it but to force-land off the island of Sylt.

"The magneto was beyond repair, but I could still 'have a go' on the one which fired the right bank of cylinders. Since I could not take off, I began to taxi my machine at about four knots in the direction where I hoped the *Vindex* would be.

"After three hours of rough-riding the waves of the open sea I saw a motor-boat filled with soldiers approaching us at top speed. Then I heard the drone of aeroplane engines, and spotted two seaplanes diving towards us. They landed near the Short. But the crews of both aircraft and motor-boat were Huns. And so ended our thrilling adventure."

It was not the end of Squadron Leader George Reid. On the way to prison camp in a fast-moving train, he gave his escort the slip by indicating that he wanted to go to the lavatory. Carelessly, they let him go alone. Whereupon George, ignoring the speed of the train, opened a carriage door and jumped out on to the embankment. Unluckily, he broke his leg in the attempt. He was recaptured, after many hours of freedom, in great pain. George made other attempts at escape later. On his release from captivity at the end of the war, he was awarded the Distinguished Flying Cross—a most deserved honour and a most unusual award after so many years.

This was the man who in 1935 bought many fields near

Desford, Leicestershire, and turned them into an aerodrome which became famous for the efficiency of the instructors who trained the newly-formed R.A.F.V.R.

By 1939, the firm of Reid and Sigrist had five aerodromes, and a large number of similar aerodromes were run by other famous firms, like De Havilland, Flying Training, at Hamble, Blackburn and Duncan Davies. The pupils were short-service officers entering the R.A.F. for five years and week-end Volunteer Reserve men holding the rank of sergeant. When war came, this big reserve became the backbone of the R.A.F. during the Battle of Britain and afterwards. For example, even in 1940, the pilots of Tiger Squadron—with the exception of Squadron Leader White—were all initially trained in the civilian-run aerodromes.

I remained with Reid and Sigrist until I was unexpectedly recalled to service on August 25, 1939. It happened this way: I was awakened at five o'clock on that morning by thunderous knocking on the front door of my house, accompanied by the prolonged ringing of the door bell. I jumped out of bed and rushed to the window to see who was causing the commotion. Down below, in the grey light of dawn, I could see the figure of the village policeman and postman.

"What the devil do you want at this hour?" I called.

The policeman looked up. "Are you Squadron Leader J. I. T. Jones, D.S.O., M.C., D.F.C., M.M.?" he asked solemnly.

"Of course, I am," I snapped. "You've seen me often enough."

Unperturbed, he continued: "Well, please come down to the door. The postman has an important letter for you."

Putting on my dressing-gown, I went below and opened the front door. The postman handed me the letter. Puzzled, I asked the policeman: "What's all this about? Does it take two of you to deliver the post now?"

For the first time he smiled. "You've got to put on your uniform and shoot down some more of them old Huns," he said. "Good luck, sir."

I went into my newly furnished lounge. I had only bought the house three months earlier. I opened the letter which was to put me back into harness again.

It instructed me to report immediately to Training Command Headquarters, Market Drayton, Shropshire. I was appointed to be the Chief Signals Officer.

A deep hatred for Hitler and all he stood for welled up inside me. Between the tears of my wife and myself, because we had to break up our first-ever and only newly occupied house and home, I asked God to give me health to assist in the destruction of this vile beast and his followers. That prayer was answered, however small my contribution to victory turned out to be. I immediately wrote to the Air Ministry, requesting that consideration be given to my taking over command of Tiger Squadron. I pointed out that I had kept in touch with the pilots of the squadron through the years of peace, and had drilled into them the offensive spirit and the will to conquer. I stressed that in my opinion (which was in opposition to that of many senior officers), the fighting would revert to dog-fights, as in World War I, whatever the "top" speed of the aircraft engaged, and in this I was proved to be correct. While on this subject, I predict that should a third war come, the main fighting casualties will again be the result of dog-fights. Young pilots, remember these words! And remember that superior height is essential in attacking fighters, but *not* twin bombers.

But to revert to my application. I was politely informed that my "fighting spirit" was appreciated, but owing to my age (forty-three) and "the new technique" of fighting, such a posting was out of the question. I was not versed in the radio control of squadrons. In other words, I was to be a good boy and attend to the job picked out for me. But my heart was not in signals (nowadays called radar). It was in flying. Despite my forty-three years, I was fighting fit. To fly Hurricanes and Spitfires became my supreme ambition. Determinedly and proudly, I eventually achieved my goal.

Don't think for a minute that I am decrying the value of signals. In World War I, we had neither radar nor radio-telephony.

If a pilot wished to draw his leader's attention to any Huns he had spotted, he flew close up and just in front of him and waggled his wings. When the leader waggled *his* wings to tell him to give further information, the pilot would lift his arm if the Huns were above or point downwards if they were below. He would then turn his machine in their direction and dip his nose up and down! How amateurish it all sounds *now*.

We would never have won the Battle of Britain without the help of Sir Robert Watson-Watt, who invented the type of radar whereby we could "fix" the approximate position of Nazi aeroplanes approaching our coasts. Radar gave our fighters the necessary time to meet their foes as they crossed our shores; or, if they had done so already, to make contact with them before they reached their targets or scurried homewards.

Tiger Squadron

I was in charge of the Electrical and Wireless Flight at the Royal Aircraft Experimental Establishment, Farnborough, in 1930–1, when Watson-Watt was beginning his earliest experiments. Everything concerning them was very "hush-hush." We know now that he was using a cathode-ray tube—the main component of a television set. He noticed that when an aeroplane was flying overhead, there was a disturbance on the cathode-ray tube. This was the beginning of the invention which so greatly helped to destroy the might of Goering's Luftwaffe and Hitler's dream of sleeping in Buckingham Palace.

We must also give praise to the Royal Observer Corps for their efficient and untiring co-operation with Fighter Command. When war was declared, we had radar stations, ten to fifteen miles apart, all along the south-east coast of England. There were observer posts all over the area. Telephones of the radar stations and observer posts were linked with the "filter room" and Observer Corps plotting room at Fighter Command Headquarters, Stanmore. The Observer Corps also had telephone communication with groups and sectors. We were not quite so deeply asleep or so defenceless as the Nazi High Command assumed.

One name which must always be linked with the Battle of Britain is that of the late Lady Houston. It was she who, when the British Government of the time refused, continued to finance the Schneider Trophy race. The late Mr. R. I. Mitchell designed the Spitfire from his aircraft which, in 1931, won the Trophy outright. The Hurricane, designed by Mr. Sydney Camm (Hawkers' brilliant chief designer), was also a direct result of knowledge gained in battling for the Schneider Trophy.

Both the Spitfire and the Hurricane mounted eight guns and were equipped with radio telephony. They were the first types of R.A.F. fighters to be fitted with retractable undercarriages. The Spitfire was the faster of the pair, and faster than either of the German fighters, the Messerschmitt 109 and 110.

The Spitfire could outdive the German fighters and catch them up. Frequently, when diving after a "runaway" 109, the pilot registered 550 m.p.h. By the autumn of 1940, modifications of the 109 had improved its performance to such an extent that it was comparable with the Spitfire mechanically. But it is the fighting spirit of the pilots that matters, and, as in World War I, our pilots found only one "Schitz-ot" type in 100 Huns.

The Hurricane's speed was around 300 m.p.h. It was highly manœuvrable, being able to turn inside the Messerschmitt 109, which had only four guns and a 20-mm. cannon to pierce the armour plate at the back of our pilots' seats.

Tiger Squadron was one of the very few chosen to be equipped with the Spitfire I.

The German bomber types most commonly used during Dunkirk and the Battle of Britain were the Heinkel, Dornier and Junkers 87 and 88. These machines had no gun turrets and only a token rear ward defence. The Germans increased the speed of their aircraft through sacrificing a good defence. The world now knows how foolish this policy proved. I am surprised that not more were destroyed. The bomber crews' efforts at defence were almost childish at times. They even resorted to throwing overboard all sorts of junk, such as coils of wire, in the hope of damaging our fighters' propellers.

The German bombers relied mainly on their fighter escorts, but not infrequently the 109 pilots were heard over the radio shouting "*Achtung*, Spitfire!" before turning for their aerodromes in northern France at top speed, noses down and tails between legs, leaving their unfortunate comrades to their fate.

We heard a lot, at first, about the Junkers 87 or Stuka, the dive-bomber type which created such material and, particularly, moral damage during the Germans' initial onslaught through the Ardennes, France and Belgium. Their accuracy of bombing was certainly more effective than that of other bombers, but they were so slow that the Spitfires and Hurricanes tore the guts out of them with their eight guns. Indeed, one squadron which attacked Croydon during the early phase of the Battle of Britain was completely destroyed; just as, later in the war, the only Italian fighter squadron (biplanes) to approach these shores off Harwich was almost completely wiped out by Hurricanes.

There is some argument about the number of Huns we shot down during the Battle of Britain. I am with the gallant, legless Douglas Bader, who said he would see the Channel dried before he accepted any German figures. The Huns have always been liars in my lifetime—from Kaiser Bill to Adolf Hitler.

Book Two

DUNKIRK AND THE BATTLE OF BRITAIN

17

At the outbreak of World War II, four groups—10, 11, 12 and 13—comprised Fighter Command for the purpose of command and control. Each of these consisted of a number of sectors which, in turn, had their own principal stations and operation-rooms, which were smaller than the big one at headquarters, but worked in the same way. Every sector station had its advanced aerodromes and small landing-grounds where aircraft could be dispersed in the event of the parent station being heavily bombed.

No. 11 Group, of which Tiger Squadron was a component, was by far the most important of the four. Its area was defined by drawing a line from Norwich to Poole and passing to the north-west of London. Consequently, it took in London and the south-western coast-line. Its commander was Air Vice-Marshal Sir Keith Park. I feel, in company with many of the great aces of the Battle of Britain, that Sir Keith has never had his fair share of recognition in the Honours List. When I compare the services to his country of this great New Zealander with that of some other knighted Air Force officers, I cannot help thinking that the least he deserved was a baronetcy.

At the opening of hostilities 11 Group had seven sector stations and twenty-two squadrons. Tiger Squadron's sector station was Hornchurch, in Essex. Fighter Command Headquarters was at Stanmore, Middlesex. Here, approaching aircraft were identified. If they were Huns they were given a label, and the information was passed to the appropriate group. Doubtful aircraft, labelled "X raid," were also passed on—just in case! The group would then issue orders to sectors as to the number of squadrons which should participate. The sector commander on duty decided which squadrons should scramble. Once off the ground, the tactics were left to the squadron leaders.

There were four states of readiness for the squadrons at a sector aerodrome: Stand-by (two minutes); readiness (five minutes); available (twenty minutes); released. When the two minutes of the stand-by period were up, the order "Scramble!" came over the "blower."

A squadron at "readiness" eagerly awaited the order to scramble, which meant that pilots had to get off the ground at once. (What joyous music was the roar of a squadron of Spitfires taking off!) While awaiting the signal, a mechanic would be in the pilot's seat, keeping the engine warm, and as soon as the order to "Scramble!" was received, he would start up and move over on to the wing to help the pilot do up his belts. In that way the machine could taxi from the dispersal point to take-off position in minimum time. Actually there always were three mechanics to each machine: one to keep the engine ready for a quick start, another in charge of the self starter, and a third to help the pilot don his parachute quickly. They were all very important men in the scheme of a quick take-off. Often, however, the pilot himself had taken his place in the cockpit before the stand-by period was over.

A squadron of twelve aircraft usually flew in sections of three or four (very occasionally in pairs, depending on the C.O.'s tactics, which naturally differed), with one section acting as "weavers." The latter were the pilots whose very important responsibility was to inform the Leader of any Huns above and behind his squadron who were ready to "jump" (i.e. stage a surprise attack).

The squadron in the air was controlled by radar from the sector, but the leader decided on the fighting tactics. The operations-room relied on information supplied, but it could never be absolutely correctly apprised of every Hun in the air, together with their accurate positions. Hence the necessity for "weavers."

There was usually strict radio-telephone silence, unless something really important cropped up. For example, if one of the "weavers" spotted Nazis above and behind, he would break wireless silence to pass on the information.

To ensure secrecy, the sections were known by colours—red, yellow, blue and green—and the Leader was always No. 1.

Similarly, the other pilots in a section of three would be numbered, say, Yellow 2 and Yellow 3. If the section were one of four, then there would be a Yellow 4. It was an excellent idea, and prevented the Hun from knowing the leaders he was up against.

Pilots always used these secret code numbers when making out their combat reports, but later, in describing air battles, I shall give the fighter's name whenever possible.

Dunkirk and the Battle of Britain

Radar information from ground to aircraft was also in code. Probably the hardest-worked words were "bandits" and "angels," which signified "enemy" and "height." Thus, "Bandits fifty, angels twenty" meant fifty Huns at 20,000 feet. The direction of the enemy aircraft was given as a compass vector. These, of course, were signals from the operations-room to the fighters. But from aircraft to ground we had the famous code signal for which the operational chief was always waiting. It was "Tally-ho!" And it meant that the leader could see the enemy. At any moment the stuttering machine guns and cannons would be tearing the guts out of the Nazi formations.

Sometimes, sitting in the sector corps-room, you could hear for split seconds the rattle of those guns. Once, listening in at the Biggin Hill operations-room, I heard "Sailor" Malan's voice over the R/T: "Tally-ho!" A few seconds later, he was calling loudly to the Tiger boys following him: "Let 'em have it! Let 'em have it!" Then I heard the chatter of his guns as they fired at the rate of 1,000 rounds a minute. Two Nazis died in those few seconds.

The inactive periods at dispersals, when the pilots played cards or restlessly roamed about awaiting the "Scramble!" order, were often a greater strain on the nerves than the few tense moments of battle. This hanging about for the scramble and the subsequent combat, after months of intense and nerve-racking fighting, caused a type of "nerves" which left an indelible mark on the pilots. They themselves often failed to notice the insidious change in their personalities which was so clear to the doctors—a change which gave a public uneducated in psychology the idea that all air fighters were wild and irresponsible men.

The civilian only saw those heroes when they were relaxing, enjoying "fun and games" off duty, and not in the grim battle for their lives and their country's safety tens of thousands of feet up, where the sky was literally the limit as they juggled with death.

Occasionally pilots broke down under the prolonged stress and strain. They developed what the psychiatrists called a psycho-neurosis. A long rest was the only cure. But frequently a man would be sent for a "rest" as instructor to an operational training unit (O.T.U.). This was quite wrong. It was no rest whatever, as I, having commanded a Spitfire O.T.U., know only too well. Teaching formation flying to fledglings in Spitfires was more nerve-racking than facing an oncoming, hate-breathing Messerschmitt. You could get out of the way of the 109 and shoot him down. But with the pupil—Oh, la, la! You had to "pull your finger out".

As will be well remembered, Britain expected enemy bombing to commence, with London as the main target, as soon as war was declared. On September 3, 1939, only a few minutes after Mr. Neville Chamberlain had told the nation over the wireless, "We are now at war with Germany," the first wailing siren was heard. Many people donned their gas masks and kept them on until the "All Clear." I was not one of them. I never thought Hitler would have the guts to use gas. He had already been a victim of it in the 1914-18 war. Once bitten, twice shy! The siren proved to be the first of many false alarms. The "enemy" was a machine carrying Dutch refugees, which had crossed the coast without having notified Fighter Command.

Tiger Squadron was involved in a similar abortive job next day. Flight Lieutenant Adolph "Sailor" Malan led A Flight (Red Section), with Flying Officers Measures, Byrne, Freeborn, and Sergeants Hawkin and Flinders on a patrol by sections to intercept enemy raiders approaching the coast from Holland. The "enemy," this time, turned out to be our own bombers. Incidentally, it was on September 4 that another pilot for whom I had "worked a posting" joined the Tigers from the Fleet Air Arm. Flying Officer J. C. Mungo-Park, a Yorkshireman, proved himself worthy of the valiant fold into which I had got him. Gay and gallant, he won the D.F.C. and bar and commanded the Tigers before he was killed in 1941.

My experience of air fighters in the 1914-18 War had taught me how to pick a "good probable." Usually, though not invariably, your fighter has to be a mildly psychopathic personality, with a naughty twinkle in his blue-grey eyes. Brown-eyed pilots seem less boisterous by nature and more at home in bombers. I wonder why this is? Of course, there are exceptions. Wing Commander Norman Ryder is one. He was the first Spitfire pilot to shoot down a Nazi and the first of our fighters to be shot down in the sea.

Tiger Squadron opened its illustrious war record tragically, even though the incident was indicative of its efficient gunnery training and marksmanship, which augured well for future air battles. It happened during the first complete squadron patrol on September 6.

A Flight, led by Malan, and B Flight, led by Treacy, were ordered to scramble to intercept an enemy patrol. Malan led the squadron towards an approaching formation of fighters, but, realising that they were Hurricanes, turned away. Paddy Byrne and Freeborn mistook the aircraft for Germans and opened fire, each pilot shooting down his "enemy." Pilot Officer Halton-Harrop, flying one of the shot-down Hurricanes, was killed. The other pilot escaped injury. Both men were promising pilots of 56 Squadron. Rightly, Byrne and Freeborn stood their court-martial. Equally rightly, both were honourably acquitted.

In October, 1939, the Squadron moved to the satellite aero-drome at Rochford, where formation practice, fighter attacks, D/F homing, Ack-Ack co-operation, dusk landings and night-flying training were carried out during the "phony war" period. The fighting tempo of the Spitfire was to be three times as fast as that of the S.E. 5 in World War I. The Spitfire was con-structed of duralumin, not wood and fabric which broke up in the air.

Dark, curly-haired, blue-eyed, stockily built Flying Officer W. G. Measures shot down a Nazi and so achieved the first of nearly 150 victories which were to be recorded on the squadron board and show the Tigers leading the fighter field on October 30, 1940, when the Battle of Britain ended.

The great day was November 20, 1939. Accompanied by Pilot Officer Temple-Harris and Sergeant Flinders, Flying Officer Measures attacked a Heinkel 111 at 27,000 feet, fifteen miles over the sea, east of Southend. The time was 12.45 p.m. Measures ordered his Yellow Section line astern before attacking and opening fire from 800 to 300 yards with a one and a half seconds' burst. The estimated speed of the enemy was 270 m.p.h.

The Heinkel dived at about 400 m.p.h. to 6,000 feet before going into a cloud. Diving after him, Measures' Spitfire got into his slipstream and broke off the attack, but Temple-Harris carried on the good work and small black objects were seen to be breaking off the Heinkel before it was lost in the cloud. The following day, the pilot and observer were picked up in a rubber dinghy. Both were wounded. The dark green camouflaged Heinkel rested where hundreds more of the vaunted Luftwaffe were to find their last home, at the bottom of the sea.

When Measures landed after this fight, he told me he had perforated his eardrums during the long dive after the Heinkel. I have met other pilots with similar disabilities as a result of diving steeply in Spitfires which were clocking more than 550 m.p.h. Pulling out from such dives sometimes caused black-outs.

Tiger Squadron

From this time on, the Squadron worked only on Home Defence. Lord Dowding rightly refused to send any of his seven Spitfire squadrons to France to be a part of the Expeditionary Force. Besides the risk of losing a Spitfire over the German lines, it was not good policy to allow Luftwaffe pilots to become familiar with the aircraft's tactical abilities in battle before Goering's air armada launched its attack on Britain as the first stage in "Operation Sea-lion."

Tiger Squadron concentrated its training at Rochford Aerodrome, Southend, and after December at Hornchurch, on night flying, formation flying, tactical attacks, D/F homing, anti-aircraft co-operation, cine-camera work, and—most important of all—air firing. Malan was very hot at the latter. He admits, as all successful air aces do, that air firing practice is the key to success. Even on the ground, he practised deflection shooting.

Once, in 1941, while I was visiting him at Biggin Hill, he asked: "Do you like jugged hare, Taffy?"

I replied: "Very much."

"Well, drive my car," he said. "I know where there is a hare on the aerodrome. I saw it when I was flying this afternoon."

Into his car we got. Sailor, armed with a double-barrel gun, opened the sun roof and guided me to a certain spot on the aerodrome. Suddenly a hare got up near the centre of the drome and about 40 yards ahead of us. I put my foot on the accelerator and went flat out after it.

When we closed up with the hare, it began to zigzag. I followed, keeping formation with it. When I got to within 25 yards of the target, I was doing between 50 and 60 m.p.h., and the car was jolting a good deal. Sailor lifted the gun to his shoulder. There was a bang—and in front of us was a dead hare. Having picked it up, Sailor said: "Taffy, I think there is another one over there." He pointed out the direction in which I was to drive. Sure enough, up got another hare, and I did some more dirt-track driving. Again Sailor waited until we got to within 30 yards before firing. And once more we picked up a dead hare.

We were now at the far end of the aerodrome, the opposite end from the officers' mess. As we were driving back, Sailor asked: "Do you like plovers, too?" Smiling, he pointed up at a small covey flying across the aerodrome. I knew by the twinkle in his eye that he wanted me to drive under them. I obliged. Believe it or not, he got a left and a right!

I was so amazed by the exhibition that all I could say was: "Good God, Sailor! How do you do it? I just can't believe it."

OUTSIDE THE OFFICERS' MESS, CLAMARAIS, ST. OMER,
SEPTEMBER, 1918

Back Row: L. A. Richardson (New Brunswick); F. E. Luff, D.F.C. (Clarland, Ohio, U.S.A.); H. G. Shoemaker, D.F.C. (Bridgetown, N.S., Canada).

Middle Row: P. F. C. Howe (Bremersdorf, Swaziland); H. G. Clements (Leicester); C. H. Matthiessen (New York, U.S.A.); E. Roxburgh-Smith, D.F.C. (Romford); J. Adamson (Bournemouth); R. H. Gray (Wellington, N.Z.); H. C. Goudie (Moose Jaw, Sask.); S. T. Stidolph (Wellington, N.Z.); F. S. Gordon, D.F.C. (Auckland, N.Z.).

Bottom Row: R. Spiers (Glasgow); A. G. Kiddie, D.F.C. (Kimberley, S.A.); G. W. G. Gauld, D.F.C. (Mimico, Ontario); L. Harrison, D.F.C. (South Africa); F. J. Hunt, D.F.C. (Basingstoke); J. Venter, D.F.C. (South Africa); S. Carlin, D.F.C. (Hull); Harry Coverdale (Blackheath).

From Top Left: Sqd/Ldr. A. G. Malan, D.S.O., D.F.C.; Sqd/Ldr. A. A. McKellar, D.F.C.; Sqd/Ldr. Max Aitken, D.F.C.; F/Lt. H. S. L. Dundas, D.F.C.; Sqd/Ldr. W. P. F. Treacy; F/O W. Urbanowicz; F/Lt. J. Cunningham; W/Cdr. John Peel, D.S.O., D.F.C.; F/Lt. B. E. Finucane, D.F.C.

When we got back and carried our "bag" into the mess, Al Deere said: "Where did you get those?"

"On the aerodrome," Sailor replied with his pleasant smile. "We've been ferreting."

I then knew one of Sailor's secrets as an air fighter—a steady aim and good deflection shooting. I used to think I was quite a useful deflection shot, but I was "not at the races" compared with Malan.

18

THE GLORIOUS DEEDS OF the pilots of 1 and 73 Squadrons with the Expeditionary Force in France will rank in history with the grim heroism of the men who fought and won the Battle of Britain, which was really the turning point of the war. In Hurricanes, they valiantly bore the brunt of the fighting with the numerically superior Luftwaffe, who were throwing out tactical feelers to probe our fighting strength and the location of our aerodromes.

The Hawker Hurricane, our main fighter in France, was powered by a Rolls-Royce Merlin engine of 1,100 h.p. and had a speed of 330 m.p.h. (The S.E. 5, the "Spitfire" of World War I, was powered by a 180 h.p. Hispano-Suiza engine and had a maximum speed of 130 m.p.h.!) The Hurricane's eight Browning guns, disposed in two groups of four, were fitted in the wings and fired outside the radius of airscrew rotation. Each gun fired at the rate of 1,200 rounds per minute. So that, on pressing the "tit," a stream of bullets poured towards the enemy at a total rate of 9,600 a minute. These sudden bursts—usually of two to three seconds' duration, to conserve ammunition—temporarily reduced the speed of the aircraft by thirty miles an hour, but did not affect the manœuvrability.

The Spitfire I was similarly armed, but had a speed in excess of 350 m.p.h. Never was the claim "I am the captain of my soul" more applicable to any human being than to the man who flew alone against an enemy, many miles up, at speeds like these.

The greatest care was taken by the Royal Air Force to prevent "line shooting" in connection with the claiming of air-fighting victories. Here, for the record, is the official "gen" on the subject:

Definitions of Enemy Casualties

Destroyed

(*a*) Aircraft must be seen on the ground or in the air destroyed by a member of the crew or formation, or confirmed from other sources, e.g. ships at sea, local authorities, etc.

(b) Aircraft must be seen to descend with flames issuing. It is not sufficient if only smoke is seen.

(c) Aircraft must be seen to break up in the air.

Probables

(a) When the pilot of a single-engined aircraft is seen to bale out.

(b) The aircraft must be seen to break off the combat in circumstances which lead our pilot to believe it will be a loss.

Damaged

Aircraft must be seen to be considerably damaged as the result of attack, e.g. under-carriage dropped, engine stopped, aircraft parts shot away, or volumes of smoke issuing.

I strongly recommend the reading of two stirring books about the fighting of the Air Component (Fighter Squadrons) during the early days in France. They are *Fighter Pilot*, by Wing Commander Paul Richey, D.F.C. (who was to command Tiger Squadron in 1942), and *Squadrons Up*, by Noel Monks, the genial Air Correspondent of the *Daily Mail*. I consider *Fighter Pilot* the most vividly descriptive book ever written about air fighting during World War II.

Fittingly, the first Nazi machine shot down in France, a Dornier 17, fell to the guns of a pilot of 1 Squadron. It was on October 30, 1939, that Pilot Officer P. W. C. ("Boy") Mould found the Dornier at 19,000 feet over Toul and destroyed it in flames. Born at Hallaton, Uppingham, in 1917, Mould joined the R.A.F. as an apprentice in 1934. He was awarded a Cranwell Cadetship in 1937 and passed out to be commissioned in 1939. He later was awarded a D.F.C. and destroyed several other Germans.

During these early days in France, the aerodromes were frequently attacked. Typical was the raid on Vitry Aerodrome on May 18, 1940. Eight aircraft were employed. It was thought that they were Me. 110s, but owing to the element of surprise and the speed at which the attack was carried out definite identification was not possible. At about 6 p.m. four Me 110's appeared at approximately 7,000 feet to the north-west of the aerodrome. The fighter patrol over the aerodrome immediately engaged them. Immediately, the eight bombing aircraft appeared out of the sun to the west of the aerodrome, at about 6,000 feet and possibly three miles away.

Almost as soon as they were seen, the formation made an almost vertical dive to ground level. Flattening out to about 50 feet above the ground, they flew at this height straight across from west to east in open formation. They crossed the aerodrome, stick-bombing, while the rear-gunners machine-gunned aircraft and buildings. Then, still at a low height, they flashed out of sight in an easterly direction. Their speed across the aerodrome was in the neighbourhood of 350 m.p.h. Although the ground defence crews around Vitry were fully alert and had had considerable practice in engaging enemy aircraft, the raid was carried out so swiftly, and with such surprise, that they had not time to bring their guns to bear before the aircraft passed over the aerodrome and were out of range.

Eight Hurricanes, one Blenheim, one Moth, one petrol bowser, one ammunition dump and one Nissen hut containing photographic equipment were destroyed. The bombs used appeared to be light, and no serious damage was caused to the aerodrome surface. Most of the bombs were fused with only a few seconds' delay, but some were fused with delay periods ranging from a quarter of an hour to three and four hours. Raids of this kind were a serious problem. Similarly, the success of the German advance was due to the heavy and incessant bombing of our ground forces. Particularly harassing was the dive-bombing by Ju. 87s.

The advance of the German tanks was preceded by violent bombing attacks, which were requested by wireless by the enemy whenever he encountered any resistance. The dive-bombing attacks took our troops by surprise and lessened their powers of resistance. The tanks then took advantage of the wavering to penetrate the gaps made.

Whenever our fighters were in sufficient strength to oppose these bombing attacks, the Hun armoured units, having to act unaided, were unable to register any marked success. It was essential, therefore, that a strong body of fighter aircraft should be sent with all speed to the sectors attacked by the enemy.

The German bombers frequently operated in large formations of thirty to fifty aircraft, escorted by a number of Me. 110's and Me. 109's, which penetrated to a considerable depth over our territory. Certain bombers—in particular, the He. 111—had increased their fire power in the rear and lateral sectors of fire. Under these conditions, fighting tactics had to be adapted to correspond with the material and tactics employed by the enemy. Attack in succession in line ahead on an enemy formation would encounter the maximum concentration of fire, and had to be changed to angle deflection fire.

Dunkirk and the Battle of Britain

It was a common occurrence to see one Hurricane challenging a formation of from fifty to sixty Nazi raiders. Before the *blitzkreig* had started on May 10, 1940, the men of 1 and 73 Squadrons— the R.A.F.'s advance air guard—had proved the superiority of British pilots and machines over their opponents of the Luftwaffe. These two squadrons had at least one representative from each of the chief member-countries of the Commonwealth of Nations. Leslie Clisby was an Australian. E. U. ("Cobber") Kain, the ace of them all, was a New Zealander. "Hilly" Brown hailed from Canada, and I. J. Le Roux from South Africa. A. ("Taffy") Clowes, a Welshman from Cardiff, eventually rose from sergeant-pilot to wing commander, wearing the D.S.O., D.F.C. and D.F.M. Kilmartin was a Scot; while P. J. H. ("Bull") Hallahan, who led 1 Squadron with Celtic fervour, was an Irishman.

Of course, the majority were English-born, like Paul Richey, Billy Drake, Lorrimer, Prosser Hanks, Peter Mould, Johnny Walker, Demozay, Stratton, Peter Brett, "Ginger" Paul and "Fanny" Orton, No. 2 ace of 73 Squadron. Then there were other fine fellows, like Dickie Martin ("the Prisoner of Luxembourg"), and Sergeants Payne, George Berry, R. E. Lovett, J. G. Perry and Winn. These boys struck terror into the hearts of the Nazis, some of whom were seen taking to their parachutes at the approach of the initial "Few." They had the measure of their opponents and it was an encouraging prelude to what was to follow.

It was while serving with the Expeditionary Force that British pilots first used parachutes in war to save their lives when aircraft were in flames or unmanageable. And two facts immediately emerged. First, pilots were able to fight again—some as soon as they got back to their aerodromes, others when they had recovered from their injuries. Second, pilots did not jump "unnecessarily," as a chairborne senior officer had once predicted they would.

The Tiger boys were fast asleep in their beds when Hitler unleashed his armoured Panzer divisions, Stuka (Ju. 87) dive-bombers and parachute regiments against the Western Front before the crack of dawn on May 10, 1940. He was allowed to choose his own zero hour by the ineptness of those in France and Britain who were responsible for Allied air strategy and tactics. He could not have shouted louder that he was moving his victorious troops and air squadrons from the Eastern front to the west. The movements went on for months, but there was no strategic bombing of railway junctions or aircraft factories. Don't ask me who was personally to blame. Ever since the tragic day, senior officers on both sides of the Channel have been passing and re-passing the "buck."

The Dutch had to resist the paratroops, used for the first time in any major war. It was at 4 a.m. that the barracks and aerodromes in Fortress Holland were attacked with bombs and paratroops. By 5 a.m., three aerodromes near The Hague had been captured by paratroopers dressed in Dutch and even British uniforms. This typical Nazi trick bluffed the Dutch sentries, who held their fire and were themselves mowed down. If Hitler's dream of "Operation Sea-Lion" had ever materialised, no doubt we in Britain would have been up against a similar deception. The invaders would have used the uniforms of our men captured before and after Dunkirk. Once a Hun, always a Hun.

General von Sponeck, in charge of operations, had special orders to capture The Hague. He did not succeed. He and his white horse, travelling by special aeroplane to make a triumphant entry into The Hague, were killed when the machine was shot down by a Dutch pilot in one of the 248 Dutch military aircraft. Before they lost all their aeroplanes, that heroic handful of Dutch fighters brought down more than 100 Nazis.

The Nazis used tactics in Holland similar to those employed in Norway. They surrounded the Royal Palace in the hope of capturing the Queen and the Royal Family. But they failed. Paratroopers dropped in the Palace grounds were killed instantly by the Royal Guards. At 10 a.m. the capital was bombed heavily, and paratroops landed in the afternoon. They were soon mopped up, and The Hague defences stood. British Wellington bombers and Hurricane and Blenheim fighters assisted the Dutch until the evacuation. Casualties were heavy. On May 13, Queen Wilhelmina, accompanied by Princess Juliana, Prince Bernhard and their children, crossed to Britain in a British destroyer. The air escort was provided by Tiger Squadron. It was indeed an honour.

Next to be rolled up was the overwhelmed Belgian army. Whether King Leopold, its commander-in-chief, was right in throwing in the towel will be argued in Belgium for centuries to come. But again British bombers and fighters did their damnedest in most disheartening circumstances. And again many good men died. From May 13 onward, the Panzer divisions, aided by Stuka dive-bombers, poured through the Ardennes to breach the line of the French Ninth Army between Sedan and Dinant.

Dunkirk and the Battle of Britain

They crossed the Meuse and fanned out into the wide-open, defenceless spaces of France and Belgium. The right flank of the attack wheeled north-west and gradually forced back the British "Contemptibles" of World War II.

At first, when the odds were not too great, the British not only held their own; they made a successful counter-attack on May 21–22 near Arras, and narrowed the gap during the next few days, but the French failed to carry out their part in the operation. This counter-attack was made without air support for the simple reason that no aircraft were available. Lord Dowding has told us since that pre-war planning had made no provision for fighters as part of the Expeditionary Force!

I do not know the names of the high-ranking strategists of the time, but it is obvious that, unlike Goering, they had not learned the lessons of World War I. My friends and I always thought that during the period 1918–39 there were too many high-ranking officers with little *practical* experience of air warfare at the head of the R.A.F. Neither were our peacetime generals as tank-minded as their Nazi "opposite numbers." Hence Dunkirk! If Hitler had not given that amazing order to halt the Panzers which were about to advance on Calais and Dunkirk, there would have been colossal slaughter instead of the successful evacuation of 338,226 soldiers. God has indeed been kind to Britain in the two world wars.

It was during the retreat to Dunkirk that Fighter Command aircraft, based on Home Defence aerodromes, made their first great effort of the war. Every day about 300 sorties were carried out. Nearly 500 Nazis were shot down in the Dunkirk area. That figure does not include the 350 Huns accounted for further south by the pilots of 1, 3, 17, 73, 79 (regular R.A.F. Squadrons), 242 (Canadian) Squadron, and 501 (Gloucester), 504 (Nottingham), 607 (Durham) and 615 (Surrey) Auxiliary Air Force Squadrons. The latter were nicknamed "the week-end playboys." *Some* playboys!

It has been estimated that the Home Defence squadrons, while covering the Dunkirk operation, flew more than 2,000,000 miles from their South of England aerodromes. Of every twenty machines which went on patrol, nineteen came home. That "thin blue line" of patrolling aircraft was holding back, at the very least, a numerical superiority of from six to ten to one from the overcrowded beaches. Naturally, a few bombers were able to sneak through, and the defenceless troops, some armpit-deep in the sea, patiently awaiting rescue developed an anxiety state which was reflected in their antagonistic attitude to Air Force personnel when they got back to England.

At that time, as O.C. Flying at Stormy Down Aerodrome, I was sleeping at the Sea Bank Hotel, Porthcawl. There I was accosted by a tired Army captain, who, on seeing my row of medal ribbons, shouted to his comrades: "Look, chaps! Here's one of the Dunkirk heroes." He then spat on the floor and laughed uproariously, like an insane person. His friends cheered and made peculiar and uncomplimentary noises.

I informed the General in charge of the evacuated troops, who was also staying at the hotel, and he ordered the offenders back to camp. As far as I was concerned, that was the end of the incident. I, too, have been bombed and fired at by aircraft, and even though I was not waist-deep in water, I must say I did not like it. I understood, therefore, that the captain was suffering from severe and prolonged strain.

All pilots, whether they were on the Dunkirk operations or not, were relieved to read Mr. Winston Churchill's words to Parliament on June 4, the last day of the evacuation:

"We must be very careful not to assign to this deliverance the attributes of a victory. Wars are not won by evacuations. *But there was a victory inside this deliverance, which should be noted. It was gained by the Air Force.* Many of our soldiers coming back have not seen the Air Force at work; they saw only the Nazi bombers which escaped its protective attack. They underrate its achievements. I have heard much talk of this; that is why I go out of my way to say this. I will tell you about it.

"There was a great trial of strength between the British and the German Air Forces. Can you conceive a greater objective for the Germans in the air than to make evacuation from these beaches impossible, and to sink all these ships which were displayed, almost to the extent of thousands? Could there have been an objective of greater military importance and significance for the whole purpose of the war than this? They tried hard, and they were beaten back; they were frustrated in their task. We got the Army away; and they have paid fourfold for any losses which they have inflicted. All of our types and all our pilots have been vindicated as superior to what they have at present to face.

"When we consider how much greater would be our advantage in defending the air above this island against an overseas attack, I must say that I find in these facts a sure basis upon which practical and reassuring thoughts may rest. I will pay my tribute to these young airmen. The great French Army was very largely, for the time being, cast back and disturbed by the onrush of a few thousands of armoured vehicles. May it not also be that the cause of civilisation itself will be defended by the skill and devotion of a few thousand airmen?"

The world now knows that Fighter Command pilots, inspired by Lord Dowding and Sir Keith Park, fought and defeated the might of the Luftwaffe with tigerish ferocity, even when physically and mentally fatigued almost to the point of sickness. I salute them!

Tiger Squadron, then based at Rochford Aerodrome, was first detailed for a Dunkirk patrol on May 21. These patrols encircled the Dunkirk area, starting over Boulogne to about twenty miles inland, making St. Omer the peak of the bend before proceeding east of Dunkirk. From May 21 to May 28, the squadron carried out four patrols a day. Then, with many casualties and aircraft riddled with bullets, it was taken out of the front line for re-equipment and rest.

Both men and machines were fatigued. Malan told me that on one or two occasions, when making the last landings of the day on May 27, his eyes were so tired that the aerodrome was in a sort of haze and he "just threw the old Spitfire on the ground." He said he did not know why he had not crashed. Pilots of all squadrons concerned in the strenuous operational flying of the time reported similar experiences.

Except for Malan, Sergeant W. M. Skinner, R.A.F.V.R., was the only pilot to serve continuously in Tiger Squadron from the declaration of war until March, 1941 (when he came for a "rest" to "the Brave Old Fifty-Third, the Fighting O.T.U.," which I was commanding at Heston Aerodrome). This is his account of the first Dunkirk patrol:

"We found, as the pilots of Air Component had done earlier in France, that after the initial formation or line astern attack the fighting developed into a series of dog fights, and it became a stern man-to-man scrap which gave the pilot with height over the enemy fighter the initiative.

"I had a feeling of trepidation as I crossed the Channel and saw the black smoke curling high into the sky from Dunkirk. I wondered how I would feel when I got into a scrap. As Malan was leading, I had complete faith in him, and had no terror of being 'jumped' by a Nazi formation.

"Well, we got into a fight, all right. Malan went into it with the initiative in our favour. Over the blower [radio], Sailor called out: 'Let 'em have it! Let 'em have it!' as he squirted a 109, which commenced to emit blackish smoke. I picked out my man, but failed to keep as cool as I should have done, so was off my target. However, when it was all over and I was on my way home I came to the conclusion that it was not so frightening as I had expected."

I think Skinner's feeling were those of the majority of pilots after their first taste of "pressing the tit" and having a go. Slim, dark-haired Skinner was nineteen years of age when he joined Tiger Squadron. He was educated at the Merchant Taylors' School, and before the war worked in the Midland Bank in London. He had the right blood in his veins, for his grandfather was a Welshman from Tregaron, Cardiganshire, and his father was a Royal Flying Corps pilot in World War I. He eventually destroyed nine Nazis and was awarded the Distinguished Flying Medal and commissioned. He was shot down and taken prisoner in June, 1941, while Tigers were escorting Stirlings bombing St. Omer.

Telling me that story, he said: "It was a very tame affair. First thing I saw was a line of bullet holes appearing across my port wing, and then a white cloud of glycol [engine-cooling liquid] coming out of the engine. The engine seized up. I pancaked in a field and was picked up immediately by a couple of Jerry soldiers. The only thought in my head at the time was that I had a date with a girl for that evening, and wouldn't be able to keep it or phone her.

"I was taken to Dulag Luft, the transit P.O.W. camp for aircrew, and to my delight was greeted by Paddy Byrne and Sammy Hoare. Later, I joined up with Boulding, Sandeman and Parkes—all Tiger boys. Paddy Byrne came up to scratch, as usual, and produced some home-made booze hidden away from the watch-dogs."

Some of the greatest air fighters began their careers as sergeant pilots. Names which come readily to mind are G. Allard, J. M. B. Beard, S. A. Burnell-Phillips, F. R. Carey, H. Chandler, A. V. Clowes, J. Frantisek (ace of 303 Polish Squadron), F. W. Higginson, H. M. Kitchener, D. E. Kingaby, J. H. Lacey, A. McDowall, C. Whitehead, G. C. Unwin, A. S. McKay and Hamlyn. Sergeant pilots had a fine record in the Battle of Britain, and Tiger Squadron sergeant pilots fought with tenacity and courage. There were Tony Mould, Flinders, Bushell, Hawkin and Ayres—all grand scrappers. Mould, Bushell and Ayres were killed later in the war.

19

DURING THE SECOND MORNING patrol over Dunkirk on May 21, Paddy Byrne—a short, thick-set irrepressible, devil-may-care Irishman, with the natural-born offensive spirit of the Celt —became a casualty. Malan commanded A Flight and Treacy B Flight. On this patrol Malan was leading his flight, which was flying in two sections of three. Paddy Byrne was leading the second section.

The patrol headed from Ostend to St. Omer—"to find some Jerries," as Malan announced over the R/T when instructing Paddy to close up on his section.

Malan led his flight at about 300 feet above the heads of our retreating army. As they passed over Clamarais Wood, which the enemy held, they ran into anti-aircraft fire. Panzers and Hun troops looked up with astonishment as the Spitfires screamed over their heads. When the patrol time was up, and still no Nazi planes could be seen, Malan wheeled his formation homewards, squirting his ammunition at suitable targets. The boys all enjoyed themselves until they flew back over Clamarais Wood. Then the Ack-Ack guns opened up again, and Paddy Byrne's machine was seen to be hit. Malan saw him going down to land with black smoke streaming from his engine.

We learned later that one shell had come up through the cockpit and wounded Paddy's leg. Another hit the engine, and another smashed into the tail section, putting the aircraft out of control. Paddy crawled out of the smashed plane with his face smothered in blood. "For you the war is over," said the Nazi soldier who took him prisoner.

After having his face cleaned up in a nearby farmhouse, Paddy was taken to a temporary "prisoners' cage." It consisted of a large field with a single strand of barbed wire around it, guarded by Nazi machine gunners. Here, in the open air, the seriously wounded were being treated on an improvised operating table. Most of the victims died of pneumonia later. The amputations appeared to Paddy to be most callous. It made him sick to watch them.

Tiger Squadron

It had been arranged in the mess at Rochford that every Tiger boy should have a go at escaping if captured. Paddy, who came from County Wicklow, put his quick Irish wits to work as he examined the position. A single strand of wire and a few not very alert sentries seemed to offer some encouragement. Then he noticed that a young Belgian boy was carrying into the camp buckets of water for the prisoners to drink. When the buckets were empty, the youngster would go outside to fetch more water. The problem was solved. Spitfire pilot Paddy Byrne would become a water-boy!

The sun blazed down on Paddy's second afternoon in the camp. Picking his time carefully, he followed the Belgian and asked for a drink. Because of the heat, the boy took off his coat before serving the water. Then, as Paddy drank thirstily, he walked off to attend to another prisoner.

It was Paddy's chance, and he snatched up the boy's coat and struggled into it before picking up one of the empty buckets and walking boldly out of the camp to freedom. Up, the Tigers! Paddy made for the British lines. Entering battle-scarred villages, he searched the empty houses for old clothes. At last he found a suit which fitted him. What was more, he picked up a road-worthy bicycle and a torch. His gallant heart now full of the songs of Killarney, he whistled his way past Panzers and ground troops. Had they but known!

Paddy's scheme was to cross the River Somme at some convenient point. It would not take long then to rejoin the British forces. After three days he reached the little village of Bray-sur-Somme, where he saw Nazi machine gunners firing across the river. This was obviously the spot for making his swim to safety under cover of darkness.

On his way to the point of embarkation, he passed a lonely house. There was a chance it might contain the food he needed so badly. Switching on his torch, he tried the back door. As he lifted the latch, a dog inside the house began barking furiously. Almost simultaneously came the sound of Nazi soldiers approaching at the double. Paddy dashed upstairs and hid under a bed. Up came the Germans. They rushed into the bedroom, threw back the bedclothes, swore, and then clattered down the stairs again. Paddy listened to them searching the ground floor. Then they moved out into the road and their footsteps died away.

Taking no more chances, Paddy made a bee-line for the Somme embankment, where he lay "doggo" for some time. Looking up at the moon in the heavens, he thought: "How splendid! I'll soon be back with the Tigers." At last, convinced by the silence that nobody was around, he slid down the side of the embankment—right into the arms of a Nazi machine-gun detachment. Such is the luck of escapers.

He was roughly manhandled and taken to the local barracks for interrogation. There he described himself as a French farmer who was looking for his wife. He said he had heard she had been seen crossing the Somme. The Jerries did not swallow this touching domestic story. Paddy came clean and admitted he was a British airman. He was put in a small cell for the rest of the night.

In the morning he was taken before a general who refused to believe he was anything but a spy. When he found himself being marched from the barracks between three fully armed Nazi thugs, he said to himself: "Well, Paddy, this is *it*." He expected to be shot against the nearest convenient wall. But he was only being taken on the first stage of the journey to the Dulag Luft at Oberursel, where he was overjoyed to meet other Tiger boys.

Later, in a camp near Frankfurt, Paddy became a leading light in the tunnelling game. One night in July, 1940, he was one of the twenty-four prisoners who escaped from the camp. The "brains" of this Frankfurt escape was my old and valued friend, Squadron Leader Roger Bushell (601 Auxiliary Squadron),who —like his great pal, Flight Lieutenant Michael Peacock, who was killed in France—was a junior counsel in the chambers of the famous English Rugby International and barrister, G. D. (khaki) Roberts, Q.C.

All twenty-four of the Frankfurt escapers were recaptured and interned in Stalag Luft III, located between Berlin and Breslau. This was the largest, most efficiently guarded Air Force officers' camp in Germany, with a total population of 10,000, including several thousand Americans.

Paddy Byrne, still undaunted, jumped from the train which was taking him from Barth to Stalag III. As he hit the ground his previously wounded ankle gave way, and the searching troops did not take long in finding him. He was put into the dank, dark, insanitary punishment cell for weeks as a result of this escapade, and was released only when it looked as if his damaged leg might become gangrenous.

When he recovered, his Irish heart continued to beat for freedom. He became one of the exclusive 500 prisoners of Stalag III who took part in the "Harry" tunnelling operations organised by South African, Roger Bushell. Of the seventy-six men who escaped through "Harry" tunnel on the night of

March 24, 1944, fifty were murdered and cremated by the vile Gestapo. The others were recaptured, with the exception of two Norwegians, who spoke German, and one Dutchman. Roger Bushell was among the murdered. The selection of those to make the attempt was made by putting into a hat the names of all who had helped in the tunnelling. Paddy was unlucky in the subsequent draw, and so lost his last chance of escape. But though the god of chance had forsaken him, his Tiger spirit remained with him until his eventual release. He would have made a great air fighter, worthy of the Fighting 74.

The Dunkirk air fighting was unlike the previous battles over Belgium and with the Air Component over France. The latter were fought in support of the swaying armies; the Dunkirk battle was a Homeric bid for air supremacy. Its object was to prevent the Luftwaffe bombers and fighters from shooting up the defenceless thousands of British soldiers waiting patiently in line formation, on the beaches and in the sea, for relief to reach them.

Had the position been reversed and the Germans been in the water and on the beaches, the Royal Air Force fighters alone would have massacred them. So much for Herman Goering's precious Luftwaffe.

The air fighting flared to a crescendo. On May 22, 11 Group destroyed twenty-seven Nazis and had ten "probables." Tiger Squadron took its full share of the toll. Indeed, Malan had an appetiser before breakfast. His three sections were donning their parachutes just after the break of dawn. He was instructed to patrol over the Channel in the Dover area at 12,000 feet, and soon sighted a Ju. 88 steering north-east in a clearing of a cloud. He instructed his Red section to form line astern (i.e. the aircraft flew one behind the other as they approached the enemy) and attempt to cut the invader off from the cloud.

The Ju. 88 dived for the Channel at a very steep angle, with an indicated air speed of 400 m.p.h., and dropped four bombs which fell harmlessly into the sea. Malan delivered No. 1 attack at 250 yards' range. After a two-second burst, the Nazi air gunner stopped firing his twin guns from the top turret, and the pilot took avoiding action by skidding and turning. Malan saw his incendiary bullets smash into the port engine and all around the fuselage. White vapour was streaming from both motors. When he first opened fire the Spitfire's air-speed indicator was showing 480 m.p.h., but after the fifth burst the Nazi's speed suddenly decreased. Malan's windscreen was covered with white vapour. He broke off the engagement to observe the result of his shooting.

Red 3, whose R/T had failed, attacked from 200 yards, expended all his ammunition and broke off. Then Red 2 (Tony Mould) went in, but after his first burst the Ju. suddenly lost height as though both engines had stopped and broken up. A couple of seconds later, there was nothing left but a dinghy floating forlornly in the sea. Malan searched for the Nazi crew, but the Channel had engulfed them with their Ju. 88.

May 23 saw fierce fighting, with the Canadian ace, Squadron Leader John Kent, leading the merry warriors of 92 Squadron into scrap after scrap. When they returned wearily to their mess at the end of the day, their score was twenty-four bombers and fighters.

In World War I, Squadrons 74 and 54 shared the same aerodrome at Clarmarais, near St. Omer. They frequently fought side by side over the Lille area against Baron von Richthofen's specially chosen warriors, the Red Devils, and their friendship on the ground was firm. By a curious chance, 74 and 54 shared Hornchurch Aerodrome at the beginning of World War II. And on May 23, 1940, they supported each other in the Battle of the Beaches. Often outnumbered by ten to one, the Spitfires of the old partners plunged into the fray. Eighteen Nazis went down to the guns of 54 Squadron. The Tigers shot down a further thirteen.

Tiger Squadron spread its successes throughout the day. The pilots shot down a Henschel near St. Omer before breakfast, a Condor near Ostend before lunch, Dorniers and Junkers also before lunch, more Junkers before teatime, and two Me. 109's before dinner. But the four patrols of the day were a great strain. After the last, they flopped into the mess chairs and settees and immediately fell asleep. Soon the arms and legs of some of the men were twitching. Occasionally a pilot was heard to say "Hold this, you bastard!" as he refought in dreams the battles of the day. Other, more placid fighters, like Malan, slept peacefully until the dinner-bell sounded.

May 23 is memorable too, in the history of Tiger Squadron, not only for the fighting, but because on that day the Squadron Commander (Squadron Leader F. L. White) was shot down in the Calais evacuation area. He was leading a section at dawn in the Calais-St. Omer area, and, flying at about 2,000 feet in and out of low clouds, he spotted a Henschel 126 floating around. It was a German army co-operation machine, a slow two-seater. The gunner saw the Spitfire approaching and opened fire just as White cut loose with his eight Brownings.

White's fire was deadly and the Henschel went tumbling earthwards to crash. But the Nazi gunner's aim had been equally accurate. His bullets had pierced the radiator of the Spitfire, causing a glycol leak. The smelly vapour poured on to the windscreen and into the cockpit, choking the pilot. Squadron Leader White kept cool and, picking his spot, landed safely on pothole-scarred Calais Marcke Aerodrome, a few miles outside Calais. The aerodrome was being shelled occasionally, and low bombing was expected, so White's first thought was to get his machine into a sheltered position. Workmen engaged on filling up shell-holes and bomb-craters helped him to pull it under the cover of a hedge.

The Spitfire was a new one and now all it needed was a new engine. White, eager and enterprising, hitch-hiked into Calais and made for the R.T.O.'s office. There he explained who he was and what had happened. The R.T.O. asked to see his identity card, but White was on operational patrol and carried no papers, in case he was captured. Throughout the area, however, Germans were known to be masquerading in all sorts of uniforms, and he found himself under arrest.

Nevertheless, the R.T.O. was a good type and using the only remaining telephone line to England, he got through to Fighter Command Headquarters and made some inquiries. Then he put White on the telephone and listened to the conversation. When it was over, he took the transmitter and asked whether Fighter Command accepted White as O.C. 74 Squadron. The answer being satisfactory, he gave White a car to take him back to the aerodrome.

The Huns were fast approaching the Calais perimeter. No one seemed to know where their advance guard was. But White had asked for an engine to be sent over and for a machine to come and pick him up. Fighter Command informed 11 Group, which in turn, got through to Group Captain Boucher, who commanded Hornchurch. Now, 54 Squadron possessed a Miles Master trainer. Boucher ordered Flight Lieutenant Leathart to fly it over to Calais Marcke Aerodrome after lunch, taking an escort of two fighters.

When Malan was informed, he immediately submitted that Tiger Squadron should be allowed to pick up its own C.O., and asked that Sergeant Skinner, who had been an instructor on Miles Masters, should fly the plane. Group Captain Boucher would not agree, and I don't think Sailor Malan ever forgave him. I know his squadron never went back to Hornchurch, once it had left there.

Dunkirk and the Battle of Britain

Well, Leathart chose as his escort Pilot Officer John Lawrence Allen and Pilot Officer Allan ("Al") Deere. Allen had drawn Nazi blood before this exciting day, and loved nothing better than a scrap. Now, proud and unashamed, he rests in the Valhalla of heroes. Al Deere was a tough New Zealander of the Grid Caldwell type. I can pay him no greater compliment. Indeed, he and Grid were similar in athletic build, strong face and determined jaw, and a fiery temperament. Al was a fine boxer and Rugby footballer. His air fighting successes were many before the end of the Battle of Britain, and though he had to take to his parachute on seven occasions he still kept smiling.

Malan decided that pilots of 74 Squadron should carry out a high escort for the rescue party, which took off at 12.30 p.m. It was a lovely day, with clouds at 5,000–6,000 feet. Al Deere flew below the clouds and Allen above them. When the party reached Calais Marcke, Leathart was seen by Deere to land safely and to speak to some people and taxi to the perimeter before getting out to make further inquiries into White's whereabouts.

Deere called up Allen on the R/T to ask if all was well above the clouds. "O.K.!" Allen replied confidently. Both aircraft were then circling the aerodrome, but just as Deere was watching Leathart's machine taking off again, Allen's voice came urgently over the R/T: "Twelve Me. 109s approaching at 6,000 feet." Deere dived towards the Miles Master. To his disappointment, he could see that it was carrying no passenger. Attracting Leathart's attention, he indicated that he should land, as there were Nazis above.

Leathart put his nose towards the aerodrome. As he did so, Deere spotted an Me. 109, which had dived through the clouds, firing cannon shell at the Master from 500 to 200 yards. Luckily, his shooting was ragged and he missed his target. Pouncing on him as he pulled away upwards from Leathart's machine, Deere got the 109 well in his sights. He gave him a brief squirt. Toppling over, the Nazi dived into the sea a few yards from the shore near Calais, his tail sticking well vertical.

Just as the Master landed, Squadron Leader White was seen dashing towards it. He had missed it only by seconds when it took off the first time. Though he and the workmen had waved frantically to attract the pilot's attention, Leathart unfortunately did not happen to be looking in their direction.

The air now seemed to be filled with Spitfires. The Tiger boys had come down to join in the schemozzle, while the 109s played hide-and-seek up in the clouds at 5,000 feet. The rattle of the guns, as the Brownings blazed away, was music in the ears of White and Leathart, who were sheltering in a ditch. They saw a Nazi join his pal in the sea while another burst into flames. Al Deere was having a whale of a time. He saw a 109 on Allen's tail. The Nazi was too intent on shooting Johnny down to spare a quick look behind (as all good fighters should). He paid the price. Al Deere, after taking the steady aim which is so important, gave him a longish burst. The arrogant Nazi went down in flames.

Now Al was attacked. Tracer bullets whistled past his machine. He went up in a climbing turn, pulling his throttle back. The Nazi flashed past him. Then Al opened his throttle to full bore and got on his enemy's tail. Coolly getting the 109 in his sights, he pressed the "tit." His guns roared briefly, then no more. He had run out of ammunition. Still, it looked as if the Nazi was groggy. He was diving earthwards.

Turning for home, Al called Allen over the R/T: "How did you get on, Johnny?"

"One destroyed and two probables," came a joyful voice. "Wasn't it great fun?"

When the sky had cleared of friend and foe, Leathart took off with the rescued commanding officer of Tiger Squadron. After their previous records had been taken into account, Flight Lieutenant Leathart was awarded the D.S.O. and Pilot Officers Al Deere and Johnny Allen the Distinguished Flying Cross.

Just for the record, contemporaries of Al Deere who also became famous air fighters were Johnny Gibson (New Zealand), R. R. S. Tuck ("the Fighting Fury"), Archie McKellar (Scotland), Max Aitken (son of Lord Beaverbrook), J. C. and H. S. L. Dundas, John Cunningham ("Cat's-Eyes," the night-fighter ace), Paddy Finucane (Ireland), J. H. Lacey (Bristol), R. G. Kellett (O.C., 303 Polish Squadron), Michael Robinson, W. M. Churchill (Birmingham), E. S. Lock (Leicester), Peter Townsend, H. N. Tamplin (Canada), R. F. Boyd and Jamie Rankin (Scotland), F. R. Carey, D. O. Findlay (world-famous hurdler), Sir Archie Hope, J. Peel, J. W. Villa, Charlie Beamish, the Donaldson brothers, John, Edward and Oliver (who were all awarded the D.S.O. for air fighting), Peter Powell, and R. Malfroy (the tennis star).

"Cast thy bread upon the waters and it shall return unto you," says the Bible. It often works out like that, too. On May 24 Malan had just destroyed a Heinkel east of Dunkirk after leading the Tigers into a bunch of Me. 109s and 110s which were protecting thirty He. 111s and twenty Do. 17 bombers. Nazis all over the place were yelling "*Achtung!* Spitfire!" as they toppled out of the sky one after another. The bombers soon jettisoned their loads and dived in the direction of their aerodromes, their escorts having deserted them. Treacy, Freeborn, Skinner, Cobden, Stevenson and Mould each scalped a Nazi during the scrap.

When the fight with this bunch of thugs was over, Malan found himself with some ammunition left.

One of the secrets of a good air fighter is to conserve his ammunition by firing only in two-second bursts. If his aim is correct, the enemy will fall to a short burst. If it is faulty, any burst is a waste of ammunition. Few realise that when the firing tit is pressed continuously in a Spitfire, all the ammunition is expended in sixteen seconds. Hence the importance of getting your man with the least possible delay.

Well, there was Malan, with still some shots in his locker. Looking round for a possible target, he spotted a dog-fight in progress some distance away. Leading his sections to the scene of the fray, he found six Spitfires battling it out with thirty Me. 109s and 110s. The Nazis dived away to safety when they spotted the arrival of reinforcements, but a good time was had by all for the few seconds before the Messerschmitts made for home. When Malan landed at Hornchurch, he found to his joy that he had gone to the aid of none other than Al Deere and the brave old 54th.

Similar friendships to that of 74 and 54 were struck throughout the R.A.F. wherever squadrons shared aerodromes. One station which comes readily to mind in this connection was Tangmere, which I sometimes visited in my Spitfire during the Battle of Britain.

Tangmere was the home of 43 Squadron, commanded by Squadron Leader Tommy Dalton-Morgan, the fiery Welsh fighter from Penarth, who was an exceptionally fine leader with an impressive personal record of victories. On the same aerodrome was 1 Squadron, commanded by an equally aggressive and lovable character, Squadron Leader M. ("Hilly") Brown, who was later killed in Sicily. Brown was a Canadian with a very keen sense of humour and an astonishing vocabulary. He and Tommy Morgan were forever pulling each other's legs, but they and their squadrons were linked in indissoluble comradeship.

20

TIGER PILOTS WERE INVOLVED in three amusing incidents on that exciting day of May 24, 1940. As one of the Spitfires came down from patrol and taxied along the perimeter track to its dispersal point, the pilot was seen to be standing up in the cockpit, waving frantically. Thinking he was in distress, the ground staff went after the machine at the double. Getting closer, they could see that the pilot was wearing a red glove on one hand and a green glove on the other.

"It's Paddy Treacy," one mechanic shouted to his mate.

Paddy had now reached his dispersal point. He had stopped his propeller and they could hear him making noises like the blaring of a huntsman's horn when the hounds are in full cry. When the mechanics reached the Spitfire, he shouted in his delightful Irish brogue: "I got two of the b——s!"

Paddy hated the Nazi with the same intensity as Air Marshal Sir Basil Embry, and as bitterly as his great compatriot, Mick Mannock.

Sergeant Skinner was in one of the sections following Malan on the early patrol. Sailor had led the sections in line astern into a shower of Me. 109s and 110s. The Nazis were at least ten to one. Sailor called out over the R/T: "Let 'em have it! Let 'em have it!"

It is wonderfully inspiring to the less experienced to know that the leader is courageous and knows his job. Into the fray went the confident Tigers. Soon, flaming Messerschmitts were tumbling out of the sky in all directions. When Skinner could see no more Nazis anywhere (it is remarkable how soon an air battle area becomes clear of machines in these days of high-speed fighting), he flew towards a Spitfire over the water. The pilot turned out to be Malan, who called up Skinner on the R/T, and asked: "Have you got any ammunition left?"

Skinner, thinking his leader had asked if he had *no* ammunition, replied: "Yes." Whereupon, Malan led him ·in the direction of one or two Me. 110s which he had not spotted. Says Skinner: "I stood in such awe of Malan, who was a stern leader who feared no foe, that I kept quiet. I went off and did some dummy attacks of dives and zooms until the Nazis saw me and ran for home. I then rejoined Sailor again."

Skinner was also involved in the third incident. "One of the Ju. 88s shot down that day crashed in a field and tore through a herd of cows, tossing some of them in the air," he recalls. "The Nazi crew were seen to get out of their machine and proceed to shake their fists at us. That proved too much for Freeborn. He promptly shot them up and consigned them to their Maker!"

On Malan's second patrol of the day, he destroyed a Do. 17 east of Calais. His report is interesting:

"The Squadron was on offensive patrol off Calais," he wrote. "Sighted Do. 17 five miles to sea below 8/10th cumulus at 3,000 feet. Enemy made off towards cloud at very high speed. Delivered short bursts at enemy whenever opportunity occurred, i.e. when he emerged into clear air between clouds. Most of my bursts were delivered at 400-300 yards, owing to the difficulty of closing up quickly in spaces. Broke away after enemy dived below cloud base and I expended my remaining ammunition and had his starboard engine on fire. I then saw Sgt. Mould and P/O Stevenson firing from astern. The enemy burst into flames and crashed. I filmed the crash and wreck with my cine-gun. The pilot got out and dragged a wounded member of the crew out. At one time I saw what appeared to be flaps falling off whilst I was firing."

Such was the fate of dozens of Nazi machines making individual reconnaissance of the shipping evacuating the British Expeditionary Force and our Allies.

The fighting was now getting ferocious, and 74 and 54 Squadrons had a busy day. The Tigers shot down seven aircraft and damaged four more; while 54, patrolling the French coast during the afternoon, met a large force of Nazi machines and destroyed eleven and seriously damaged three without loss to themselves. The Tigers were not so lucky in their last fight of the day. Aubert and Mould were missing, and Mungo was wounded.

Malan got a He. 111 on the afternoon patrol. His report is of special interest:

"I was leading four aircraft of Yellow Section on offensive patrol, Dunkirk-Calais-Boulogne. Spotted A.A. fire at 12,000 feet over Dunkirk when at 500 feet off coast, west of Dunkirk. Climbed in line astern to investigate and saw three vics of mixed bombers (approx. 9-12-9). Intercepted second vic at 12,000 feet and passed through very heavy and accurate A.A. barrage. Attacked starboard flank in echelon port from astern as Me. 109 and Me. 110 were observed above and into the sun, turning on to our flank for attack. Observed about eight of these, although probably more were about. Delivered three 1-second bursts at both engine and fuselage of He. 111 from starboard flank, 250 to 150 yards. I was then hit on starboard mainplane and through fuselage by A.A. fire, which severed electrical leads near my seat and extinguished reflector sight. As I broke off I observed one Me. 110 coming up on starboard quarter and one Me. 109 astern. I executed some very steep turns into sun and lost sight of the two fighters. I changed bulb in reflector sight, but as it failed to function I concluded that wiring had been cut. By this time the battle had gone out of sight and I hadn't enough petrol to give chase. Whilst climbing into sun I observed crew of He. 111 I had shot take to parachutes and aircraft gradually lose height on zigzag course. Whilst climbing up to the attack I observed one bomber badly hit (presumably by A.A.) with port engine stopped and left wing well down and dropping out of formation."

Imagine the coolness of this young fighter! When the reflector sight went out of action, he proceeded to change the bulb—with angry Nazis all around him, waiting for the chance to get a bead on him! It is obvious that Malan always kept cool and had complete confidence in himself in the toughest situations.

Here is a sergeant pilot's view of Malan, even that early in the war. It comes from Sergeant Skinner:

"He was a born leader and natural pilot of the first order," he writes. "Complete absence of balderdash. As far as he was concerned, you either did your job properly or you were on your way. He inspired his air crews by his dynamic and forceful personality, and by the fact that he set such a high standard in his flying. Weather never bothered him. He would frequently take off when the birds were grounded. On occasion, notably at Rochford, he would give a spontaneous display of aerobatics fully equal to the demonstrations of Supermarine's own test pilots, which were acknowledged to be in a class of their own.

"Another example of Malan's supreme flying ability and powers of leadership was shown by the fact that when occasion presented itself at Hornchurch or Manston he would take off and land the whole squadron in perfect formation. When it is realised that the twelve machines in vics of three occupied the whole width of the aerodrome, and the complicated cockpit drill allied to the high landing speed of Spitfires, it will be appreciated that, to put it mildly, a very nice sense of judgment and timing was involved."

That jovial Yorkshireman and keen warrior, Mungo-Park, who loved life and was fond of a party, was in fighting temperament midway between Sailor Malan and Paddy Treacy. Of Malan, whose prowess and personality he adored, he once told me: "What I like about Sailor is his quiet, firm manner and his cold courage. He is gifted with uncanny eyesight and is a 'natural' fighter pilot. When he calls over the R/T, 'Let 'em have it! Let 'em have it!' there's no messing. The b——s are for it, particularly the one he has in his own reflector sight. Mannock and Malan have made 74. Up, the Tigers!" With which, Mungo gave a loud "Whoop-ee!" I was very sad when I heard of his passing. He had the real fighter-boy's spirit and outlook.

All through the nine days from May 26 to June 3, the fighting became fiercer and ever fiercer, with air battles raging from 5.30 a.m. until 9.30 p.m. On an average, we were shooting down four or five of the enemy to one of our own. The actual figures were 377 Nazis destroyed for a loss of eighty-seven of our machines. So ended the first rearguard air action in history. And our pilots had proved they had the measure of the Nazi fighter pilots.

During those few days the Tigers lost a number of men, but the irreparable loss was that of the O.C. B Flight, Flight Lieutenant W. P. F. (Paddy) Treacy, who was missing on May 27. No one saw him go down. There was slight but not undue depression in the mess that night. The "new" 74 Squadron followed the example set by the original Tigers in not allowing casualties to play on their minds. The thing to do was to hope that they were all right. Other pilots of the squadron (indeed, pilots of most squadrons) had been posted missing during the Dunkirk fighting, had found a boat to bring them home, and had turned up in the mess all smiles. And Paddy Treacy was a Dubliner—a typical hot-headed Irishman, who didn't give a damn for anyone and who had the true spirit of the Tigers. He had been shot down previously in France, and he had got away from the Nazi lines. Why shouldn't it happen again?

The confidence of the boys was justified. History repeated itself. And later in the war, I got the whole story from Paddy himself. It all began when a flight of 74 sighted three Do. 17s off Calais. Two of them were soon shot down, one by Treacy and the other by Skinner.

Tiger Squadron

Treacy chased the third far into the enemy's lines, the Nazi going lower and lower in a steep dive. Paddy watched it go to earth with its port engine on fire. Then he noticed a smell of glycol in his own cockpit and made for the beaches at Dunkirk.

Unfortunately, he made for Calais by mistake, and meanwhile his engine was slowly seizing. Flak flustered him, and he was hit. He made a "wheels-up" landing near Gravelines, on the Belgian coast. Unhurt, he was taken prisoner. As usual with the Nazis, he was kicked up the posterior several times by a Hun sergeant. Paddy was taken to be interrogated at the German Air Force H.Q. near Dunkirk. Being a good airman, he would give only his name, his number and his rank. He told me he was treated quite well, and was informed of the impending air attack on Britain, which—according to the Nazis—would bring our people to their knees, crying for peace. France, they said, would soon be overrun and would give in. Then Italy would stab her in the back. How right they were about France and Italy, but, Oh! how wrong about the Britisher when his back is to the wall—as it was in April, 1918.

Treacy was sent, after this indoctrination, to the prisoners' camp at Desvers football field. It held 1,000 British prisoners from Dunkirk and about 5,000 others. Some of them looked ill. They had had no food for days. The most famous inmate of the camp was Wing Commander (now Air Marshal) Sir Basil Embry. On the afternoon that the two men met they were transferred, with a number of other prisoners, to Hucqueliers, which they reached the same night. They were told they would be on the move again at 5 a.m. next morning, and Embry and Treacy decided to escape when the column got under way.

In order to prevent prisoners escaping while on the march, the Nazis stationed a lorry, with machine guns mounted, every hundred yards along the column. It was a fairly efficient method, but hardly proof against the will-to-win of British airmen. Awaiting the appropriate moment, Embry dived into a ditch. A few minutes later, Treacy followed his example. They failed to connect up after the column had disappeared, and each man went on his way on what are now accepted as two of the finest escapes of World War II. (Sir Basil's account of his subsequent adventures has already been published.)

Paddy remained free for about a week. By day, he hid in hay-barns and outbuildings which were sometimes visited by Huns. At night, he ventured into farmhouses, where he was fed and given ill-fitting civilian clothes. The British people owe a great debt of gratitude to the brave men and women of the French Resistance movement for the unstinting help they gave to our men on the run.

Eventually, Paddy reached Beire-le-Sec and went on to the Bay of Authie. But there, accompanied by three soldiers of the Black Watch, he was spotted by some Nazis. He was again taken prisoner and escorted to the Exhibition Ground at Lille.

Two hours later, he was on his way to freedom once more!

He told his story to a Frenchwoman. She hid him in her house for a week. Again the Resistance came to his aid, and he was given a passport, food, money, and a bicycle to help him on his way. His next adventure is an epic. He made for the Bay of Authie, through an area well occupied by Germans. There he bought a boat from a farmer for 50 francs and, showing courage typical of the Tiger boys, rowed it that night past Nazi sentries, and headed out to sea in the direction of England.

At dawn, he was spotted and fired at by machine guns. When he got out of their range, artillery guns opened fire. Shells or no shells, Paddy Treacy rowed for his life towards the white cliffs of Dover. Now, a couple of Me. 110s came searching for him. They found him and sprayed the boat with lead. Paddy jumped over the side and hid under it. Eventually, a motor-boat went after him. Paddy Treacy went back to prison.

Irish, determined and always undeterred, he found still another way to escape. This time he made for Spain, which, after hiding in the back of a car, he reached safely. However, he was arrested almost at once and appeared to be in worse trouble than ever. He was told that he would be treated as a neutral prisoner. He would have to remain in Spain until the end of the war.

That did not suit bold Paddy. He demanded to see the Eire Consul in Madrid. When he was taken before that gentleman, he announced that he was an Irishman from Dublin. Giving his home address, he said he had been employed in Brussels when the war started, and that he now wanted to go home. Believe it or not, he was put on a cargo boat for Dublin, but, needless to say, he did not remain in that city once he had reached it. After a few days of good food and much-needed baths, he reported— clad in a new uniform—to the Air Ministry.

Paddy Treacy never returned to Tiger Squadron. He was honoured with the command of Douglas Bader's old squadron, 242. But his happiness was short-lived. An aircraft of his section collided with his machine over the Channel off Dungeness, and into the "ditch" went a great Irish fighter. Another guest-night in Valhalla.

Skinner, who was in Treacy's flight in 74 Squadron, said of him: "Like Mannock, he hated the guts of the Germans because of their callousness. He could not get at grips with them quickly enough. He was impulsively generous, but would not tolerate slap-dash pilots. He was a man of quick decision, right or wrong. Unlike Malan, who weighed up every position before going into the attack, Paddy Treacy was individualistic by nature. Sailor Malan was cool and calculating."

And so, as the pilots of Tiger Squadron saw the little ships make their last trips across the Channel on June 4, 1940, the Battle of Dunkirk ended. We had to leave in France during the evacuation all our valuable stores and equipment, with the exception of one complete R.A.F. unit—No. 2 Air Stores Park, commanded by Wing Commander S. W. Thomas.

This officer showed great initiative. His unit was mobile and consisted of eighty vehicles. He took the convoy from Lillers (Pas de Calais) on May 21 to Cherbourg via St. Pol, Abbeville and Rouen. At 6.30 p.m. on May 22 the vehicles were dispersed outside Cherbourg, and later that evening the personnel were embarked for Southampton, and arrived the following morning. Next day, the vehicles were loaded on to the S.S. *Floristen* and two smaller craft, and taken to Southampton. Their commander then informed the amazed senior officers at the Air Ministry of the arrival of his unit, and was instructed to take it to Henlow, the station where it had been formed.

Wing Commander Thomas, a Welshman, was very deservedly awarded the Order of the British Empire. I have seen the C.B.E. awarded to officers with less ability and initiative.

2 1

With the inevitable collapse of France, shortly after Dunkirk, we awaited with quiet confidence and stern determination the beginning of Hitler's "Operation Sea-lion." But Hitler made a mistake similar to that of von Kluck in World War I. Instead of concentrating on the massacre of the British Army, his vanity could not resist the capture of Paris, with all its attendant glory. He was eager to drive in triumph down the Champs d'Elysee and past Napoleon's Tomb. The balcony of Buckingham Palace could await his pleasure. August would be a good month for entering the Royal residence!

While Hitler savoured triumph in France, the question in every Briton's mind was whether he could, and would, invade our country. There were two reasons that convinced me that Britain would survive such an assault.

The first essential for an operation of this magnitude was to have air supremacy over the Channel and south-east England. The air operations over France and the Dunkirk area satisfied me that we had more than the measure of the Luftwaffe. Secondly, I was convinced that the Royal Navy, ably supported by the R.A.F., would tear to ribbons any sea invasion force. The few remnants which might get ashore would easily be disposed of by the Army, which was already in position and poised for their destruction. It is now history that "Operation Sea-lion" was the Nazis' biggest flop. The closest Hitler, like Napoleon, ever got to Buckingham Palace was Cap Gris Nez.

Licking their wounds after Dunkirk, the Luftwaffe took a breather in June, reforming, re-equipping and reorganising their units for the impending fighting over Britain. Their main activity during this month was an advanced rehearsal for night raids on a big scale, raids which were actually to begin in September, 1940, when their day raids had been routed. Some of the night attacks during June were landmarks in this type of tactical operation.

Tiger Squadron

Goering launched his first large-scale attack on the night of June 18–19 and it was in the nature of a probe to test our defences. About 100 bombers crossed our coast between Yorkshire and Kent on a bright, moonlit night, and the raid cost the Nazis seven aircraft shot down.

The honour of destroying two bombers in one night fell to a Tiger Squadron pilot, Sailor Malan. His report of the combats, in which he fired 2,800 rounds of ammunition, is typical in its simplicity of Malan's detached outlook on the destruction of an enemy. Sailor had none of Mannock's viciousness and hatred of the Hun. He fought, like Victor Beamish, as a Crusader, and was determined to do his duty by assisting in destroying Nazi tyranny.

"During an air raid in the locality of Southend," he wrote, "various E/A (enemy aircraft) were observed and held by searchlights for prolonged periods. On request from Squadron I was allowed to take off with one Spitfire. I climbed towards E/A which was making for coast and held in searchlight beams at 8,000 feet. I positioned myself astern and opened fire at 200 yards and closed to 50 yards with one burst. Observed bullets entering E/A and had my windscreen covered in oil. Broke off to the left and immediately below as E/A spiralled out of beam. Climbed to 12,000 feet towards another E/A held by the searchlights on northerly course. Opened fire at 250 yards, taking good care not to overshoot this time. Gave five 2-second bursts and observed bullets entering all over E/A with slight deflection as he was turning to port. E/A emitted heavy smoke and I observed one parachute open very close. E/A went down in spiral dive. Searchlights and I followed him right down until he crashed in flames near Chelmsford. As I approached target in each case, I flashed succession of dots on downward recognition light before moving into attack. I did not notice A.A. fire after I had done this. When following second E/A down, I switched on navigation lights for short time to help establish identity. Gave letter of period only once when returning at 3,000 feet from Chelmsford, when one searchlight searched for me. Cine-camera gun in action."

Both the enemy bombers were He. 111s. The first spun into the seashore, the three occupants being killed. For them not only the war but life itself was over. The second aircraft fell inland.

While Sailor was taking part in these epic fights for the safety of our hearths and homes, his charming wife was in hospital, awaiting the arrival of the baby who was to become Sir Winston

Churchill's godson, and who was himself to be christened Winston.

All Fighter Command pilots were now trying to get some night-fighting experience. Malan's "double" had made them confident that, given bright moonlight and the co-operation of A.A. searchlight batteries, the spotting of enemy aircraft should not be too difficult. Once the enemy had been seen, it was a test of the pilot's determination to get close and take a steady aim. It will be noted that Sailor had opened fire at 200 yards and 250 yards respectively. Very close!

A few nights later, the Nazis visited Scotland, and an Auxiliary pilot—Flight Lieutenant H. K. McDonald—shot down a He. 111 near the Firth of Forth. The night was dark, and bursting anti-aircraft shells and searchlights guided McDonald to his target. "The Heinkel pilot was mesmerised," he said later.

Lord Beaverbrook's gallant son, Squadron Leader Max Aitken, an Auxiliary pilot of 601 (County of London), had a thrilling scrap on the night of June 26-7.

"I took off and climbed through the clouds," he wrote. "I was excited, for I had waited for this chance for the previous three nights; sitting in a chair all night, dressed in my flying clothes and yellow-painted rubber life-jacket, which we call Mae West. I had waited from dusk to dawn, but nothing whatsoever would come our way. This night, they obviously were coming.

"I climbed to my ordered height and remained on my patrol line. After about an hour I was told by wireless that the enemy were at a certain spot, flying from N.W. to S.E. Luckily, I was approaching that spot myself.

"The searchlights, which had been weaving about beneath light cloud, suddenly all converged at a spot. They illuminated the cloud brilliantly, and there, silhouetted on the cloud, flying across my starboard beam, were three enemy aircraft. I turned left, and slowed down slightly. One searchlight struck through a small gap and showed up the whole of one plane. I recognised the plane as a He. 111. One of the enemy turned left, and I lost sight of the other.

"I fastened on the last of the three. I got about 100 yards behind and below, where I could clearly see his exhaust flames. As we went out of the searchlights and crossed the coast, he went into a shallow dive. This upset me for a bit, for I got rather high, almost directly behind him. I managed to get back and opened my hood to see better. I put my firing button to fire, and pressed it. Bullets poured into him. It was at point-blank range and I could see the tracer disappearing inside, but nothing seemed to happen except that he slowed down considerably. I almost overshot him, but put the propeller into the full fine and managed to keep my position.

"I fired again, four bursts, and then noticed a glow inside the machine. We had been in a shallow dive and I thought we were getting near the sea, so I fired all the rest of my ammunition into him. The red glow got brighter. He was obviously on fire inside. At 500 feet I broke away to the right and tried to follow, but overshot, so I did not see him strike the water. I climbed and at 1,000 feet pulled off a parachute flare. As the flare fell towards the sea, I saw the Heinkel lying on the water. A column of smoke was blowing from his rear section. I circled twice, but there was no movement. No one tried to climb out, so I turned and flew for home."

Max Aitken shot many more down at night.

Night fighting during 1940 was much more difficult than later, when radar became a companion of the pilot. As may be imagined in 1940 it was most difficult to judge distances at night. Many were the occasions when a collision between our fighters and their opponents was missed by inches.

Let me run a couple of months ahead of my narrative to illustrate this point.

In August, 1940, my old friend, R. S. S. (Bob) Tuck, who became one of the great air aces of the war, was with 92 Squadron at Pembrey, near Llanelly, Carmarthenshire. One night, searchlights led him to a Do. 17, which was bombing a ship off Swansea. After firing a three-second burst he saw pieces from the Dornier, which was emitting unusually large exhaust flames. The enemy went into a cloud, and Bob went after him.

Suddenly, his Spitfire seemed to be making a cracking sound. Puzzled, he tilted the aircraft; and there, a few feet below, was the Dornier. Pulling back his throttle, Bob got behind him and gave him the works from about 25 yards. The Dornier plunged into the sea. The Spitfire was damaged, and Bob Tuck just managed to make land by crash-landing on the cliffs.

John Cunningham, the brilliant ace of 604 Squadron and now the famous De Havilland test pilot and Comet expert, proved the value of radar to the night fighter. I was in the operations-room of 10 Group, Rudloe Manor, Bath, when he was up one night.

There was a Nazi in the air. John was being guided steadily up to it from a rear approach. I heard his voice coming over the radio: "I can see his exhaust." Then, a few seconds later: "Hello! I've fired, and I think I got him." He spoke as coolly and matter-of-factly as if he were swotting a fly.

The Nazi was down, all right. The report came in next morning: "Crashed in flames."

King George VI, of beloved memory, visited Hornchurch Aerodrome on June 28 to present Sailor Malan, J. C. Freeborn and Al Deere with the Distinguished Flying Cross. Freeborn, who was developing into a good fighter and leader, had proved his courage when he force-landed among the Nazis in the Dunkirk area and made a fine escape. Having made a safe landing, he found he was short of petrol; so he hid the Spitfire under branches while he stealthily searched the area for more "juice."

For three days he wandered about, often having to jump smartly into ditches on the approach of enemy patrols. Local Frenchmen could not help him, but he found a Nazi supply tanker loaded with petrol. Jumping into the driver's seat, he was able with some difficulty to get it moving. His heart leaped for joy, but not for long. He found he was driving straight into the path of an enemy column. He had to ditch the tanker and make a quick getaway. In the end, he got to Calais and was flown home.

By the end of June, the Luftwaffe and the R.A.F. had time to clear the decks (to mix a metaphor!) for real action. Despite the efforts of dynamic Lord Beaverbrook at the Ministry of Aircraft Production, the loss and damage to Spitfires was worrying commanding officers, among them Squadron Leader White of 74.

Tiger Squadron lost a Spitfire and its pilot in a most unusual way on July 3. Sergeant White was carrying out an operational patrol in the Dover area when his machine was struck by lightning. It crashed in flames.

The Luftwaffe were still carrying out tip-and-run raids on Channel shipping and on the towns of Dover and Folkestone and Tiger Squadron was kept very busy. Early in July, I flew over to Hornchurch to visit Sailor Malan. I found him in his office. He had just landed from a patrol, somewhat depressed. His instructions to "scramble" had arrived a little too late. He could see the Ju. 87's dropping their bombs on Dover Harbour while he was still a few miles away from them.

"They always run away, Boetie," he said gloomily. "What would you do to catch them?"

I suggested that if he went on "full boost" towards the French coast, keeping an eye on the Junkers as they screamed for home, low over the Channel, he might be able to intercept them and give the "tail-arse Charlies" the works. Some time afterwards he told me that on several occasions those tactics had been a success, particularly on the "tail-arse Charlies."

There was some enemy activity on July 8. Before lunch, Blue Section, led by Flight Lieutenant Measures, took off from the Tiger Squadron satellite aerodrome at Manston. Measures was accompanied by Pilot Officer Dowding, the dashing young son of the A.O.C. Fighter Command, and Sergeant Bill Skinner.

Measures spotted a He. 111 over the Channel. He was soon under its tail, and his bullets were seen to enter its fuselage. After firing, he turned off. Then down came young Dowding on the Heinkel's tail. After a three to four seconds' burst, the back-gunner in the bomber ceased to return the fire. Now, Bill Skinner came in after the diving aircraft. Another short burst, and the Heinkel crashed into the Channel in flames.

During the afternoon, Sergeant Mould (Red 1) and Pilot Officer Stevenson (Red 2) had an enjoyable five minutes when they went on patrol over Manston. At 4 p.m., they spotted four Me. 109s. Sergeant Mould dashed in to attack. After a four seconds' burst, one of the Messerschmitts spiralled earthward. It landed at Eltham, where the uninjured pilot was made a prisoner. Meanwhile, the 109 which Stevenson had picked as a target was also showing signs of distress. Another couple of Nazis were chalked up on the Squadron score-board.

Although the weather was summery, there was nothing to report on July 9; but the following day our defending fighter squadrons met the first horde of Nazi bombers and fighters over England and Wales. Indeed, the raid on Cardiff on July 10 was unopposed because there were no fighters to spare to guard the Principality. At this time, as I have already hinted, I was O.C. Flying at Stormy Down Aerodrome, Porthcawl—a position I owed to Air Marshal Sir Arthur Longmore and Air Vice-Marshal de Crespigny, who had arranged my transfer from Flying Training Command H.Q. At Stormy Down I had been given command of No. 7 Bombing and Gunnery School, with the rank of Wing Commander. Under my wing, I had about sixty aircraft, ranging from Whitleys to Harvards, and some forty pilots, whose duty it was to fly aircraft across the sea from Porthcawl to Ilfracombe. (Looking at a photograph of those youngsters, the other day, I realised sadly that thirty-two of them are now dead.)

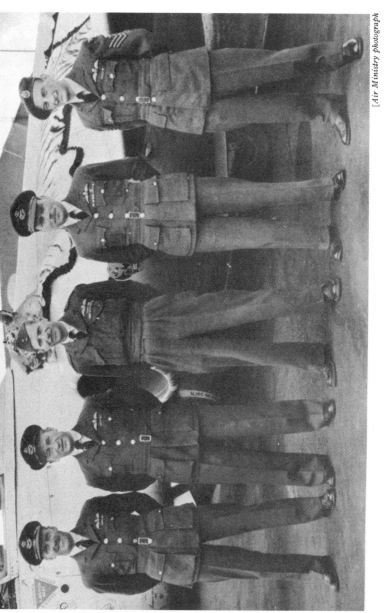

The tiger skin on the cowling of the jet in this picture was presented to 74 Squadron by the father of one of the "Tiger" pilots. Members of the squadron's aerobatic team seen here are (*left to right*): F/Lt. D. L. Edmonds; F/O. P. Wilson; Sqdn/Ldr. H. R. de L. Inniss, D.F.C.; F/Lt. B. Beard and Sgt. A. Nisbet.

From Top Left: W/Cdr. J. Rankin, D.S.O., D.F.C.; F/Lt. R. F. Boyd, D.F.C. (and bar); F/Lt. H. N. Tamblyn, D.F.C.; F/Lt. P. H. M. Richey, D.F.C.; F/Lt. C. B. F. Kingcome, D.F.C.; W/Cdr. Peter Townsend, D.S.O., D.F.C.; W/Cdr. G. R. McGregor, D.F.C. (and bar); F/Lt. E. S. Lock, D.S.O., D.F.C. (and bar); Sgt. Josef Frantisek.

Dunkirk and the Battle of Britain

The aircraft worked in pairs, and the air-gunners were trained to shoot at towed targets. When the gunners, who were all sergeants, had qualified, they were posted to bombing units. None of my aircraft had suitable armament for fighting. Consequently, I was both frustrated and annoyed whenever the sirens began to wail.

One lunch-time the Observer Corps kept on ringing up to tell me there was a Nazi over Swansea. I could see the blighter through my binoculars, and a maddening situation he was putting me in. I could not tell the Observer boys over the telephone that since all my aircraft were used for drogue-towing, I had no suitable machine for air fighting.

At last I got fed-up with that ringing telephone. Jumping into a Henley (a two-seater of the Hurricane type), I fairly leapt into the air and climbed for a position in which I could approach the Nazi out of the sun, so that it would be difficult for his gunner to spot me. The enemy was a Ju. 88, obviously on photographic duties over the dock area. The sun was south of Swansea, so I flew out to sea and made for Mumbles Head before turning round to approach the bomber, which was flying at 12,000 feet. I climbed to 15,000 feet and made a steady dive at 300 m.p.h., with my throttle full on. When I got near enough to see the black crosses on the Hun's wings and rudder, I felt the old joy of action coursing through my body, though my only armament was a Very pistol which fired a cartridge of varicoloured lights.

A bare 100 yards in front of the bomber, I pressed the trigger of the pistol. Then I turned gently to the left. The lights went floating prettily down in front of the Junker, and the pilot made a sharp flick turn towards the open sea. He put his diving flaps into action and nosed vertically into billowy clouds at about 8,000 feet. I screamed along the top of the cloud, just to have the fun of seeing him run away.

After passing Mumbles Head, the aircraft came out of the cloud about 300 yards ahead of me. The gunner was obviously looking out for me. I could see the flashes from his guns as he fired. When a bullet hole suddenly appeared in my port wing, I decided it was time to turn back. Flying back to base at Stormy Down, the Henley developed a tail flutter which frightened me much more than the Nazi bullets. In fact, I undid my shoulder straps and prepared to jump. However, I got back safely and quite enjoyed my lunch. *Cymro glan!*

22

AND NOW BACK TO the real air war on the south and south-east coasts, fought tenaciously by young pilots from every part of the Commonwealth of Nations. The battle was waged in four phases. The first phase began on July 10 and went on until August 8, 1940. Goering confined his Luftwaffe in an attempt to drive our convoys from the Channel area as far south as Bournemouth, and to attack ports of importance, such as Dover, Portsmouth, Portland and Weymouth.

The Nazi tactics were to scour the sea in large formations from about 10,000 feet, using Ju. 87 and 88, Do. 17 (the "flying pencil") and He. 111, escorted by Me. 109 and 110. The fighters did very little to protect their charges, a fact which, not un-naturally, made the bomber pilots furious. There are stories of a duel between the commanders of a Ju. 88 outfit and a Messerschmitt squadron. The latter "hero" claimed to have shot down 200 R.A.F. machines. No doubt the Junkers commander had told him what he thought of his fictitious claims before the first blow was struck.

The air fighting was mostly below 10,000 feet. Our fighters would nip into the bomber formations, shoot down a few, then come screaming home at sea level. The high-flying fighting did not start until the second phase of the battle opened on August 8, when the first series of mass air attacks were launched on Britain. Tiger Squadron's heavy fighting during the first phase is matched by the experience of other squadrons; but it is quite possible that the boys of 74 were the first to shoot down a Nazi.

At 3.45 a.m. on July 10, a formation of Spitfires took off from Manston Aerodrome on dawn patrol, and at 9,000 feet over Dover Flight Lieutenant Measures, who was leading, sighted an enemy formation about 100 strong flying over the centre of the Channel. Without delay, the Tigers got stuck into the Dorniers and Messerschmitts. Tracer bullets began to fly in all directions, and very quickly Nazis were seen to tumble away from the fierce fighting area.

Dunkirk and the Battle of Britain

The first to be definitely destroyed—perhaps the first in the Battle of Britain—was a Dornier "flying pencil." It fell to Mungo-Park, whose three-second burst sent it into the Channel in flames. Pilot Officer Cobden, a fine rugger player from New Zealand, drew his first blood when he damaged another Dornier, and Pilot Officer Stevenson, who later won a D.F.C., crippled two Me. 110s after his own machine had been shot up. Pilot Officer St. John, enjoying himself thoroughly, badly damaged a 109, and Measures, in a hectic ten minutes, badly damaged a Dornier and two Messerschmitts.

There were so many machines circling round that collisions were inevitable. Two Messerschmitts dived earthwards in swift, vicious spins, with their wings buckled upwards. Neither of the pilots took to their parachutes. They must both have been semiconscious when death ended their war. Measures told me afterwards it was the first collision he had ever seen.

Eight Tiger pilots played hell in that fight with 100 Huns. Splendid!

Next to enter into the fun and games on this historic day were Red Section (Freeborn, Stevenson and Mould) and Yellow Section (St. John, Draper and Cobden). In the second squadron patrol, they scrambled off the ground at 10.30 a.m. from Manston and, with full boost, climbed steeply for the skies over Margate. As they approached the area, Freeborn's voice came over the R/T: "Tally-ho! the Tigers." His section in line astern, with Yellow Section following suit, he made for a formation of about thirty Me. 109s which were escorting a single Do. 17. The latter, judging by its escort, was undoubtedly on a photographic and reconnaissance mission of some importance.

Freeborn decided to break up the fighter formation. He knew that if he succeeded the Dornier would forget its job and dive for home, while the Messerschmitts would become confused and make their usual hasty exit for their aerodromes in northern France. He picked out the leader of the formation, opening fire at 300 yards and closing in to 50 yards. The torrent of bullets from his Brownings tore the Messerschmitt to ribbons. "It just dropped out of the sky, Taffy," he told me. "What a thrilling sight!"

Cobden, the dashing All Black and Barbarians Rugby winger, gave another Me. 109 all his ammunition. "It went diving vertically earthward in flames," he said afterwards. Like all New Zealanders and Welshmen, air fighting and Rugby football were bred in Cobden's bones. He fought hard and he played hard, enjoying both experiences. He was a grand type.

Tiger Squadron

The fight had now developed into a good old dog-fight of the 1918 vintage, when formations of sixty Fokkers and Pfalz would be chased and scattered, some in flames and some in pieces, by the game little S.Es. Stevenson was showing great promise. Now, flying skilfully, with coolness and determination he held his fire to within 100 yards before destroying two of the 109s. Draper and St. John added to the squadron's "bag" by each damaging a Messerschmitt.

The Tigers' proud record on the opening day of the Battle of Britain was two destroyed, four crippled, and eight damaged. And they had no casualties.

At Clamarais on April 12, 1918, the pilots of 74 Squadron were congratulated on their fighting prowess by General Sir John Salmond. History repeated itself on July 10, 1940, when Air Vice-Marshal Sir Keith Park "called in" at Manston in his Hurricane to compliment the youngsters who were so gallantly carrying on the squadron tradition.

Two days later, Sailor Malan, accompanied by Mould and Stevenson, took off from Manston at 4.30 p.m. to intercept raiders in the Margate area. Sailor could see spouts of water in the sea off Margate where a ship was being bombed. Soon he was heard calling over the R/T: "Tally-ho! the Tigers." In a few seconds Red Section was scattering the Messerschmitts, who promptly deserted the old He. 111 that was doing the bombing.

In line astern, Malan and his section made after the Heinkel, whose rear-gunner was firing with all he had. Sailor got the bomber in his ring sight; then, opening fire at 300 yards and closing in, silenced the opposition guns. Pulling away, he let Mould and Stevenson have some practice. Battered and defeated, the Heinkel went down into the sea. The sailors in the bombed ship waved frantically as Red Section, led by Malan, dived past them in salute. So were forged the links of friendship and admiration between the gallant merchant seamen and the air fighters.

Daily throughout July and early August, the fighter boys' main efforts were exerted in driving off and shooting down the Nazi bombers who were trying to drop their "eggs" on our ships, with their valuable war cargoes, and on the radar stations, which were the eyes and ears of the Air Force.

At 3.45 p.m. on July 19, Tiger Squadron, led by Malan, took off from Manston to intercept enemy aircraft over Dover. To Sailor's dismay, his scramble order had not been received quickly enough. Approaching the Harbour, he could see high spouts of water where the bombs were exploding. Already, the Nazis were scuttling at sea-level for the French coast. But a brave Hurricane pilot was holding two Me. 109s in mortal combat. Diving into the fray, the Tigers rescued the lone-hand scrapper from the tight circle in which he was fighting. Malan took on one of the Messerschmitts. Stevenson tackled the other. After a short burst from the Spitfire guns, both the Nazis were seen to be in distress as they tumbled into low cloud over the Channel. Since neither reappeared, they were probably destroyed.

The dogged Hurricane pilot came from the famous 242 (Canadian) Squadron, commanded by the incomparable legless fighter, Douglas Bader. Born in the neighbourhood of Regent's Park, Bader was educated at St. Edward's School, Oxford, and entered the Royal Air Force College, Cranwell, at the age of eighteen years. There he had his grounding in the theory of flight, giving every promise of becoming a masterly aerobatic pilot. He was a fine Rugby footballer, and played at outside half for the Royal Air Force and for the Harlequins. Had he not crashed, I think he would have played for England, too. He had that extra little touch of daring in going through the defence at full throttle and boost. This dashing spirit proved to be his downfall. While doing low aerobatics, he misjudged his height and crashed so badly that both his legs had to be amputated. His life was despaired of, and, in fact, most men in his condition would have died. But not Bader. He was too tough, too determined to live.

Most of his flying friends and the general public thought he would never sit in an aircraft cockpit again. Yet he not only flew, but became a most daring and skilful fighter pilot and one of Britain's outstanding aces, ranking with Malan, Mungo-Park and H. M. Stephen of 74 Squadron, John Kent, D. E. Kingaby and James Rankin of 92, John Cunningham of 604, R. G. Kellett and Jozef Frantisek of 303 (Polish), Standford Tuck of 46, Al Deere of 54, M. L. Robinson of 29, Johnny Johnson and J. H. Lacey of 501, Dalton-Morgan of 43, Archie McKellar of 602, J. A. F. Maclachlan and A. V. Clowes of 1, E. A. McNab of 1 (Canadian), J. B. Nicholson, V.C., and John Peel of 145, Victor Beamish, Eric Lock, Michael Crossley, Hallowes, H. G. Lewis, Villa, Allard and R. G. Dutton.

Bader was not only a great scrapper. Like Malan, he also excelled in leadership. Though he ended his war as a prisoner, before he was captured he had been awarded the D.S.O. and bar, D.F.C. and bar, and had reached the rank of Group Captain. And as he used to say, with a wicked glint in his blue eyes, he had "shot down more than twenty Nazis out of the perishing sky." As an example of courage and a pattern for British youth, Douglas Bader is in a class of his own. For he proved that a man can conquer the most frightful handicap if the determination and the will to win are in his soul.

Even as a prisoner, Bader was more than a handful for the Nazis, for, in spite of his disability, he managed to escape. After his recapture, he was transferred to a special punishment *stalag*, where his artificial legs were taken away nightly by the guards. Bader held in high esteem the young Canadian pilot whom Malan and Stevenson rescued from the two Messerschmitts. He was Pilot Officer Hugh Tamblyn, an old pupil of mine. After gaining the D.F.C., he was killed while fighting three Messerschmitts single-handed.

The weather during July 20 and 21 was "affirmative" (as we used to call good flying weather in our reports). But typical of the squadron activities during this month, when the enemy attacked our convoys at various points, the Tigers had "nothing to record." The strain of fighting during those days, and particularly on July 21, fell heavily on the "Fighting forty-third," whose achievements rivalled those of Tiger Squadron during the Battle.

Like the Tigers, 43 Squadron was formed in World War I, when it covered itself with glory. No doubt the personality of its first commanding officer played a big part in ensuring its success. He was Major (now Marshal of the Air Force) Lord Sholto Douglas. His machines were Sopwith two-seater fighters, and later Camels. The famous pilots of the Squadron included Woollet and John Trollope, who shot down six Huns in a single day. Wilfred Giles, a member of the original Tigers, and nowadays the manager of Alliance Assurance in Bristol, was an observer-gunner with the "Fighting forty-third," and has a fund of thrilling reminiscences of the period.

In World War II, 43 Squadron had a galaxy of intrepid fighting men. In the first year its pilots shot down nearly 100 Nazis and suffered the loss of thirty-six. A fine achievement. I knew several of the pilots who made a name for themselves. Two very proud youngsters were V. C. W. ("Tubby") Badger and Cæsar Hull. Both rose from junior rank to command the squadron.

Tubby Badger, who was shot down over England on August 30, 1940, had just taken over the command. He never flew again and died about a year later. The Nazi-strafer, Cæsar Hull, took

over from Badger, but had only a week of violent fighting in
which to enjoy the honour. On September 8, he was found in
the wreckage of his Hurricane in a poppy field in Kent. He was
last seen downing a couple of Dorniers. Their wreckage lay
strewn over the Kentish fields not far from Cæsar's Hurricane.

Tony Woods-Scriven was killed on September 2, after winning
the D.F.C. Tommy Dalton-Morgan, who was later to command
the Squadron, was shot down on September 6, but was only
wounded. A typical Welsh air-fighting type, Dalton-Morgan had
dash and solidarity in combat. His personality in battle resembled
that of another famous Welshman, Oliver ap Williams, *alias*
Oliver Cromwell. On September 8, the Squadron had another
serious loss when Dickie Reynell, a fine test pilot who had been
attached to 43 for a few weeks of combat experience, was killed.
Dickie, a lad with a keen sense of humour, had been with the
Hawker Company, makers of the Hurricane. God rest his soul.

One of the brightest pages in the annals of the "Fighting
forty-third" is concerned with the battle of six pilots of the
Squadron against forty Do. 17s, and an equal number of Me. 109s
and 110s. This Homeric contest—which parallels the eight Spitfires of Tiger Squadron who fought 100 Nazis at dawn on July
10—took place over the English Channel, in the Tangmere
sector; on the afternoon of July 21.

It was a Sunday afternoon, and Tubby Badger was leading a
patrol of six Hurricanes, being in charge of the lower section of
three. Tom Dalton-Morgan was leading the upper section at
about 12,000 feet. Suddenly, Tom called over the R/T: "Huns
ahead!" Sure enough, when Tubby looked up, there they were,
stepped up in escalator pattern. Ordering their sections into line
astern, Tom and Tubby darted in to attack the tightly packed
formations of Dorniers and Messerschmitts, regardless of the
inequality of the odds against them. Morgan's section took on
the 109s and 110s, leaving the bombers to Tubby's boys.

Tubby had a crack at two or three Dorniers before his Hurricane was badly damaged, forcing him to return to Tangmere.
One of his pilots was shot down. Tom Morgan picked on a 109
which was flying with others in a defensive circle. He saw one
of its ailerons tear away and float in the air. Too busy tearing
into the other 109s to watch his victim, he only claimed a
"damaged." I have no doubt that the Nazi pilot took to his
parachute and that the Messerschmitt was destroyed.

Now, this happened at a time when the American Press was
throwing doubts on our pilots' claims of Huns "bagged." By a

lucky chance, the fight of six against eighty was watched by American reporters. Their glowing reports of the fray thrilled their readers, who, it is to be expected, probably changed their minds about the accuracy of Fighter Command's arithmetic. At any rate, the aggressiveness of the "Fighting forty-third" gave the journalists a sample of the tactics and valour of British fighter pilots.

Lord Dowding has told us of his retort to Americans who doubted the Fighter Command scoreboard. "If the Germans were correct," he pointed out to them, "they would be in England now." According to Goering's falsified figures (revealed in captured documents), the Luftwaffe won the Battle of Britain. No wonder the Reichmarshal and his Führer had to commit suicide!

On July 24 Flying Officer Measures was posted from Tiger Squadron to 57 Operational Training Unit at Hawarden, near Chester. The O.T.U. was commanded by Wing Commander Hallings-Pott, D.S.O., D.F.C., who led the famous raid on Sylt Island early in the war. I was attached to 57 at the time, giving pep talks to the pupils. Later, as I shall explain in another chapter, I took over the Unit, flew my first Spitfire, and had the joy of pressing the tit and enjoying the rattling music of its eight Brownings.

At 5.20 p.m. on July 24 Red Section, led by Sailor Malan, with Mould and Stevenson, and Yellow Section, led by Freeborn, with Cobden and Hastings, took off from Manston to patrol the Channel. Five minutes later, Sector Ops. gave the information that Raid 45 was near Dover. With full throttle on, Sailor made for the area. His war cry came over the R/T: "Tally-ho! Huns ahead. Three bandits, sea-level." Looking ahead, the other pilots saw three Do. 215s skimming the waves. The 215 was a new type, with a cruising speed of 266 m.p.h. and a maximum speed of 310 m.p.h.

The Nazis spotted the approach of the Spitfires and, making for the French coast at top speed, opened fire at more than 1,000 yards in an attempt to scare them off. They little knew the pilots they were hoping to frighten were Britain's greatest air ace and his Tiger boys. Closing in to 300 yards, Sailor, Freeborn, Cobden and Sergeant Hastings shot up two of the Dorniers in workman-like fashion.

Next day Blue Section, with Kelly leading Gunn and Eley, and Green Section, with Mungo-Park leading Flying Officer Boulding and Sergeant Skinner, took off on convoy patrol over the Thames Estuary. Sailor Malan and Freeborn were detailed to intercept raiders over the Dover area.

There were various groups of machines over Dover, but all were Hurricanes. Then Sailor investigated another group of aircraft nearing Calais. They were 109s, going home. By screaming flat out, Sailor was able to get within 150 yards of the tail of the "arse-end Charlie" and give him the works. He could see his tracers going into the fuselage. The squadron returned without loss. But once again the instructions to intercept had been just too late. A scared Nazi flies very fast.

During July, Tiger Squadron had forced down one 109 which landed without damage. It was taken to Farnborough to be made serviceable and flown by our own pilots. Their general opinion was that while the aircraft's top speed was around 360 m.p.h,. after 250 m.p.h. the controls suddenly became very heavy because of the weight of the elevator. Neither the Hurricane nor the Spitfire showed this fault. It was also found that at 400 m.p.h. recovery from a dive became difficult. Manœuvres in the looping plane, including steep climbing turns, were very difficult, too. In general, the 109 was inferior to the Hurricane and Spitfire at all speeds and in all conditions of flight. It did not possess the control which permits good quality flying, and this was particularly noticeable in aerobatics.

All this was comforting news to our pilots, who were advised to take advantage of the 109's peculiarities if they were "jumped." By pulling up fairly steeply, it was pointed out, they should be able to evade their attackers.

Sailor and his flight proved this when he was ordered to intercept a formation over the Channel. He found a Do. 17 being used as a decoy for some thirty 109s, which were in three layers of ten aircraft high above it. Summing up the situation quickly, Sailor made a sharp dart at the Dornier and sent it down in flames. The 109s were now diving down at more than 400 m.p.h. Sailor ordered his flight to do climbing turns in towards the Nazis. The Nazis' shooting was hopeless. So were their efforts to pull out of the dive to keep height and initiative. Three of the 109s were seen emitting smoke.

Ever since the early days of World War I, the German has been keen on employing decoy tactics. Our pupils at the O.T.Us. were impressed with the necessity of carrying out a thorough search, particularly above and into the sun, before attacking solitary enemy aircraft. The fighter pilot of the future might also remember this tip. Some day, it might save his life.

233

On another occasion, 74 Squadron, led by Malan, intercepted two Do. 17s which were acting as decoys for twenty or more high-flying Me. 110s. The latter made no attempt to go to the aid of the bombers, which were being shot down. Stephen, Mungo-Park, Freeborn, Skinner and Mould all had a squirt at the Dorniers after Malan had broken away. Each pilot went in close before pressing the tit. The 110s stayed above in formation, circling round and round in a left-handed turn. They refused to come down and fight, even when the Spitfires climbed up to attack. They ran for home instead. The incident was yet another example of the low morale of Messerschmitt pilots when opposed by Spitfires. Later, the Me. 110s became fighter-bombers which usually carried out tip-and-run raids.

Goering now produced two new fighters, the He. 112 and 113. These machines mounted two machine guns and one cannon firing through the propeller. They had a maximum speed of 360 m.p.h. Sailor Malan told me they were often mistaken for Spitfires, to which—except for a fatter fuselage—they were very similar. In combat, they were usually handled in an inexperienced manner. The pilots frequently opened fire at 1,000 yards or more. They would then break away and run for it. They never engaged our Spitfires seriously. Cannon fire at long range is inaccurate.

Although they had their casualties, chiefly in aircraft, the opening of the Battle of Britain had been a vintage month for the Tigers. The fighting on the last few days of July was even more glorious than that of July 10 and onwards. On July 28 the Tigers had a real show-down, when the squadron of twelve Rotol Spitfires won a resounding victory over three times their number of Me. 109s.

At four o'clock in the afternoon Sailor Malan, cruising at 6,000 feet above Dover in good weather, received orders to climb the Squadron to 18,000 feet, where he would intercept bombers and fighters. The Spitfires were to attack the fighters, while Hurricane squadrons were detailed to deal with the bombers. The Spitfires, which could outclimb any 109, were soon tangling with the Messerschmitts. And what a hectic dog-fight it was!

Sailor started the destruction by blowing a 109 to smithereens. Later, he damaged another. Others were destroyed by Freeborn, Stevenson, Kelly, Gunn, St. John and Stephen. It was in this fight that Pilot Officer Stephen, who was to make a name for himself, drew his first blood. The Tigers suffered two casualties, one of them fatal, when Pilot Officer Young was shot down. Sergeant

Mould, a very aggressive scrapper who had been Sailor's No. 2 for some time, was wounded when his machine was set on fire. He successfully took to his "umbrella," and ended up in Dover Military Hospital.

Malan's combat report on his two fights is a model of conciseness. His tactics, an example to pilots, were to go in close—100 yards—before firing. It was the only way to make certain of the enemy's destruction.

"I was Dysoe [A Flight] Leader on interception patrol on reported enemy raid, Dover Area," he wrote. "Climbed to 18,000 feet, having been ordered to engage enemy fighters and leave bombers to Hurricanes. Met up with 6 or 9 Me. 109s at 18,000 feet coming from sun towards Dover to attack some Hurricanes. Turned on to their tails without being observed and led Red Section into attack.

"Gave one E/A about five two seconds' bursts from 250 yards, closing in to 100 yards. He attempted no evasion tactics except gentle right-hand turns and decreasing speed, by which I concluded he had at least had his controls hit.

"I then turned on another Me. 109 which had turned past my nose and delivered three deflection bursts at 100 yards' range. He went down in pieces.

"I then returned, as my ammunition had run out."

July 31 was a memorable day in the Tigers' hard month of fierce fighting. Flight Lieutenant Kelly, a new flight commander with little operational experience, was given command of B Flight after Measures' departure. He slipped badly in this fight due to over-eagerness to engage the Nazis, instead of first gaining height initiative before attacking.

During the afternoon, Malan led A Flight to orbit Manston Aerodrome at 20,000 feet. This was about the greatest operational height during the early part of the Battle. Hostile raids were plotted at Sector Ops. room, where the gallant W.A.A.F. were efficiently carrying out their exacting work. (How I admired those beautiful, unemotional young things as they did their stuff!) As the number of enemy aircraft increased, B Flight was sent to reinforce Sailor and his boys. The Squadron was then despatched to Dover to engage the fighters of the enemy raiding formations.

B Flight were on their way up to 20,000 feet when they glimpsed a number of Me. 110s in the distance, away over the sea and out of reach, but at 18,000 feet they sighted about fifteen 109s, 2,000 feet above them, and approaching on the port bow. The Flight formed line astern and continued to climb on the sunny side of the enemy, turning towards them. The Messerschmitts split into two groups of six and nine, both in line astern, and the first group dived towards Blue section, opening fire from the beam. Green 1 saw Blue 3 (Sergeant Eley) go down in flames, and the enemy then closed in behind and Pilot Officer Gunn was then shot down.

Blue 1 (Flight Lieutenant Kelly) turned to get on the tail of an attacker, only to find that another Messerschmitt had fastened on to him similarly and was firing at short range. The cowling, armour plating and port wing of Kelly's machine were damaged and the upper petrol tank pierced so that the machine became difficult to control. Pulling out of a short spin, Kelly found himself in the company of a couple of Messerschmitts, on either side of him and just above. He gave one of them a burst, but as he turned to the other he again went into a spin. He recovered only to find himself sandwiched by a couple of the enemy. The machine below did a slow roll and dived away, as if to act as a decoy, while the second stayed up in the sun, ready to attack. Ignoring the first, Blue 1 climbed towards the second, but the damage to his aircraft prevented him from getting within range, and Kelly dived towards Hastings and returned to Manston.

Mungo-Park, leading Green Section, saw the second formation of nine Me. 109s approaching from above, turned in towards them and continued to climb. Two of the enemy dived past, apparently as decoys, but the section ignored them and continued to climb to 23,000 feet. By this time they had lost sight of the enemy.

Green 3, who had become detached from his section during the first climbing turn, saw a wide vic section of three Me.109s 5,000 feet above him. He made a diving attack from astern on the centre aircraft and saw smoke and flames coming from the Messerschmitt, which was last seen going down in a shallow dive.

There was practically no cloud at the time of the attack, which took place miles out to sea off Dover. Ten aircraft landed at Manston after the fight. The enemy casualties were one Me.109 destroyed and one unconfirmed. Our casualties were two pilots (Pilot Officer Gunn and Sergeant Eley) and two Spitfires missing, and one Spitfire damaged. One of the Spitfires crashed in Folkestone Harbour.

The Squadron's total of enemy casualties to the end of July was thirty confirmed, nineteen unconfirmed. Our own losses were seven pilots missing, two of them (Treacy and Byrne) known to be prisoners of war in Germany, and one pilot in the Military Hospital, Dover, slightly wounded.

23

F IERCE AS WAS THE fighting in July, it increased in intensity in August. Early in the month the Nazis were varying their tactics, and pilots had to be wary of synchronised attacks from different directions. Sailor told me that while leading his section, he sighted fifteen Me.109s 2,000 feet above him, on his port bow. The Messerschmitts split into two groups of six and nine, each in line astern. The first group attacked the section from the beam and then closed from astern. One Nazi from the second group attacked Malan from below, half-rolling and diving away in front of him as if to act as a decoy, while the remaining Nazis of the group remained in the sun above, ready to attack if Sailor fell into the trap and followed the decoy. But Sailor was too wary to be caught, and after the fight he explained the decoy trick to his section.

Similar tactics were employed by the Hun in 1918. As Sailor was telling me the story, I seemed to see the smiling face of Ernst Udet, the great German fighter. I said as much to Sailor. "Taffy," he replied, in that low, serious voice of his, "I, too, remembered what you told me at Uxbridge."

It was a generous compliment, which I shall never forget.

Enemy bombers were now occasionally being escorted by two formations of fighters, one below and one above. This was because of the tactics of our Hurricane pilots who, while the Spitfires dealt with the Messerschmitts, attacked the bombers underneath. Now, the Nazis of the lower formation were expected to handle the Hurricane pilots as they broke off attacks.

Occasionally they were successful, particularly in shooting down pilots newly joined from operational training units. For this reason, I always impressed on new pupils the importance of never relaxing their look-out for the enemy, especially those approaching from the sun.

The massed attacks on our shipping mounted to their peak on August 11, and then Goering decided that his raids on the slow moving ships did not pay, either over the sea or in the Thames Estuary. However, he was able to assess the strength of our

Tiger Squadron

defences before he started the aerodrome-strafing which brought his pilots over Britain, and must have realised that casualties would become even greater, because damaged aircraft and wounded crews would have to stagger home over the Channel with Spitfires and Hurricanes on their tails. What a story the bottom of the Channel could tell!

On August 8, a convoy off the Isle of Wight was fiercely attacked, once in the morning and again soon after midday. More than 150 Nazi aircraft took part in the raid, but only two ships were sunk. In the afternoon, more than 130 bombers attacked a convoy off Bournemouth, but without success, not a single ship being sunk. During that day, sixty-odd Nazi aircraft made their final plunge into Davy Jones's locker. Most of the fighting was shared by 41, 43, 145, 238, 257 and 601 Squadrons.

On August 11, Tiger Squadron, now under the command of Squadron Leader "Sailor" Malan, D.F.C., was stationed at Manston. It was the first day on which Sailor led the squadron into battle as their commanding officer. And it was another day of days in the Tigers' heroic history. The pilots accounted for thirteen Me. 109s and ten Me. 110s destroyed, one Me. 110 "probable," and nine Me. 109s and five Me. 110s damaged. For the thirty-eight Nazi casualties, the Tigers lost only two pilots, Pilot Officers Smith and Cobden. These smashing victories accumulated during the four hectic interceptions between the hours of 7.45 a.m. and 2 p.m. Considering the short period of time which elapsed between the first and last combats, the stress and strain on the physical and mental make-up of the pilots must have been very tremendous.

The number of bullet holes in the wings of the Spitfires was a visible indication of the intensity of the fighting, and let me salute, too, those loyal and zealous air mechanics who worked like demons to get the machines into the air again as soon as possible.

The first fight took place over the sea off Dover at about 8 a.m. Sailor climbed his Squadron to 20,000 feet and surprised eight Me. 109s approaching the port. He tells the story in his combat report.

"I was Dysoe Leader when Squadron was sent off to intercept bandits approaching Dover at a reported height of 13,000 feet," he begins. "I climbed on an E.N.E. course to 20,000 feet into the sun, and then turned down-sun towards Dover and surprised eight Me.109s at 20,000 feet flying in pairs staggered line astern towards Dover.

238

Dunkirk and the Battle of Britain

"I ordered the Squadron to attack. Some of them adopted the usual German fighter evasive tactics, i.e. quick half-roll and dive. On this occasion, as the air seemed clear of German aircraft above us, I followed one down and overtook him after he had dived 2,000 feet, opening fire during the dive at 200 yards' range with deflection. He levelled out at about 12,000 feet, when I gave him two two-second bursts at 100 yards' range. He was in a quick half-roll and dived towards the French coast. I closed again to 100 yards range and gave him another two or three two-second bursts, when he suddenly burst into flames and was obscured by heavy smoke. This was at 4,000 feet, one mile N.W. of Cap Griz Nez. I did not watch him go in, but flew back as fast as I could. I did not see the engagements of the rest of the Squadron.

"N.B.—Normally I have strongly advised all pilots in the Squadron not to follow 109s on the half-roll and dive because in most cases we are outnumbered, and generally at least one layer of enemy fighters is some thousands of feet above. It was found that even at high altitudes there was no difficulty in overtaking E/A on diving apart from the physical strain imposed on the body when pulling out.

"*(Signed)* A. G. MALAN,
"*Squadron Leader*,
"*Commanding No. 74 Squadron*."

The successful Tiger pilots in the first fight of "Sailor's August Eleventh"—as the day is known in the squadron—were Malan, Nelson, Mungo-Park, Stevenson, Hastings and Smith (one destroyed each), Stephen (two destroyed, two damaged). Besides their "kills," Mungo-Park and Hastings each damaged two Messerschmitts. During this hectic affair, Stevenson's Spitfire was so badly knocked about that he baled out and landed in the Channel off Dover. By firing his revolver, he attracted the attention of the crew of an M.T.B. and was rescued none the worse for his ducking.

At this time, all pilots wore the "Mae West" watertight jacket, which could be inflated to assist the wearer in keeping afloat until rescued, usually by the very efficient R.A.F. Air Sea Rescue Service. The latter was equipped with aircraft which could land on the water as well as with fast motor-boats. The original motor-boats, by the way, had been tested and recommended to the Air Ministry before the war by Aircraftman Shaw, better known as Lawrence of Arabia.

The second squadron patrol intercepted the enemy as they approached Dover about 10 a.m. Several flights of six Nazis could be seen flying around over the Channel, and Sailor led his twelve Spitfires in their direction. Pilot Officer Freeborn and Warrant Officer Mayne made up Sailor's section. Sailor and Freeborn each destroyed one aircraft, and Mayne damaged a couple more. Owing to R/T trouble, the other three sections did not hear Sailor's orders.

"I was Dysoe Leader ordered to intercept enemy fighters approaching Dover," ran the *Maestro's* combat report. "I climbed on a north-easterly course to 24,000 feet and did a sweep to the right, approaching Dover from the sea. I saw a number of small groups of Me. 109s in mid-Channel at about 24,000 feet, and as we approached most of them dived towards the French coast.

"I intercepted two Me. 109s and dived on to their tails with Red Section. I delivered two two-second bursts at 150 yards, but as I was overshooting I went off and the remainder of the section continued the attack. I immediately climbed back towards where Blue and Green Sections were waiting above and tried to attract their attention, but owing to R/T difficulties did not manage to get them to form up on me.

"I proceeded towards Dover by myself. I attacked two Me. 109s at 25,000 feet about mid-Channel, delivered two two-second bursts with deflection at the rearmost one and saw my bullets entering the fuselage with about 15 degrees deflection. He immediately flicked off to the left, and I delivered two long bursts at the leading one. He poured out quite a quantity of white vapour. Eight Me. 109s, who had previously escaped my attention, dived towards me and I climbed in right-hand spiral, and they made no attempt to follow. I proceeded towards Dover on the climb and saw ten Me. 109s at 27,000 feet in line astern with one straggler, which I tried to pick off, but was unable to close the range without being turned on to by the leader of the formation. I circled on a wide sweep with them for about ten minutes whilst I attempted to notify the remainder of the Squadron by R/T. This proved to be impossible owing to heavy atmospherics, and in the end I gave up and returned to Manston.

"N.B.—It seems that at 27,000 feet I had no superior speed or manœuvrability over the Me. 109. This is merely an impression and is not necessarily a reliable statement."

Notice Sailor's humility in the last sentence of the report. As if he didn't know the answer!

TEN of MY RULES for AIR FIGHTING.

1 <u>Wait until you see the whites of his eyes.</u>
  Fire short bursts of 1 to 2 seconds and only when your sights are definitely 'ON'.

2 Whilst shooting think of nothing else; brace the whole of the body; have both hands on the stick; concentrate on your ring sight.

3 Always keep a sharp lookout. "Keep your finger out"!

4 Height gives <u>You</u> the initiative.

5 Always turn and face the attack.

6 Make your decisions promptly. It is better to act quickly even though your tactics are not the best.

7 Never fly straight and level for more than 30 seconds in the combat area.

8 When diving to attack always leave a proportion of your formation above to act as top guard.

9 INITIATIVE, AGGRESSION, AIR DISCIPLINE, and TEAM WORK are words that MEAN something in Air Fighting.

10 Go in quickly – Punch hard – Get out!

81 GROUP TACTICS G.506.

The original of "Sailor" Malan's rules for air fighting. Copies were in a great many air stations.

From Top Left: Sgt. J. H. Lacey, D.F.M.; Sqd/Ldr. A. H. Boyd, D.F.C. (and bar); Sqd/Ldr. Douglas Bader, D.S.O., D.F.C.; Sqd/Ldr. T. F. Dalton-Morgan, D.F.C.; F/Lt. A. V. Clowes, D.F.M.; W/Cdr. F. V. Beamish, D.S.O., D.F.C., A.F.C.; Sqd/Ldr. R. G. Kellett, D.F.C.; P/O F. W. Higginson, D.F.M.; F/Lt. W. D. David, D.F.C.

Dunkirk and the Battle of Britain

The third combat was the big fight of the day. Sailor's Spitfire had been damaged a little in the previous engagement, so young Freeborn led the squadron, which had been ordered to patrol a convoy about twelve miles east of Clacton. About forty Me. 110s (Jaguars) were spotted approaching the convoy from the east, below cloud base and in close formation. The Nazi pilots, all shouting "*Achtung!* Spitfire!", immediately formed their usual tactical defensive circle—as in World War I. This was just the job for Freeborn. He led the squadron into the middle of the circle. The Tigers soon had their teeth and claws into their opponents. Ten Nazis were destroyed and five damaged.

Freeborn, Stephen and Skinner destroyed two each. Mungo-Park accounted for one and probably a second, while Nelson, Kirk and Mayne each chalked up one destroyed and one damaged. Stephen and Skinner also had one damaged each in addition to those they had destroyed.

It was during this engagement that the squadron lost Pilot Officers Smith and Cobden. The latter was another fighting New Zealander. He was a great loss to the Squadron, for he had already a few victories to his account, and was gaining experience and confidence.

When I think of all the Commonwealth pilots I have met in two world wars, I know that for my ideal squadron I would choose first New Zealanders, then South Africans, then Canadians, and then Australians. One can rely on New Zealanders for discipline and fiery fighting, on South Africans for discipline and calculating fighting, on Canadians for a certain amount of discipline and fiery fighting, and on the Australian for little discipline but fierce fighting. (I use the word "discipline" in the sense of discipline in the air, which nowadays is so essential in formation combat.) Of pilots from the home countries, I put the Welsh on a par with the New Zealanders, the Scots and the English with the South Africans and the Irish with the Australians. If the R/T breaks down, you want the Irish and the Australians on your side.

On the fourth patrol of "Sailor's August Eleventh," he led eight Spitfires over Folkestone at about 4 p.m., got up to 15,000 feet and subsequently flew over Margate, where Nazis had been reported over the R/T. Ten Ju. 87s were sighted at 6,000 feet and twenty Me. 109s at 10,000 feet.

Sailor, Freeborn, Mungo-Park and Stephen pounced on the 109s, who were diving for the clouds through which the Junkers had just gone. A good old dog-fight ensued between 6,000 and

Q

10,000 feet. Three Nazis left their damaged machines, took to their parachutes and floated down gently into the Channel. Sailor gave the necessary information over the R/T for our Air Sea Rescue boats to try to pick them up. One of the pilots was found. He was an arrogant little beast, who spat at the airman helping him into the boat.

Malan said of the fight: "I was Dysoe Leader told to patrol Manston at 10,000 feet. I climbed through 10/10ths cloud with the eight machines in two sections of four.

"On emerging through the cloud, I spotted about 30 Ju. 87s in long lines of small vic formation; about 15 Me. 109s about 2,000 feet above and half a mile astern. On sighting us, the bombers dived towards a gap in the clouds whilst the Me. 109s closed their range with the bombers.

"I ordered Freeborn's Blue Section to attack the bombers whilst I attacked the fighters with Red Section. I closed the range with the fighters and attacked an Me. 109 as he dived through a gap. I opened up at 30 degrees deflection at 200 yards and closed to 100 yards dead astern. After the third two-second burst he burst into flames and went into the sea approximately off Margate.

"I immediately climbed towards the cloud and then dived towards another group of four Me. 109s and delivered 30-degree deflection bursts of about three seconds at about 200 yards. I saw no results.

"As my ammunition was now expended, I returned to Manston."

The outstanding feature of the day's many victories—never equalled by any other squadron in either war—was the eight victories (five destroyed, three damaged) of Pilot Officer Harbourne Mackay Stephen. Employed before the war in the advertising department of the *Evening Standard*, Stephen trained as a sergeant pilot in the R.A.F.V.R. at White Waltham.

Here, as he told it to me, is the story of his fighting on August 11.

"The first fight was over the Channel," he said. "There were so many targets, Taffy, that I was having bang after bang. I gave one blighter a bang up his Jacksie and he fell in the Channel. Then I had the leader of the formation with a short burst from close up. He exploded in mid-air, a shattering sight. After joining formation with two 109s climbing into the sun, I gave the nearest to me a burst and particles flew off his machine. He turned over and dived Channel-wards. Later, I got another Nazi damaged.

Dunkirk and the Battle of Britain

"After breakfast, the stand-by order was received. The pilots sat in their machines, strapped in and with oxygen masks, all ready for a quick take-off. Before long we were in the air. Malan led his section into a scrap and they destroyed one and damaged four. My section, led by Mungo-Park, did not receive special instructions to join the fray, as Malan's radio had got a bullet in it and we could not hear anything.

"The third fight was a smasher and developed into a hell of a dog-fight. We found forty Me. 110s in three groups, getting into position to attack a convoy. When the leader saw us approaching, he started forming into the Nazi's defensive formation circles. This suited us. Mungo-Park, who was leading, and his merry Tiger boys carried out Sailor's diving-in-and-out-of-the-circle tactics. Nazis were tumbling into the Channel, one after another. Ten went in for certain, and probably another six.

"My first Nazi destroyed went down in flames after a long burst. Then another Nazi pilot and I had a somewhat prolonged dog-fight. Eventually, a short burst put his gunner out of action. I was now able to get close to the enemy, and after a short burst the Me. 110 went down out of control into the Channel. I now finished up my ammunition on another machine. I think I hit him.

"In the fourth fight Malan was again leading. He picked up a Nazi raid to the north-east of Margate. Here, we saw ten Ju. 87s diving through clouds at 6,000 feet, and twenty 109s 4,000 feet above them. Malan attacked the fighters, who dived for the clouds. The bombers had made for home.

"I picked out a straggler and we waltzed around one another for a short time. Then, after a burst, I saw he was losing speed. He foolishly dived away. I dived after him, firing short bursts. Suddenly I saw the pilot get out of his 109 and jump. His parachute failed to open, and he fell into the water with a splash. I saw one or two other Nazis swimming around. The Me. 109 from which my victim had jumped burst into flames on crashing. Ominous black smoke curled upwards."

This story should give you an idea of the determined, cool and gallant fighter young Stephen was. Mainly because of the day's fighting, he was awarded the D.F.C. A Scot, born in Elgin, he arrived in the world on April 18, 1914—my own eighteenth birthday. This was a strange coincidence, since Stephen became my great friend. He was known in the Squadron as "Baby Tiger" and I as "Grandpa Tiger." When he left 74 for a rest period in January, 1941, I arranged for him to be posted to 59 O.T.U., which I was then forming at Turnhouse, Edinburgh. I shall have something more to say about that station later on.

The Squadron devoted August 12 to giving the pilots a well-earned rest, and patching up the bullet holes in the aircraft. On August 13, the Tigers were again in action. A fight worth recording took place over the Thames Estuary in the afternoon. The enemy raid was of forty-five plus on the operations board. Sailor, in his report, tells the story of the pattern of the individual fights.

"Whilst leading the Squadron into attack against enemy bombers, Do. 17s, in the Estuary, they came across in a vic formation on my beam. I closed to within 100 yards and raked them with machine-gun fire. I then swung into line astern and fired at No. 3 of the formation. I fired at 150 yards, using 4×2 second bursts. This machine burst into flames in mid-air and was last seen heading for the sea.

"I then attacked the leader of the formation and gave him a three-second burst at 150 yards. One of the engines was put out of action, and bits and pieces fell off. This machine could not possibly have got home. I attacked the third of the section and used my last ammunition, but did not see any results. No evasive action was taken by these three machines.

"I carried a cine-camera gun, which was in action during the combat."

Sailor carried a cine-camera gun with him as often as possible, in order to pass on the technique of deflection firing and sighting to other young pilots. I saw this particular film, along with others he had made, and there was no doubt as to the complete destruction of his opponents. He surprised this bombing formation of Dornier 17s. Victories were gained by Malan (two), Hastings (one), Mungo-Park (one), Bill Skinner (two), Freeborn (one), Nelson (one), Flying Officer Szcesny (one) and Flying Officer Brezezina[1] (two). We suffered no casualties, only holes!

Szcesny and Brezezina were Polish pilots who had newly joined the squadron. They were typical of their brother nationals who fought with such venom and hatred in other squadrons. Towards the end of the Battle, there were Poles, Czechs, Belgians and Dutchmen flying alongside the Commonwealth pilots. Fighter Command became quite a family party.

Flying Officer Brezezina said in his report of the engagement: "I followed the Squadron Leader in the attack against enemy bombers in the Estuary. We attacked the third of three formations

[1] These two Poles were promptly nicknamed "Sneezy" and "Breezy."

of bombers in line astern and were about to engage when we noticed a fourth section closing in on our tails. We broke away and came round to attack this last formation.

"I attacked No. 2 and gave him a long burst and saw him gliding down towards the sea with smoke coming from one engine. I did not see him go into the water. I then attacked No. 3 of the formation and must have got to within 50 yards when there was a sudden explosion in my cockpit and I found myself falling fast.

"I managed to get out of the machine at about 2,000 feet and made a successful parachute landing. I did not see what happened to this Do. 17, but I was at such close range that it must have been severely damaged. It has since been confirmed by eyewitnesses at a searchlight post that the Do. 17 crashed south of their post."

Pilot Officer Stevenson wrote of his experiences: "I was Red 2 when 74 Squadron was ordered to intercept enemy fighters over Dover. Red Leader dived on to a lone Me. 109 over Dover at 18,000 feet and chased it out to sea. I saw another Me. 109 high up which looked as if it was going to follow Red Leader. I climbed up to him. He must have thought I was an Me. 109, but when he suddenly dived away I followed him and gave a two-second deflection burst. The E/A lurched slightly and went into a vertical dive. I kept my height at 15,000 feet and watched. I saw the E/A dive straight into the sea fifteen miles S.E. of Dover and disappear in a big splash of water. I then climbed to 23,000 feet up-sun, and saw a formation of twelve Me. 109s 2,000 feet beneath me proceeding north of Dover.

"It was my intention to attach myself to the back of this formation from out of the sun and spray the whole formation. As I was diving for them, a really large volume of cannon and machine-gun fire came from behind. There were about twelve Me. 109s diving at me from the sun and at least half of them must have been firing deflection shots at me. There was a popping noise and my control column became useless. I found myself doing a vertical dive, getting faster and faster.

"I pulled the hood back. I got my head out of the cockpit and the slipstream tore the rest of me clean out of the machine. My trouser leg and both shoes were torn off. I saw my machine crash into the sea a mile off Deal.

"It took me twenty minutes to come down. I had drifted eleven miles out to sea. One string of my parachute did not come undone, and I was dragged along by my left leg at ten miles an hour, with my head underneath the water. After three minutes I was almost unconscious, when the string came undone. I got my breath back and started swimming. There was a heavy sea running. After one and a half hours an M.T.B. came to look for me. I fired my revolver at it. It went out of sight, but it came back. I changed magazines and fired all my shots over it. It heard my shots and I kicked up a foam in the water, and it saw me. The M.T.B. picked me up and took me to Dover."

Sergeant Skinner, as usual, was busy. He says: "Whilst patrolling in the Thames Estuary the Squadron encountered about forty enemy bombers in two big vics, line astern. The squadron attacked individually. I attacked the outside machine of the left-hand formation. Opening at 250 yards I gave a three-second burst from astern and the port engine was put out of action.

"I immediately climbed to 5,000 feet and saw five Me. 109s circling just above the cloud. I dived straight back again into the cloud and came across a lone Do. 215. This I attacked from slightly above and astern, opening at 250 yards, closing at 150 yards, firing for seven seconds. Almost before I had ceased firing the lower rear-gunner baled out, and he was followed by a second individual. The machine burst into flames at about 1,500 feet and went straight into the sea somewhere west of Eastchurch."

Flying Officer Szcesny's report reads: "I saw three Do. 17s in front of me. I went to attack No. 3 of the formation when he swung round to the right. I broke away to the left and came round behind the Dorniers and on their tails. One of the machines was out of formation and I attacked it from astern. At this point the Dornier dropped several bombs into the sea.

"I got a good burst in from very close range and the Dornier started to dive towards the sea. He tried to land there, but as he flattened out he burst into flames and toppled straight into the water. This must have been somewhere in the Estuary east of the Isle of Sheppey. I did not know where I was and managed to force-land at Maidstone with my undercarriage up, as I could not get it down."

Sergeant Kirk, a gallant fighter, said: "We were on patrol over a convoy when we met E/A. There appeared to be about thirty or forty aircraft. We attacked from dead ahead. The Squadron broke up and a dog-fight ensued. I manœuvred on to the tail of an E/A and opened fire at about 300 yards, giving a ten-second burst approximately. Big pieces fell off the E/A as it did a left-hand climbing turn. It continued to turn and slowly rolled over on its back. It went into a fairly shallow dive and went into the sea, still on its back.

"When I finished my burst, I would be about 100 yards from E/A. I dived to sea-level, did a steep turn to port and came in again. Another Me. 110 came past my nose, so I gave him a deflection shot and followed him round. Big pieces came off this machine, also, but my ammunition gave out, so I dived away and came home. In this combat I opened fire at about 300, closing to 150 yards."

Tiger Squadron was now sent to Wittering and Cottishall Aerodromes for re-equipping and training new pilots, and rest for those who had fought so hard. The old pilots hated this inactivity. Although they were permitted to do sector patrols in their area, there were, unfortunately, no bandits to squirt at. In spite of that, the squadron record board for August was twenty-nine destroyed, seven probables, and fifteen damaged.

That was the score for two days of dogged fighting—August 11 and 13. Taking into account the July fighting as well, perhaps Sir Keith Park was right to take them out of the line, much as they disliked missing August 15, the peak day of the first phase, when our pilots destroyed 180 Nazi aircraft. Had Tiger Squadron been in action, we can only hazard a guess what the score would have been. I would say, at least 200.

While I was at Uxbridge in the old pre-war days, a tall, lanky, Hampstead-born youngster named J. B. Nicholson passed through my hands. He attracted my attention because he was a very jovial type who enjoyed crooning and playing a tin whistle in the mess. On August 16, 1940, this young man, who had risen to be a flight commander in 249 Squadron, with the rank of Flight Lieutenant, won the only Victoria Cross to be awarded for air fighting during World War II.

The fight took place over the Southampton area one glorious afternoon when the sun shone brilliantly and the landscape below looked so beautiful that the deadly combat overhead, notwithstanding the high heroism that went with it, seemed an affront to Nature.

Across the path of 249 Squadron flew three Ju. 88s, and the Squadron Commander ordered Nicholson to lead his flight to the attack. He chased them, but a squadron of Spitfires got in first, and all three Nazis were shot down. Nicholson was crestfallen. "I hadn't had a crack at one of the baskets," he told me afterwards in tones of regret.

As he climbed to rejoin his squadron he was "jumped" by an Me. 110, who poured four cannon shells into his Hurricane. There was a hell of a clatter in his cockpit. One shell hit his spare petrol tank and caused a fire. Another crashed into the cockpit, tearing away part of his right trouser leg. A third wounded him in the left heel. The fourth completed his discomfiture when it burst through the cockpit hood, sending splinters into his left eye and almost severing the eyelid.

Blinded with blood, Nicholson acted quickly and carried out evasive action. Then he saw that his attacker had overshot him. The sight of the Nazi plane with the swastika on its wings and tail-fin filled him with black hate. The pain of his injured eye and foot was agonising, and his hands were a mass of angry blisters from the terrific heat in the blazing cockpit. But Nicholson was determined that no Nazi was going to do that to him and get away with it, and with matchless courage he got the enemy in his sights and pressed the fire-button on the circular hand-grip. The eight Browning guns roared their approval of his valour. By now, Nicholson's vision was failing. He could no longer see his enemy but he had his revenge all right. Eyewitnesses on ground and ships in the vicinity saw the Messerschmitt crash into the sea. Providence was with Nicholson that day, for, badly injured as he was, he somehow managed to extricate himself from his Hurricane, but so badly were his hands burned that he actually fell several thousand feet before he was able to pull the ripcord of his parachute. As he floated slowly down, on the point of collapse, a Nazi flew closely past him and Nicholson knew he was not yet out of the wood. He pretended, however, that he had "bought" it and thus escaped being fired on. As he dropped lower and lower, he noticed that blood was oozing from the lace-holes of his boots. He was now aching all over, and his hands were so painful that he was unable to remove his oxygen mask. No Victoria Cross was ever more deservedly won than that awarded to this young Flight Lieutenant, who, incidentally, had bagged his first enemy on his first flight. Later he came under the care of Sir Archie MacIndoe at East Grinstead and made a good recovery from his injuries.

24

Now began the great attempt of the Luftwaffe to destroy our fighter aerodromes and so immobilise Fighter Command. Enemy aircraft first attacked Biggin Hill, Kenley, Middle Wallop, Lympe, Hastings, Dover, Deal and Martlesham, and a few even reached Croydon. Most of them were destroyed, and Goering must have scratched his head when he saw his casualty sheets, but he persisted. Between August 16 and 18, from 500 to 600 aircraft came over, and Biggin Hill, Kenley, Croydon, Manston, West Malling, Gosport, Rochester, Tangmere and Northolt were bombed.

These attacks cost the Luftwaffe 245 machines, and Goering called a halt until August 24 to give his pilots a rest. Meanwhile, he worked out fresh tactics from those which he had employed in attacking our convoys and ports. The efficiency of the radar stations, the Observer Corps and the control-rooms at Fighter Command groups and sectors was going to be put severely to the test. The real zero hour of the Battle of Britain had arrived.

Thank God, He was on our side. Radar even informed Lord Dowding of the number of enemy raiders orbiting their bases and the approximate number in each formation (unless it was under 1,000 feet) crossing the French coast.

On August 20, Mr. Winston Churchill gave the House of Commons and the world his considered judgment of the valiant deeds of the young pilots of Fighter Command. His words will always be remembered:

"The gratitude of every home in our island, in our Empire and, indeed, throughout the world, except in the abodes of the guilty, goes out to the British airmen, who, undaunted by odds, unweary in their constant challenge and mortal danger, are turning the tide of the world war by their prowess and their devotion. Never in the field of human conflict was so much owed by so many to so few."

Even while the Prime Minister was speaking, the stuttering of Browning guns in action, high in the heavens, could be heard faintly in the chamber of the Commons. People in the streets of Westminster could see tiny specks scintillating like diamonds in the brilliant sunshine. Looking from a window of the Ministry of Aircraft Production, I saw a sight that thrilled me. A section of three Spitfires had split up to take on three Me. 109s, who were screaming down the Thames in the direction of Hammersmith. The Browning guns of the Spitfire leader could be heard, and the tracers made a pattern in the sky.

The pilot who was on the tail of the Nazi on the left was the famous Group Captain Victor Beamish, who frequently led sections, in spite of his age, as an example to his younger comrades of enthusiasm and leadership. The Beamish family has become almost legendary in the Royal Air Force. Victor was the elder of four brothers and two sisters, all of whom served in World War II. Although their father is of English and their mother of Scottish descent, they were born in Larne, County Antrim. The brothers are famous Ireland Rugby footballers and golfers.

George was Air Force Commander in Crete when the island was captured by overwhelming airborne and ground forces in 1941. Now, an Air Vice-Marshal, with the C.B., C.B.E., American Legion of Merit and the Greek Crossed Swords, he is A.O.C., Iraq.

Charles was one of the "Few." A day and night fighter of great bravery and skill, he was awarded the D.F.C. and bar, and promoted to Group Captain, before retiring to his farm in Ulster. St. John is a dental officer who uses air transport on all possible occasions. He has made a name for himself in the world of amateur golf. The two sisters were also in the dentistry branch of the Service.

Victor Francis Beamish, D.S.O. and bar, D.F.C. and bar, A.F.C., is in the finest tradition of the fighter ace with the will to conquer. Searching the skies over Britain and northern France for Nazis to destroy, he held high the torch which his compatriot, Mick Mannock, had lit. He fought with the spirit of the Crusader when other pilots of his age—thirty-nine years—had long ceased to press the button on the joystick. Early in 1942, when he was looking very flying-tired, he said in reply to a request from his aunt: "Don't ask me not to fly. We must kill all the Nazis in the air."

Like his brothers, George and Charles, Victor passed through Cranwell. He soon showed a flair for fighter aircraft. Indeed, a few years before the war he was sent to Canada to make a tour of aerodromes and advise Canadian pilots in fighting tactics. During this lengthy tour, when he flew 1,000 hours in one year, he suffered several colds and an attack of pleurisy. Probably as a result, he developed pulmonary tuberculosis, lost a considerable amount of weight, and was invalided from the R.A.F. I saw him on his return from Canada. He looked very thin and ill.

It was three years before he regained his health. Then he had to fight his way back into the Service he loved so much. Returning as a civilian adjutant at Aldergrove, County Antrim, he persuaded the authorities to let him fly a single-seater aircraft. He was posted to the Meteorological Flight, Hendon, and it was while with that unit that he was awarded the Air Force Cross for very good work in bad flying weather. Unostentatiously, Victor wheedled his way into Fighter Command. When the Battle of Britain began, his promotion from Squadron Leader to Group Captain was rapid. He hit the high-lights when he commanded North Weald and Kenley, always setting an example to his juniors and destroying many Nazis. It was then that he established his claim to rank with the greatest fighter pilots of all time.

Air Marshal Sir Trafford Leigh-Mallory, when commanding 11 Group in 1941, wrote of Victor: "He will best be remembered for his magnificent and infectious courage as a brilliant and fearless leader of the fighter pilots whose interests were so dear to him, and who loved him so well."

I have never been able to understand why Victor Beamish was never given a posthumous Victoria Cross, as in the case of Mick Mannock. It is still not too late to do justice to the memory of a very great warrior and man.

It was Victor who, on February 12, 1942, spotted the German pocket-battleships *Scharnhorst* and *Gneisenau* sneaking through the English Channel from Brest to German ports. The important discovery was due to pure chance. It was a misty, muggy day. Pilots in the Kenley officers' mess were fretting with inactivity. Boredom was written all over the Station Commander's face. He had finished his morning's office work, and there was nothing else requiring his attention. Suddenly he turned to his Wing Commander Flying.

"I'm browned off," he said. "Let's go over and beat up the Casino at Le Touquet, and bump off any sods we see."

Shortly afterwards, the "Groupy" and his "Wingco Flying" were splintering the Casino's roof with bullets. Searching the Channel at 500 feet on the way back for something else to shoot up, the visibility being very bad, they came across a couple of Me. 109s. Chasing them, they spotted the two German pocket-battleships hugging the French coast. Within seconds, the escorting destroyers and E-boats were plastering the Spitfires with flak and green, red and yellow tracers. "Hell was let loose at us," Victor told me afterwards.

Once out of the flak area, Beamish passed the vital information to Group, who passed it on to Fighter Command. The subsequent events are now history. It was a Godsend that Victor discovered those troublesome battleships. He saved us hundreds of perfectly good bombs. For it was only after the departure of the two ships from Brest that we discovered there were excellent dummies in the harbour, which had previously been bombed in mistake for the real targets.

Victor frequently led the Wing, and during a bombing raid on Le Havre, the day before he was killed, seven out of the eight Nazis shot down fell to his team. Two of them were victims of his own guns. The first, a Focke-Wolff 190, at 8,000 feet over Le Havre, exploded and dived into the sea. The second, a Me. 109, dived vertically past the cliffs off Havre.

"As the 109 was going straight down, my Wingco called me up on the R/T and said there was another on my tail," Victor reported. "I pulled up, and only just cleared the cliffs." Such was the thrill of an air fight to a man nearly forty years of age!

On the following afternoon, Beamish led his last patrol over the French coast. Said Flight Lieutenant Reg. Grant, D.F.C., D.F.M., a New Zealander: "Victor was Red 1 and I was Red 3. We were flying high and saw some F.W. 190s below us. Victor's Spitfire dived so fast that I almost blacked out. My Spitfire was clocking up 550 m.p.h. I could not get the Group Captain on the R/T, but No. 2 called up and warned him that a 190 was getting on his tail. We were being jumped. I fired at it and I saw his bullets hitting the Group Captain's machine.

"The Hun went down with a large hole in its port wing and an aileron missing. I believe it crashed. The Group Captain turned for home and I followed, as I feared he might be wounded. Another 190 dived on the Group Captain and I shot him up and he went down. The time was then about 3.45 p.m. The Group Captain was flying level at about 13,000 feet about five miles from Calais over the Channel. I then ran into a thin layer of cloud. On coming out I saw a Spitfire below, so I went and joined it. To my horror, it was not the Group Captain. I looked around in all directions, and kept circling, but I could not see the Group Captain's Spitfire."

So ends Grant's report. When he got back to Kenley, and there was still no sign of Victor, all available aircraft took off—

so anxious were his pilots—to search the Channel. They continued flying in relays until dusk. At dawn next morning they were off again, hoping to spot their hero floating in his dinghy.

It was not to be. The Great Crusader had fought his last fight. But his spirit lives on in Fighter Command. Victor Beamish, the born leader, did not ask his juniors to fight hard and stubbornly without setting them an example. In the grand manner, he passed on to Valhalla.

While at Kirton-in-Lindsey, Lincolnshire, from August 21 until September 9 (when Tiger Squadron moved to Coltishall), Malan trained his pilots to his usual high standard of efficiency. But even training can have its excitements. Sergeant Bill Skinner had his "worst moment to date" on August 30.

He says of the incident: "Flight Lieutenant Kelly, a new pilot, and I took off to carry out practice head-on attacks, with another section of B Flight acting as targets. The target aircraft flew a steady course in vic. We got well in front, then went into echelon port and proceeded to attack them head-on. The drill was to pull over the top of them and then turn starboard, coming round for a stern attack in line astern.

"As I pulled over the top of the leader of the target aircraft, I heard a scrunch. My aircraft was slowed up suddenly and I was thrown forward against my straps, my hands going into the glass covers on the instrument panel. I immediately thought 'Christ! I've clouted the target aircraft. I shall be for it.' I had no time to ponder the matter, as my aircraft, now minus its tail unit, went into a spin. For a moment I really thought my luck had run out, but the old instinct to survive automatically made me start trying to get out. In the process, I left a shoe and my R/T wire behind. I counted up to three and pulled the ripcord. A moment later I was hanging upside-down, with one foot caught in the parachute lines.

"I freed my foot and floated down the right way up. My aircraft passed me on one side and the tail unit on the other. I joined them in a stubble field. Expecting an explosion, I ran off across the field, one shoe off and blood all over my face, to be pulled up short by a couple of farmers with shotguns. They thought I was a Jerry who had been shot down. I convinced them otherwise, and they put me to bed in the nearest farmhouse until an ambulance arrived from Kirton-in-Lindsey.

"Actually, the new pilot, No. 3, had pulled into me on the break-off. He landed in a field with a bent prop. The first thing

Tiger Squadron

I did on leaving the sick bay was to seek out the man who had packed my parachute and press a pound note into his hand."

It was at Kirton-in-Lindsey that Sailor Malan wrote his famous "Ten Rules for Air Fighting," and they were to have the authority of Biblical quotations for Tiger pilots. Malan stressed that they were the crux of the sum total of his considered opinion as to the essentials of a successful air fighter. Certainly they were very similar to those which I had issued to A Flight, 74 Squadron, twenty-two years earlier. There can be little doubt that until successful robot air fighting missiles are invented, it will be the qualities of the man and not of his machine which will decide the question of air supremacy.

Here, then, is Malan's "Bible":

Ten of My Rules for Air Fighting

1. Wait until you see the whites of his eyes. Fire short bursts of one to two seconds, and only when your sights are definitely "on."
2. Whilst shooting, think of nothing else. Brace the whole of the body, have both hands on the stick, concentrate on your ring sight.
3. Always keep a sharp look out. "Keep your finger out!"
4. Height gives *you* the initiative.
5. Always turn and face the attack.
6. Make your decisions promptly. It is better to act quickly, even though your tactics are not of the best.
7. Never fly straight and level for more than thirty seconds in the combat area.
8. When diving to attack, always leave a proportion of your formation above to act as top guard.
9. Initiative, aggression, air discipline, and team-work are words that *mean* something in air fighting.
10. Go in quickly. Punch hard. Get out!

The Tigers were soon to prove the value of the rest and the training. On September 11, the squadron flew from Coltishall to Duxford, Cambridgeshire, to operate in 11 Group area. To most squadrons there, September 15 was the day of days during the entire Battle, and without doubt the stinging victory achieved by the pilots of Fighter Command over Luftwaffe was the turning-point of the war.

To the Luftwaffe, as to the British people—but for very different reasons—August 15 and September 15 were Sundays to

Dunkirk and the Battle of Britain

be remembered. They were the days when Goering ordered his air forces to "have a go" in a really big way. Apart from the heavy fighting, the main feature which historians will record of August 15 will be the strategic foresight of Lord Dowding in deploying his seven squadrons in reserve on aerodromes which would protect the North of England if it were attacked. In fact, the Luftwaffe did make a diversionary raid to the north, and Hurricane and Spitfire pilots, bored with being at rest, were delighted when they received orders to scramble. Young British pilots from every part of the Commonwealth sailed into those He. 111s. Thirty were shot down for the loss of two of our pilots injured.

As long as there are British and German historians, there will be arguments about the number of Nazi machines destroyed on September 15, but there can be no dispute over the fact, and its significance must be plain even to a dull mind, that on September 17—only two days later—after Hitler and Goering had scanned the *true* casualty lists, the Führer decided to postpone "Operation Sea-lion" indefinitely.

If the Nazi figure of fifty-six machines lost is correct, and the 185 we claimed is wrong, why did Hitler and Goering decide to call it a day? Surely neither of them was as chicken-hearted as all that. Let us use a little common sense. The Luftwaffe had undoubtedly had a good hiding, and Hitler could see the writing on the wall.

Anyway, Goering was a great bluffer. It may be that he gave secret orders to every group to fake casualty lists for Hitler's benefit, the Führer being the only Nazi maniac he really feared. Leopards do not change their spots. I had a perfect example of the inaccuracies of the German Air Ministry records in the First World War. In 1934 I was attached to the Air Historical Section in connection with the writing of an official pamphlet on air fighting tactics in 1914–18. There was an agreed exchange of information between the British and the German Air Ministries. I told the Official Air Historian (the late Mr. H. A. Jones, whose aircraft fell into the Atlantic during World War II and was never heard of again) that I placed little credence in the German information. After some discussion, we put them to the test of known facts.

On June 19, 1918, Major (later Colonel) Billy Bishop, V.C., D.S.O., M.C., D.F.C., who was then commanding 85 Squadron, shot down five Huns before breakfast, and Captain Cobby, D.S.O., M.C., D.F.C., No. 1 Australian Squadron, shot down one Hun after tea. These were the only victories claimed on that day by the Royal Air Force.

In reply to our query, the German Air Ministry said they had lost neither pilots nor aircraft on June 19. I know for a fact that that statement was a lie. Captain Cobby's victim was lying, riddled with bullets, in my hangar at Clamarais North Aerodrome, near St. Omer, on the evening in question.

So much for the accuracy of German statistics!

Tiger Squadron won fresh and shining honours on September 11 and 14, 1940. Its pilots' reports on the fighting over London on September 11 may be taken as typical, also, of the combats of other squadrons during this hectic period.

Said Malan: "I was detailed to intercept raid over London at 20,000 feet. I was leading 74 Squadron as rear squadron of 3 Squadron Wing, led by 19 Squadron, with 611 Squadron in the middle. It was arranged that the two leading squadrons should keep fighter escort busy while I attacked the bombers. We made contact with a long rectangle of Ju. 88s at approximately 16.30 hours.

"We were flying in three fours in section line astern. I gave orders for head-on attack, but before I could get far enough ahead I saw the He. 113s coming down on us and turned towards bombers immediately, in order to deliver some form of attack before engaging fighters. I could not turn in the space and quite accidentally developed a very effective beam attack at close range (150–50 yards). I saw my ammunition pouring into two Ju. 88s as I raked across formation, which was tightly packed, and because of close pursuit of enemy fighters continued down in fast spiral to 13,000 feet, and climbed into sun to 20,000 feet again.

"I then saw two thirty-fifty formations at 22,000 feet proceeding towards me turning on to southerly course, but spotted a Ju. 88 at 20,000 feet which had either engine trouble or was observing results of bombing. I delivered one head-on attack and blew large pieces from his port engine. I turned and delivered beam attack at 100 yards as enemy fighter dived down on me. I continued down, but saw port engine well on fire and aircraft going down in gentle dive. Also thought I saw one parachute open close to the Ju. 88.

"The enemy fighter, which appeared to be a He. 113, followed me down to 10,000 feet, where I did a steep left-hand turn, blacking myself out, and shook them off. As my ammunition was expended I returned to Duxford. Position of engagement was about over Biggin Hill."

Pilot Officer Hastings, who had two probables, said: "I attacked a Ju. 88 and white smoke poured out of it as it dived with its undercarriage down. I then attacked a Me. 110 from abeam and saw smoke pouring from rear after pieces had broken off. I gave him another burst, but had to break away as two He. 113 were diving on to my tail. I did a steep climbing turn to the left and shook them off. They had yellow wing-tips and camouflage made up largely of yellow."

Pilot Officer Churches saw "pieces falling off the wings" of the He. 113 which he fought. The Nazi pilot was seen to jump for his life.

Freeborn said: "I intercepted a Dornier at 20,000 feet, and attacked from ahead and completely stopped his port engine. I then did an astern attack, and the aircraft crashed near Dungeness and burst into flames. It crashed in the next field to a He. 111."

Peter St. John reported: "I attacked the formation from the port quarter and, the E/As being in very tight formation, I gave them a 5-seconds burst. I broke away downwards and then climbed back above the formation. It was then noticed that a He. 111 had dropped out from the formation. I attacked this machine, using a quarter attack again. I saw my rounds entering the E/A and I saw one engine burst into flame. The E/A then climbed steeply and fell away to port. I had no time to see what happened to this machine as I was attacked by H.E. 113s. After shaking these off my tail I returned to Duxford."

Mungo-Park, as usual, did his stuff. He said: "At 17,000 feet I sighted formation of thirty Ju. 88s. I carried out a beam attack and saw pieces falling off the bomber of the second section leader. I broke away and climbed to 20,000 feet and attacked a He. 111 from slightly above, setting the starboard engine on fire, and saw him diving steeply towards the ground."

H. M. Stephen's report reads: "I attacked, at 18,000 feet, a Ju. 88 and put an eight-second burst into him, causing his undercarriage to fall down and port engine to stop. I broke away and was about to attack again when a Hurricane nipped in front of me and finished the Ju. 88 off. I was then attacked by a 109 and he swept past me in a dive, so I turned on to his tail and gave him a burst of two seconds, when I saw my de Wilde ammunition entering his fuselage. I think he was armour-plated or he should have gone, and rather than lose too much height I broke off."

Like all Polish pilots, Flying Officer Szcesny went in close before opening fire on his Me. 110. He reported: "I sighted two bombers and delivered astern attack at 100 yards, giving 3×1 second bursts, but observed no apparent damage. I then saw two Me. 109s attacking two Spitfires, and chased to the attack. I fired at one from 200 yards, closing in to 100 yards, and the 109 dived steeply, apparently out of control, I then sighted one Me. 110 and closed to attack from astern, giving 5×1 second bursts from 300-150 yards range. The 109 dived and crashed to the ground in flames. I then returned home."

25

W<small>HILE THE TIGER SQUADRON</small> pilots were fighting it out with the Hun in the skies, I was having my own less spectacular but still interesting adventures. Early in August, 1940, I was posted from Porthcawl to Hawarden to form a transport unit; but before I could take over its active command, the unit was transferred to the administration of the Ministry of Aircraft Production. No. 57 Operational Training Unit was stationed at Hawarden, Flintshire. It had been formed and was commanded by Group Captain Hallings-Pott, D.S.O., D.F.C., one of the original flight commanders of Tiger Squadron. It was he who had led the famous raid on Sylt early in the war, a feat in which his gallantry and skill won him the D.S.O.

No. 57 was the only Spitfire O.T.U. Here, a fighter pilot spent the final stage of ten months' training before being posted on active service. As my transport job had collapsed, I smuggled myself (with the connivance of Hallings-Pott) into the O.T.U. and gave the pupils lectures and pep talks on air fighting tactics. It was great fun, and right up my street. I was having a whale of a time until I received instructions to report to 41 Group at Andover. I took the posting signal to Hallings-Pott and pleaded with him to try to retain my services. He went flat out to keep me in charge of ground training, and I was retained for a month.

At this time, we were rushing pupils through to fill the gaps caused by casualties in the early part of the Battle of Britain. Pilots who had flown Lysander two-seaters were being hurriedly trained to fly Spitfires. We were also training Squadron Leader Taylor and the other Americans who were to form the celebrated Eagle Squadron. Those American boys were a tough bunch, and just the type to make good air fighters. Squadron Leader Taylor had seen service in Norway and was full of the offensive spirit He would promise me frequently: "We'll knock hell out of those Nazi cissies, Chief." And they kept their word.

When my month's respite was up, I was amazed to receive a signal to report to Mr. (now Sir) Eric Bowater at the Ministry of

Aircraft Production, Thames House, Millbank, London. My heart was in 57 O.T.U., and the thought of leaving it made me miserable. As the train took me south, I wondered desperately: "What the hell's all this about? Are they planning to make a chairborne warrior out of you at last, Taffy?"

Bowater was engaged when I reported at the warren of a Ministry building. One of his juniors—a short, fat, podgy-faced man—took me in hand. Leading me to his room, he solemnly unrolled a large map of England, decorated with large red circles. "We have a big job for you, Jones," he said. "I want to know whether you feel happy about taking it on. You have been specially recommended."

"By whom?" I asked.

He smiled broadly. "You'd be surprised," he replied. "I'm sorry that I am not permitted to tell you." I left it at that. To this day, I've never found out who was my godfather.

"Well," said the little fat man, now very jovial, "you see these circles? They mark the locations of our aircraft factories. You've no doubt heard that the Luftwaffe recently bombed Supermarine's, Southampton, and the Bristol Aeroplane Works, destroying a large number of Spitfires and Bristols which were stored, awaiting the installation of engines. Lord Beaverbrook has decided that in future all airframes are to be taken away from the works as soon as they are completed, and stored in dispersal."

Before he could tell me more, Bowater entered the room and greeted me with a warm handshake. "I hear you are known as 'Taffy' Jones," he said with a smile. I admitted it. He turned to his junior and asked him what he had told me. Then he began to reveal the work required of me by Lord Beaverbrook.

Briefly, I was to produce an organisation wherein every aircraft firm would produce a scheme by which neighbouring buildings, such as cinemas, large garages, warehouses and storerooms, could be requisitioned for the stowage in dispersal of all completed airframes. I could see that it was going to be an important job, and that there was no time to waste. Immediately, I felt a lot happier.

Seriously and quietly, Bowater asked: "Do you feel you can take it on, Taffy?"

Without hesitation, I replied: "Yes—but on one important condition."

"What's that?"

"That I can use Lord Beaverbrook's name to cut red tape in dealing both with my seniors in the R.A.F. and any civilians who may be troublesome when I want to make a quick decision."

Bowater picked up the telephone and asked for Lord Beaverbrook's secretary. "Will the Chief see me for a couple of minutes?" he inquired. There was a pause, during which he gave me a wink. Then he said "Thank you," and put down the receiver. We waited, chatting, for some time. Then I was taken into the office of the Almighty of the M.A.P. And there I was, face to face with the wizened, flashing-eyed, staccato-voiced Lord Beaverbrook— "The Beaver" himself.

"This is Wing Commander Taffy Jones," said Bowater. "He is the officer of whom I spoke to you in connection with the dispersing of aircraft in factories."

"Ah, yes," said the Beaver. Then, looking at me: "You must be a Welshman with a name like that. Did you know Lloyd George?"

"Yes, sir," I replied.

"Well, if you are as good as he was in charge of munitions in the First War, you'll do me!" he said with a laugh. "Are you happy about the job?"

"I am, sir, if I can use your name to cut red tape when I think I should, and to help me in making decisions when I am up against awkward customers."

"You sure have my full support. Now get on with the job. We have no time to waste." He stood up and shook my hand. "Good luck, Jones."

The interview was over in a couple of minutes. This was a man after my own heart. I knew instinctively that I could trust his word if things got sticky. So I got cracking.

"Mr. Bowater," I said seriously, "after meeting the Chief, I feel as if I'd been born again. Can you arrange for me to have an aeroplane and a motor car whenever I want one to go and visit the factories?"

Within a few minutes it had been fixed that an aeroplane of the Communications Flight at Andover and a touring car from 41 Group H.Q. pool were to be at my disposal. I first tackled the airframes requiring dispersal at De Havilland's, Hatfield, and from the difficulties and the eventual organisation for the efficient working of the scheme at this famous establishment I found the answer to the whole problem.

The first morning that I flew from Andover to Hatfield, the weather was very bad and visibility poor. I had not been on the ground half an hour when I heard the firing of the Bofors guns which were defending the place. Looking out of the office window,

I saw a Ju. 88 actually releasing his bombs. He was so low and travelling so fast that his bombs were bouncing over the aerodrome surface before exploding.

I saw one of those bombs blow up a section of the works. Bodies were hurled into the air. Many people were killed. The incident inspired me to get on with my new job. It was obviously of the highest national importance, especially at this period, when aircraft were Britain's saviours.

I decided that a staff of one officer, one corporal and three aircraftmen was necessary to supervise the work at each factory. My first clash with my seniors in the R.A.F. came when I informed my A.O.C. and Air Member for Personnel at the Air Ministry that I wanted enough staff for ten factories.

"We have no officers or men to spare," said the A.O.C. at Andover.

I got into my touring car and dashed up to see Bowater. He, in turn, got on to the A.M.P. at the Air Ministry. An interview was arranged for me.

"I haven't any officers or men," said Air Marshal Sir Philip Babbington.

I knew of many friends, chiefly officers in World War I, who had tried to rejoin and had been turned down as unfit. So I told Sir Philip: "I know of a couple of officers who have been turned down medically. They will be all right for this job." And I added: "Lord Beaverbrook has told me that I *must* have them. If I don't get them, I have to report the fact to him."

The necessary staff were soon allocated for the jobs! My biggest headache was in getting the agreement of owners of buildings I intended to requisition. Many were the heated refusals, abusive remarks and threats to "put the matter in the hands of my M.P." Softly, I would reply: "I am very sorry, but I am only carrying out Lord Beaverbrook's orders. If you have a grievance, you had better write to him. Meanwhile, here is your notice of requisition." Sometimes the person I was addressing would tear up the paper. The place was requisitioned, just the same, on the appointed day. Occasionally, I would decide to be accompanied by a police officer. This was no "cushy" job, believe me.

However, I had the whole scheme working smoothly in one month. And I had organised myself out of a job! Of my efforts, David Farrer (an author I have never met) kindly says in *The Sky's the Limit*, his biography of Lord Beaverbrook as Minister of Aircraft Production: "The work was carried out under the direction of Air Force officers on the staff of M.A.P., supervised by a Welshman of splendid drive and initiative, Group Captain Ira Jones."

Air Marshal Sir Wilfred Freeman, the senior Air Force Officer attached to M.A.P., sent for me and thanked me, on behalf of Lord Beaverbrook, for my "splendid job of work." He asked me if he could help me to get another job I would like.

"Yes, sir," I replied. "I'd like to command a Spitfire Operational Training Unit."

To my great delight, I was posted to command 57 O.T.U., as Hallings-Pott was being sent to form a new O.T.U. in Scotland. My stay was brief, as Hallings-Pott returned to Hawarden, but I had had a few very interesting weeks in my first Spitfire O.T.U. command. I had flown my first Spitfire and fired the eight Browning guns into the sea off Rhyl. I was thrilled when I heard the staccato chatter of the guns. My blood tingled for an air fight, as it had done twenty-two years before. My spirit was still yearning for "just one more scrap."

It was in late September or early October that I had the exultation of scrambling to try and contact a Ju. 88, reported at 20,000 feet over Liverpool. The aircraft had been reported by the Observer Corps. I had two pilots standing by daily to intercept any such intruders over Liverpool, as there were no fighter squadrons in the area.

Sergeant Payne and another sergeant were taxi-ing out to take off as I jumped into my own Spitfire "for fun." I climbed in their direction, and at 22,000 feet, over Flint, I saw them chasing a Ju. 88. The Nazi was coming in my direction with his nose well down. He must have been diving at 450 plus. I tried to intercept him, and as he passed me I gave him a deflection squirt at about 300 yards. I don't think I even tickled his bottom.

The foremost of the two Spitfires was diving line astern of the Junker and speedily closing the range. There were clouds over the Welsh mountains at 3,000 feet. The last I saw of the Nazi, he had black smoke pouring from one of his engines as he disappeared into the mists. Later, I heard from the police that he had crashed in the hills near Machynlleth, Montgomeryshire. There was a crew of five, including a Gestapo man, aged about thirty-five years. The Chief Constable told me that one of the Nazis had said the Gestapo man was aboard to ensure that the pilot actually went over Liverpool. The destroyer of the aircraft was Sergeant Pilkington, late of 73 Squadron.

26

THE FOURTH AND FINAL phase of the Battle of Britain began on October 6, and once more Goering introduced different strategy and tactics for the Luftwaffe. Long-range bombers previously used in mass attacks had received such a mauling that the force had to be withdrawn altogether from daylight action and given the task of carrying out after-dark raids on London. In place of the long-range bomber came the fighter-bomber, mostly Me. 110s, usually accompanied by Me. 110 fighters and Me. 109s, which also carried a couple of bombs and, like the 110s, dropped them anywhere as soon as they spotted the approach of our Spitfires. The fighter-bombers usually flew at 30,000 feet, i.e. six miles up, and the tactics used were those of diversion. Infrequently, a certain number would get through the defences and drop their bombs in the London area. Fighting at 30,000 feet was a severe test for the physical and mental fitness of every pilot.

As the days passed, it became clearer and clearer to Goering that his Luftwaffe could not break the morale of Fighter Command. The casualties from the daylight attacks were too high. The brave men and women of Kent and of London noticed, as October drew to a close, that the white vapour trails forming beautiful, fantastic arabesques in the sky—so numerous in August and September that they had become part of the accepted pattern of life—were decreasing quietly but rapidly. The boys of Fighter Command had become triumphantly supreme.

On October 15, Tiger Squadron returned to Biggin Hill, Kent —the most heavily bombed aerodrome in Fighter Command. The Squadron Record Book for that day forecast: "Should now get back into our stride again." It was no idle boast. Two days later, they were making mincemeat of a small formation of 109s which ventured into the Thames Estuary, about 3 p.m., at 26,000 feet.

In his report, Malan said: "I was leading Dysoe Squadron (74) from Biggin Hill and took off at 15.10 hours to intercept fighter raids approaching London. I climbed mostly on an up-sun course to 26,000 feet and flew towards A.A. bursts over the Thames Estuary. At 15.30 hours, we suddenly saw some yellow-noses (Me. 109s) crossing our bows, and surprised them from the sun.

"I gave the right-hand one a two-second burst with quarter deflection from 200 yards and closed to 150 yards astern, and delivered another two-second burst. I then closed to 100 yards and delivered a four-second burst which appeared to damage elevator controls, as his nose went vertically downwards very suddenly instead of the usual half-roll. My engine naturally stopped when I followed suit, but it picked up again and I closed to 150 yards on half-roll and gave another four-second burst. I found myself doing an aileron turn to keep direction and delivered another four-second burst. He then started to smoke, but I blacked out completely and lost consciousness for a couple of seconds. F/O Ricalto is missing, and I think killed, as I saw a Spitfire go down."

Pilot Officer Nelson said: "Two yellow nosed 109s came in front of S/Ldr. Malan, who attacked one on the right, so I took on the other, who took no evasive action as we had come up-sun. I put in a five-second burst, with slight deflection at 150 yards, and the enemy half rolled and glycol was streaming out in white smoke colour. I could follow him easily, so gave him three two-second bursts, and thick black smoke now appeared. He dived vertically through a cloud at 2,000 feet. As I was following with my actuating gear wound fully forward, I decided to pull gently out of the dive. I did not see the enemy again."

Flying Officer Peter St. John destroyed one Me. 109 which, after two five-second bursts, went down in roaring flames. There was no doubt about its eventual end. The pilot did not jump. Several of the other pilots had some gun practice, but achieved no results deserving of a combat report.

From now on the squadron scrambled on interception flights almost daily. I have taken a few combat reports almost at random. There was a good scrap shortly after the lunch-hour on October 20. Mungo-Park led B Flight, and Freeborn A Flight, into a bunch of more than thirty 109s in the Maidstone area. The time was 1.30 p.m. Mungo-Park reported: "We intercepted a thirty plus raid on Maidstone area at 29,000 feet. The enemy aircraft were slightly below us and we dived from 500 feet above. They immediately dived away and then half of them zoomed up. I followed them up and fired a short burst of four seconds at the rear machine. He immediately spun and I followed him down to about 4,000 feet, when his tail unit broke away. I had to break off the engagement as I was being fired at from behind, and do not know whether the pilot baled out."

H. M. Stephen, who was Mungo-Park's No. 2, destroyed one and had another probable. He said: "I was Blue 2 of 74 Squadron when we engaged many 109s at 29,000 feet approximately. As I was the tail end of the Squadron, I attacked four enemy aircraft, who started to dive. They headed for Dungeness and I did not overtake or engage them until we were down to 9,000 feet. I engaged the enemy aircraft on the extreme left, and after his tail started to break up as well as the top cockpit flying off I had to break away as the other three started to try to climb and get above me. In the general mêlée that followed I got on to the tail of another, and after a burst of approximately six seconds, I saw the pilot bale out, and his machine went into a wood."

Other pilots were engaged in this scrap. Freeborn's brief report of what Sergeant Kirk told him while lying seriously wounded in Maidstone Hospital, Preston Hall, near Maidstone, is interesting.

"I, Sergeant Kirk, was followed by P/O Draper, who was Yellow 3. I was Yellow 4," the report begins. "P/O Draper attacked one Me. 109, and I attacked another. The enemy aircraft dived and I followed. Large pieces of the enemy aircraft fell off the fuselage and wings. The end of the enemy aircraft's dive was unobserved, as I was attacked and shot down."

Sergeant Hilken was also wounded and baled out.

When I think of the many hundreds of airmen who were saved by the Irving parachute during World War II, it is impossible not to remember the wastage of British lives in the first great conflict, when pilots had to fly without this protection.

On October 22, the Tigers again intercepted a large formation of 109s who were trying to break through the defences in the Thames Estuary. So good was our radar information at this time that the Luftwaffe and 11 Group pilots were usually locked in mortal combat almost as soon as Nazi aircraft were across the Channel.

Mungo-Park was leading B Flight, which was directed to Maidstone at 15,000 feet. On arrival, he was immediately ordered to 30,000 feet, and then down to 27,000 feet, to avoid making vapour trails as the red-hot exhausts streaked through the cold upper air. Mungo spotted the enemy 1,000 feet below, flying on a south-westerly course. He dived his flight astern to the attack, and fastened on to an Me. 109, which had half-rolled on seeing his Spitfire. Mungo held his fire until just under 10,000 feet, when he let the 109 have a two-second burst. The enemy went into a steeper dive, and the ominous black smoke began to pour out. Mungo had now to break off the fight to wipe the ice from his windscreen. That done, he attacked again with a further two-second burst. At 2,000 feet, the Nazi disappeared into a haze of low cloud. Mungo broke off, his windscreen having iced once more.

The 109 crashed in flames near Hastings.

Bill Skinner, who was in Mungo's flight, had a tussle with a couple of Nazis who got behind him before attacking. He spun away to lose them. Flight Lieutenant St. John, who had been doing well, was killed in this engagement.

I have noticed during my fighting career that once a pilot has survived the combats which gave him ten victories, he gains great confidence, and thereafter, with a bit of luck and if God is on his side, he goes on from victory to victory. Mungo-Park, C. J. Freeborn and H. M. Stephen had all, by this time, reached double figures, and their fame in Fighter Command was rising with that of Sailor Malan. On October 27, about 9 a.m., H. M. Stephen led A Flight above the clouds over Maidstone area. In due course, he reported: "I sighted a number of 109s at about 23,000 feet. My flight was slightly below Mungo-Park's flight, and as I saw a 109 shoot at a Spitfire, I tried to attack the enemy, but he was out of range. The 109 turned and dived. I followed, and gave him a two-second burst, then another burst at closer range, and the Nazi enemy machine burst into flames. The ranges of our attacks were 450, 300 and 200 yards."

Mungo-Park was not quite so successful as Stephen. Directed to patrol Biggin Hill Aerodrome at 30,000 feet, at 9 a.m., he intercepted a small 109 formation at 22,000 feet. He attacked two machines which had become detached from the main body. Pressing the tit, he found that, owing to freezing, only one of his guns was working. Typically, he then closed the range to 50 yards. If the Nazi pilot had looked round, Mungo certainly would have seen the whites of his eyes. After firing, he saw pieces of the tail unit falling off. He then broke off the attack because he was running out of ammunition.

Blue 2 (Sergeant Bill Skinner) attacked the other 109. Mungo saw it diving seawards steeply, with black smoke trailing behind. Fighting at great speeds leaves no time for watching the difficulties of other pilots. Neither Mungo nor Skinner saw Sergeant

Scott disappear from the scrap. They heard later that he had been killed. His death was a great loss, for he had been showing promise worthy of the Tigers.

Flying Officer H. Nelson followed Malan's first rule of air fighting. He went in so close that he not only saw the whites of his enemy's eyes; he saw pieces of the 109 hitting his Spitfire. He said: "I was No. 2 to S/L Malan detailed to patrol Biggin Hill at 07.50 hours. We intercepted 30 Me. 109s over Ashford. Two of them came across my bows, heading into the sun. I followed and closed to 150 yards on the port side of the enemy and opened fire with a three-second burst which caused the 109 to smoke badly and half-roll down. I followed easily and the enemy, after a sharp dive, pulled steeply into the sun. I could only follow him with the smoke trail. After two minutes I closed once more in the climb and gave a continuous burst of ten seconds at point-blank range. The 109 shed bits of machine which hit my aircraft and damaged the spinner and propeller. The enemy then wallowed in a shallow dive, and I formated on it down through the clouds. I saw the whole central portion of fuselage was shot away and no pilot to be seen. He did not jump, so I assume he was slumped in his cockpit. The machine crashed a couple of miles to the south of Rochford Aerodrome."

Pilot Officer Peter Chesters destroyed a 109. He reported: "The enemy which I attacked was diving down to the clouds and I followed him. He saw me and tried to get on to my tail. I managed to turn inside him and put a burst into his engine, causing it to stop. I jockeyed him earthwards, and he landed on Penshurst Aerodrome with his wheels in the up position. I landed on the same aerodrome."

This case of victor and vanquished landing on the same aerodrome must be unique in World War II. On this day, the Squadron received information that the courageous and irrepressible Treacy had arrived in Marseilles. Not long afterwards he paid Malan a visit and dropped his "visiting card" in the C.O.'s tray. His address was given as "c/o Gestapo, Europe." What a broth of a boy!

Tiger Squadron's last fight within the official dates of the Battle of Britain took place on October 29. Mungo-Park was leading the squadron at 5 p.m. over East Grinstead, the village made famous during and after the Battle by Sir Archie McIndoe, the plastic surgeon. Sector Operations Control called Mungo on the R/T and ordered him to join Gannic Squadron at 25,000 feet over Biggin Hill. He contacted Gannic, and saw them dive to attack. Mungo climbed to 26,000 feet and saw about thirty Me. 109s at about 25,000 feet. He gave the "Tally-ho!" and half-rolled on to the 109s. Selecting his man, he gave him two short bursts. The Nazi blew up in flames. The pilot was obviously killed, as he did not take to his "umbrella."

Mungo then followed the runaway 109s and caught up with one of them at 18,000 feet. His speedometer was showing 550 m.p.h. After a couple of two-second bursts, he saw that the Nazi was in distress. Glycol was pouring out, and the machine went into a vertical dive. He was given another quick burst for luck and then began to disintegrate. It was the end of a perfect day for the arrogant Nazi pilot and for genial Mungo-Park.

Pilot Officer R. L. Spurdle got a probable when, "after delivering a full-deflection three-second burst at a 109, the machine rolled on its back and spiralled into a cloud inverted." Flying Officer W. H. Nelson destroyed his opponent after getting him into the sights for the kill with some difficulty. Nelson got on his tail and gave him a three-second burst at 150 yards, another at 100 yards, and finally, a two-second burst at 50 yards. This fight began at 25,000 feet and ended almost at ground-level, until at last the Messerschmitt crashed in a field near East Grinstead Hospital. How the patients cheered!

Pilot Officer E. W. G. Churches and Sergeant Morrison also gained victories in this engagement. And so we come to October 30, but the fighting continued at the same tempo in November.

27

In spite of the changed tactics of the enemy and the ebbing tide of the Battle, November was a busy month for the Tiger boys. On the second day, the squadron was ordered to patrol Biggin Hill at 15,000 feet, in company with 92 Squadron, commanded by the ace fighter leader Jamie Rankin.

Rankin and Malan, who were great friends, climbed side by side to 24,000 feet. Then, 4,000 feet below, they sighted more than sixty Me. 109s over the Isle of Sheppey. The squadrons then attacked. Mungo-Park fired two three-second bursts into a 109 before his windscreen iced up. He wiped it clean and fired another three-second burst at 200 yards, but again met with the same difficulty and had to break off the engagement. The enemy aircraft was last seen low over the water, emitting white smoke.

Pilot Officer Churches attacked a Me. 109 which was heading south. He caught it up between Dungeness and Cap Gris Nez, firing a two-second burst at 150 yards. Large pieces were seen to fall off the wing and fuselage of the enemy. It did a half-roll and dived vertically into the sea. Sergeant Morrison dived out of the sun for a stern attack on a 109. After firing two three-second bursts from 200 yards, he saw pieces of wing-roots and engine breaking off, followed by flames. Morrison's windscreen was covered with glycol from the crippled Nazi, which dived vertically into the Channel between Dover and Calais.

Bill Skinner sighted three Me. 109s flying above him at 20,000 feet. He attacked the nearest, firing short bursts of 1,600 rounds. Pieces fell off the enemy aircraft. It went down in flames, and the pilot joined his vanquished comrades in the Channel off Dover.

Pilot Officer Spurdle was a little luckier than Bill Skinner, and was able to obtain a souvenir from the 109 which he attacked at point-blank range. It fell in a field outside Ashford, Kent. I am told that the farmer took little notice of the crashed Nazi aircraft. He had become accustomed to that sort of arrival on his property.

Twelve Spitfires of 74 took off from Biggin Hill at 13.45 hours on November 14 to patrol Maidstone, in company with 66 Squadron, at 15,000 feet. Almost immediately, the two squadrons were ordered to Deal at 18,000 feet. Visibility was poor to fair, with the cloud base at 16,000 feet. An enemy formation was sighted approaching Dover from the north-east at 12,000–15,000 feet under heavy A.A. fire. The formation was made up of some fifty Ju. 87s in tight vics of five, line astern, at 12,000 feet, with an escort of approximately twenty-five Me. 109s circling above. The Tigers attacked the port flank. Mungo-Park went for one Ju. 87, giving it a three-second burst at 75 yards range. It blew up and burst into flames.

H. M. Stephen engaged a section of three Junkers. After firing a five-second burst into one of them, he was amazed to see it roll into the aircraft flying next to it. The wing of one of the pair came off. The other went down out of control, starting to disintegrate as it fell. Stephen then attacked a third machine, which was last seen flopping towards the Channel in a blaze of glory.

Pilot Officer Draper had ten minutes of glorious thrills. He first gave a Ju. 87 a short deflection shot. Pieces fell from the enemy's port wing root and engine cowling, and the machine went down almost vertically to crash just behind Dover. Next, Draper's guns put paid to another Junker, which burst into flames after a two-second burst, and he then had a go at a third bomber, which was seen to crash into the Channel. Still not satisfied, Draper followed on to a 109. It escaped with slight damage and sought shelter in a cloud.

Pilot Officer Churches evaded the attacks of two 109s, and then sighted a lone Messerschmitt at 16,000 feet. He promptly attacked with a four-second burst. The 109 gave out thick black smoke; pieces flew off his wings before it rolled over and went straight down to burst into flames.

Flying Officer Franklin pumped lead into another Ju. 87. It too burst into flames and dived into the Channel. Sergeant Glendinning picked out the leader of three Ju. 87s and closed in for a head-on attack, opening fire at 250 yards. The enemy aircraft dropped from its section with clouds of smoke pouring from it. Pieces of the machine flew in all directions and the wreck dropped into the sea. Glendinning then made another head-on attack. His second enemy was last seen diving in a fierce blaze. The third machine to receive his attentions went down with pieces flying from its wings. That sergeant was certainly good!

Flying Officer Spurdle and Sergeants Skinner and Freese each bowled over a Nazi; but it fell to the lot of Pilot Officer Armstrong to receive the greatest share of the day's excitement. To begin with before he could fire a shot, a Ju. 87 Armstrong had closed in to attack jettisoned its bombs and then the enemy rear gunner opened fire without effect. Armstrong silenced him with a four-second burst at 300 yards, while a further three-second burst from 100 yards tore pieces from the bomber. It flicked over and went into the Channel. A second Junker followed suit in short order.

Attempting to rejoin the squadron, Armstrong's Spitfire was unlucky enough to receive a hit from a cannon shell and later, an explosion in the engine caused flames to pour from the exhaust manifold. Armstrong had to take to his parachute, returning eventually to join the other Tigers who were celebrating their joyful fighting day. Needless to say, they toasted Sailor Malan, the *maestro* of fighting tactics, who had taught them their stuff. They knew how true it was that, no matter how good a pilot was before coming to the squadron, Malan would find ways of improving him still further.

On November 15 Stephen was Blue Leader, B Flight, when he intercepted numerous Me. 109s over Bognor Regis. Very unusually, several Messerschmitts made attacks on the Blues, so Stephen got his section on one flank and began to carry the fight to the enemy. He had to break off, as some of the Nazis were approaching head-on, but he succeeded in damaging one machine with a quarter attack before the fighting became too hot for him to watch its eventual fate. Sergeant Skinner, however, saw pieces flying off the 109.

Sergeant Glendinning heard a shout over the R/T: "Snappers behind!" His section was about to be jumped. He reported: "An Me.109 went past me on my port side. I delivered a beam attack. He flipped over on his back and, for a few seconds, seemed to hang in the air. I again closed in and gave him another burst. Pieces flew in all directions, and he went down in a series of rolls. Still not being satisfied, I gave another burst and something seemed to explode inside the machine, and the tail came away. The Me. 109 disappeared into the sea four miles east of Bognor Regis."

Bill Skinner had a warning of "snappers," and saw several Me. 109s going overhead, out to sea. He followed, and gave a burst to the nearest one. Smoke belched out, the front half of the fuselage burst into flames, and the Nazi went down vertically. Skinner opened fire on another aircraft and gave it two short bursts. A thin trail of smoke came from the 109, and a glow appeared in the region of the cockpit. It eventually disappeared in a cloud.

Patrolling over Littlehampton at 20,000 feet, Pilot Officer Draper led A Flight on to about twenty Me. 109s which appeared out of a cloud layer. He reported: "I played about for a few minutes, but no targets offered themselves. By this time I had lost height to about 6,000 feet, when I saw below me an Me. 109 travelling south very low. I dived down and got on his tail at 4,000 feet about fifteen miles off Littlehampton, and put a steady burst of five seconds into him; after which he rolled slowly over on to his back and went into the sea in a vertical dive."

On November 17 Freeborn and Stephen alternately had shooting practice on an Me. 109 just off Brighton Pier. Spectators on the promenade were able to enliven their constitutionals with the sight of one of Goering's "invincibles" plunging into the waves with a mighty splash.

Now, for a final example of the offensive spirit and the will to conquer, I quote from Malan's report of November 23:

"I was 'Knock-out' Leader, and took off with twelve aircraft, following 92 Squadron at 12.25 hours," Sailor wrote. "After patrolling Maidstone at 25,000 feet, we were ordered to sweep Dover area. We met various groups of Me. 109s off Dover, but we could not make contact because they did not apparently want to fight.

"Eventually two Me. 109s were met at 27,000 feet midway between Dover and Cap Gris-Nez. I climbed 500 feet to engage and delivered short bursts with half deflection. The enemy immediately emitted white smoke, but whether from artificial sources or from radiator trouble I don't know. After circling through 360 degrees, the enemy commenced diving towards Cap Gris-Nez and I followed. For the first few thousand feet the 109 drew away slightly, and I gave him several bursts at 500 yards. Eventually, I drew in to 150 yards, then 50 yards, and gave him all my ammunition. His hood tore off and heavy black smoke took the place of the white smoke. The Messerschmitt then commenced to burn as I broke away over Cap Gris-Nez." It tumbled earthwards on to French soil with the flames licking the fuselage as if it were a burning coffin. The poor old pilot must have been badly wounded or he would have taken to his "umbrella."

Malan's report provides a perfect example of the way to destroy an enemy. You must get closer and closer until—to quote Malan's rules—you can see the whites of his eyes. You must keep cool, be determined, and take steady aim. The will to conquer must predominate over all other emotions. These are the keys of success. Let young pilots, and embryo pilots of the Air Training Corps, take notice.

On November 27 Malan led the Tigers over the Isle of Sheppey at 25,000 feet to investigate anti-aircraft bursts. He spotted two Me.109s steering south, about 500 feet above. The squadron was turned and gave chase. The Nazi pilots had also seen Malan. The oft-heard air alarm, "*Achtung!* Spitfire!" came over the R/T. They dived steeply towards the haze below, but pulled out at 18,000 feet. Malan closed in on them to 800 yards. The two Nazis again started diving steeply, 200 yards apart. Sailor opened fire at 300 yards. He thought he saw tracers passing the enemy machines, and broke off. He lost distance on his target, which was now at 5,000 feet over Dungeness, but at last closed to 150 yards and opened fire once more. Getting even closer, he expended the rest of his ammunition on the machine on the right, which was slightly above and to the rear of its pal. The range was not more than 50 yards. The Nazi's engine blew up, the aircraft disintegrated, and the wreckage fell into the sea thirty miles from our coast.

The other Messerschmitt, which Malan had also fired on, was smoking badly. Sailor said afterwards: "To judge by its gyrations, either the machine was badly damaged or the pilot was badly frightened." He ordered Squadron Leader Wilson, who had been attached to Tiger Squadron from the Royal Aircraft Establishment for operational experience, to finish it off. And Wilson, like a good pupil, obeyed.

While over Chatham during this scrap, Pilot Officer Chesters, a member of one of the other sections, was fired at by a machine he did not see. His controls were badly damaged, and he had to take to his "umbrella." Floating earthwards, he felt a pain in his leg. When he landed, he found he had been slightly wounded.

While Sailor Malan and the Tigers were fighting over the Isle of Sheppey, Malan's great friend, Michael Robinson, was leading 609 (West Riding of Yorkshire) Squadron in the Isle of Wight area. He saw, about eight miles south of the Needles, a formation of Messerschmitts. Robinson made a beeline for them; but the Messerschmitts' leader, Major Helmuth Wieck, had spotted his approach. He split up his squadron to meet the attack.

During the brief encounter, Robinson heard an excited yell

over the R/T: "Whoopee! I've got a 109." He recognised the voice of his ace flight commander, John Charles Dundas, D.F.C. and bar. He called Dundas, and told him and the other pilots to re-form as quickly as possible but received no answer. Robinson looked around the sky anxiously. He called the flight commander again, but there was still no reply. Then a section leader called Michael and said he thought he saw a parachute floating in the sea below the area where the fighting had taken place. Michael led the Squadron low over the water, but could find no trace of Dundas or his dinghy.

It is now known that when Dundas had called so excitedly over the R/T, his victim had been none other than Wieck himself, the pride of the Luftwaffe, whom Hitler had decorated with the Knight's Cross of the Iron Cross with Oak Leaves, and to whom Goering had given command of the well-known Richthofen Squadron. Wieck was reputed to have shot down about sixty Allied aircraft at the time of his death. The gallant Dundas was attacked from the rear in the very act of vanquishing Goering's ace of aces.

November 30 was another great day in the history of Tiger Squadron. Pilots who had flown from Biggin Hill Aerodrome since the commencement of the Battle of Britain had formed the cream of Fighter Command. On the last day of November, 1940, the Station score-board showed 599 enemy aircraft and the pilots and ground staff of the various squadrons stationed on the aerodrome subscribed for a handsome present to the pilot who could bag the six-hundredth Nazi. The honour, and the prize, as it turned out, were shared by two pilots of Tiger Squadron, who showed commendable initiative and determination. They were, as might have been expected, the gay Mungo-Park and the placid H. M. Stephen—a fine combination.

There were four squadrons on the aerodrome at the time and, as can be imagined, everybody was pretty keen to have the winning hit. Mungo-Park and Stephen stole a march on their illustrious comrades on that damp and muggy morning, for, having obtained Sailor Malan's permission, they stealthily climbed into their Spitfires and taxied quietly from their dispersal point to the nearest runway. Suddenly, the half-asleep aerodrome was awakened by the roar as the two Spitfires took off. They were in the air on a voluntary patrol.

Pilots inside the mess rushed out on to the lawn. Someone shouted: "Who the hell are they? They must be crackers." Sailor Malan laughed softly. He looked at his watch, got into his car, and drove to the Sector operations-room. "Has Mungo called up?" he asked the controller.

"Yes," was the reply. "We've informed Group that they are up."

The controller had scarcely finished speaking when an eight plus raid appeared on the board. It was coming over from the direction of Cap Gris-Nez. Mungo was contacted over the R/T and sent to patrol a convoy off Deal at Angels 30.

For the rest of the story, let us refer to the reports of the two heroes.

"I was Blue Leader sent on patrol to convoy off Deal," Mungo wrote. "I was informed by operations that many 'Snappers' were in the close vicinity, so I climbed to 29,000 feet and sighted eight plus raid coming in from the south towards the convoy.

"We (Stephen and myself) climbed to 34,000 feet and engaged the 'Weaver.' I opened fire with a two-second burst at 150 yards approximately, and enemy aircraft immediately dived. I broke off as I was overshooting, and Stephen went in to attack. The 109 then half-rolled, and I followed him down, giving a further two-second burst at 100 yards, and saw the hood of the 109 fly off. I broke away to avoid being hit by the hood and Stephen attacked again. The 109 was over the vertical when I last saw him going through a cloud."

Pilot Officer Stephen reported: "I was No. 2 to Mungo-Park who volunteered to patrol convoy off Deal, when we sighted several Me. 109s above us. We climbed to 34,000 feet and we engaged the enemy at that height. I opened with a two-second burst of fire on a deflection attack. Then Mungo-Park fired, and I came in again from dead astern of the 109 and got another three-second burst and pieces flew off it. The enemy rolled and I got in another burst of deflection, and ended up dead astern, closing to 20 yards. By this time the enemy was out of control and beginning to smoke. I broke off as the 109 went into a cloud, upside down, beyond the vertical, doing at least 450 m.p.h. The clouds were about 4,000 feet on top."

Oberleutnant Schmidt, the unfortunate pilot, must have been too windy to bale out, for he made an almost out-of-control crash landing near Dungeness. He died fifteen hours later, and was buried with military honours. This victory brought the squadron score for the month to thirty, without casualties to the Tigers.

As a result of the splendid month of fighting, as well as previous personal successes, there were awards and recognitions. Squadron Leader Malan was awarded the Distinguished Service Order for

Dunkirk and the Battle of Britain

"commanding his squadron with outstanding success over an extensive period of air operations. By his brilliant leadership, skill and determination, he contributed largely to the successes obtained. Since early August, 1940, the squadron has destroyed at least eighty-four enemy aircraft and damaged many more."

Next came the supreme honour of the first-ever immediate award in the field in Britain of the Distinguished Service Order to Pilot Officer H. M. Stephen. The citation in the *London Gazette* read: "One day in November, 1940, Pilot Officer Stephen led a section of his squadron in an attack against an escorted formation of enemy bombers, three of which he destroyed. Later in the month he undertook a voluntary patrol in company with his flight commander and destroyed an Me.109. This success brought the number of enemy destroyed by members of his home station to the magnificent total of 600, and at the same time increased his own score to nineteen. His exceptional courage and skill have greatly enhanced the fine spirit shown by his squadron."

For a pilot officer to be given an immediate award in the field of the Distinguished Service Order was not only a very great honour to H. M. Stephen himself. It shed new lustre on Tiger Squadron as well.

In recognition of their fine service and fighting qualities, Pilot Officer Draper was awarded the Distinguished Flying Cross, and Sergeant Skinner received the Distinguished Flying Medal. A little later, Sailor won a bar to his D.S.O., and so became the first fighter pilot to win a double D.S.O. and D.F.C.

Early in December, 11 Group H.Q. published a list for November of enemy casualties inflicted by squadrons in the group. Tiger Squadron topped the lot, and shortly afterwards, the Squadron received a congratulatory message from the Minister for Air. It was forwarded through the A.O.C., 11 Group, and read:

"Please convey my congratulations to No. 74 Squadron on their brilliant fighting over the last four weeks, during which my records show that they have had the destruction of 33 enemy aircraft confirmed and have only lost two machines themselves.

"This is a splendid achievement.

"ARCHIBALD SINCLAIR."

That was high praise indeed. Up, the Tigers!

It is fitting before ending the story of Tiger Squadron's valorous deeds in 1940 to point out that, in the opinion of Sailor

Malan and other famous Squadron commanders, the high morale of the fighter pilots of all ranks was due mainly to the fine example and encouragement of the Air Officer Commanding 11 Group, Air Vice-Marshal Sir Keith Park. I well remember how the late beloved King George VI appreciated Sir Keith's magnificent efforts.

28

In DECEMBER, 1940, I was posted from Hawarden to Turnhouse Aerodrome, Edinburgh, to form 59 (Hurricane) Operational Training Unit. Turnhouse Station was commanded by the Duke of Hamilton, to whom, on May 10, 1941—the anniversary of Hitler's attack on the Low Countries—Hess made his sensational flight across the North Sea.

I have often been asked why Hess was not shot down when he crossed our coast. The answer is simple. The controller at the group sector did not think that an Me. 110, with its limited range, could possibly be flying in the area. He did not know that this particular 110 had been specially prepared for the secret flight which Hess and his cronies hoped would end in Britain's throwing up the sponge.

My chief flying instructor at Turnhouse was Flight Lieutenant "Fanny" Orton, of 73 Squadron fame. There were many heated discussions among pilots of 73 as to whether he or "Cobber" Kain was the better fighter ace. "Fanny's" face was slightly disfigured, due to burns received when he had to leave his blazing Hurricane after a scrap in France. On that occasion, his parachute got caught up in a tree. He hung, suspended from the branches, for some time while trigger-happy French troops potted at him. Luckily, he only sustained flesh wounds before being rescued by British soldiers. Orton sported a D.F.C. and bar under the wings on his left breast.

As I have already recorded, another famous pilot to join my unit was Flight Lieutenant H. M. Stephen, of Tiger Squadron.

Since forming a new operational training unit of some 3,000 men and more than eighty aircraft was a slow business, there was time for occasional relaxation in the evenings, and we found the luxurious North British and Caledonian Hotels in Edinburgh "just the job" for our celebrations on Saturday evenings. An incident occurred while I was at dinner one night which threw a revealing light on the alleged "irresponsibility" of fighter pilots and on the blindness and intolerance of some civilians.

Tiger Squadron

A very brave young officer, who was not over-fussy about the absolute correctness of his Service attire, came into the dining-room and greeted me. Naturally, I invited him to my table for a drink. As he was sitting down, the waiter said: "Very sorry, sir. I can't serve you. You are not properly dressed."

"What?" snapped the youngster. "Rot! Get me a drink."

"Very sorry, sir. I can't. I've got my orders."

This was too much. I pointed out that the officer was my guest, and demanded that he should be served. The waiter stolidly shook his head. "He's not properly dressed," he repeated.

The young pilot got to his feet. "Don't worry about it, Taffy," he said to me. He stumbled across the room, his face red with anger. Then, at the door, he turned.

"I hope your whole bloody city gets blown to hell before morning," he shouted to the startled diners.

Early next morning, while I was in bed, drinking the first cup of tea of the day, the door of my room opened and the youngster walked in. "I've come to apologise for my rotten show last night," he said. And with that he broke down and cried like a baby.

I soothed him down, talking to him like the proverbial Dutch uncle. And when he left me, he went straight round to the Manager of the hotel and made his apologies. Now, to those who had witnessed the ugly incident of the previous evening, that officer was merely another "drunken, irresponsible" fighter pilot, making a scene in a public place. They did not realise that his nerves, strained to breaking-point by months of bitter air fighting in defence of his homeland, had finally let him down. He was another victim of what the psychiatrists call a psycho-neurosis. It is a more dangerous and more insidious enemy than any Nazi.

To return to more mundane matters, the formation of 59 O.T.U. was completed towards the end of May, 1941, and I was then ordered to proceed to Heston Aerodrome, Middlesex, to form "the brave old Fifty-third, the Fighting O.T.U." For this new outfit, I wrote a unit song which was sung once a week by all 120 officers as they stood around the walls of the mess. It was sung to the tune of "The Brave Old Duke of York," and here it is:

> The brave old Fifty-third,
>   The Fighting O.T.U.
> We send our pupils up so high
>   They don't know what to do.

Dunkirk and the Battle of Britain

Their oxygen's turned on.
　Their R/T's working well.
The boys are spoiling for a fight
　To knock the Huns to hell.

They used to overshoot
　The marker aeroplane,
But since the C.O. ramped and raged
　They all go round again.

Their undercart comes up.
　Their flaps are raised as well.
The C.F.I., he shouts and cheers,
　And Satan cries: "Oh, hell!"

The course is over now;
　The boys are fighting fit.
And everyone is itching
　To meet a Messerschmitt.

They've kissed their girls goodbye.
　They've spoken their last word,
And now they're going to prove their worth
　To the Fighting Fifty-third.

I used to concentrate on developing a high morale in the pupils, and in my lecture to them, as commanding officer, on their arrival at the unit, I would give them the works on the dangers of air fighting. I would point out that although the Spitfire had armour plate to protect the pilot from bullets coming from dead astern, a deflection shot from abeam could produce a bucketful of bullets, which could be very painful to the pilot's guts. Having said so much, I waited for the laughter which was a good sign of morale. If I spotted a man who did not laugh, I knew that his mind was troubled. At the end of the lecture, I would say: "Now, if there is anyone here who is not keen on air fighting and would prefer to be in bombers, please come and have a chat with me in my office. Now is the moment, so that you don't waste our time in trying to train you. There will be no disgrace. It takes a very brave man to be a bomber pilot." I found that in a course of thirty-odd men there were always one or two who did not fancy a "bucketful of bullets in their guts." Usually, these men had brown eyes.

Stressing the importance of flying discipline, I warned pupils of the consequences of disobeying orders in the air. I "decorated" the walls of the lecture hut with photographs of crashes and of the funerals of the deceased pupils. Referring to these, I would say: "Inside those coffins are nice fellows, just like yourselves. They threw away their precious lives to satisfy a foolish desire to do a 'shooting up' for the benefit of some blue-eyed blonde or deliberately to break flying orders.

"Now, don't *you* join this tragic gallery. Think of me, having to write a sad letter to your next-of-kin, and, worse still, having to pay half a crown towards your wreath!" If the pupils merely tittered at my quip about the wreath, I knew my advice had soaked in—temporarily, at least; for there is always one naughty boy on every course who ignores flying orders and tries to break his neck, often with success. I would end my lecture: "Anyway, don't worry about death. You die every night.".

Early in 1941, a number of American pilots trained secretly in 53 O.T.U. Among them were First Lieutenant P. H. Greasley, Second Lieutenant G. E. Hubbard, Second Lieutenant D. R. McGovern, First Lieutenant D. J. Clapham, First Lieutenant J. A. Kelly, Second Lieutenant J. A. Wilson, Second Lieutenant W. H. Merriam, Second Lieutenant D. J. Green, Second Lieutenant R. L. Faurot, Second Lieutenant L. A. Viar and Second Lieutenant W. D. Greenfield.

This was more than a year before America came into the war, and the Director of Training sent for me one day and said: "Taffy, I'm sending you some American fighter pilots who are here to be taught to fly the Spitfire and to get experience of our operational training. It is a strict secret that they are here. They must not appear in uniform outside the aerodrome. For God's sake, don't kill any of them. I've specially chosen your O.T.U. I understand from Leigh-Mallory that you've got the game wrapped up."

"I'll do my best," I replied. "Unfortunately, I can't sit in their laps in a Spitfire."

As luck would have it, all the pilots completed the course without difficulty. They were exceptionally keen, and were very obedient to "Grandpa Tiger's" lucid orders. When the course had ended, and they were awaiting further instructions, First Lieutenant P. H. Greasley, the senior pupil, came to me and asked whether it would be possible for them to meet the King and Queen before they returned to America. This was one out of the bag. However, since I could see the propaganda significance, I promised to make inquiries.

Mr. (now Lord) Harold Balfour, then Under-Secretary of

Dunkirk and the Battle of Britain

State for Air—an old friend and a great air fighter in my day—came to my aid. He arranged a visit to Windsor Castle, where the pupils met Their Majesties and were entertained to tea. Wing Commander John Kent, the Canadian ace who was my O.C. Flying, accompanied the party. We were met by a guide at the King Henry VIII Gate at 3 p.m., and shown over the famous St. George's Chapel, where the Kings of England are buried. Then we proceeded to the main entrance of the Castle to await the arrival of the King and Queen.

The day of our visit was Sunday, June 22, 1941—the day on which Hitler invaded Russia. I asked the King what he thought of the Führer's latest venture.

"Thank God!" he replied, smiling.

On the lawn, where we were taken to listen to the band playing, there happened one or two incidents that I feel are worth mentioning. For instance, as soon as the party came in sight, the band struck up "God Save the King." Everybody stood to attention except the King and I. His Majesty, however, was so engrossed in discussing Hitler's Russian adventure that he did not hear the music that was being played. I kept halting in my stride, feeling very embarrassed, as the King plodded slowly forward, with his head bent. At last, he abruptly halted, stood at attention, and said under his breath: "Good gracious! They are playing 'The King'!"

As we sat listening to the music later, a roar of laughter came from the direction of the Queen's party. The joker of the bunch had said to Her Majesty: "Just think. Two years ago, I was waving a flag as you drove past me in New York. Now I'm near enough to enjoy your beauty and your lovely smile." To which another voice added fervently: "Atta boy!" It was then that the laughter broke out.

I first met King George VI shortly after Armistice Day, 1918, near Lille, in northern France. He was then the Duke of York, and was accompanied by his elder brother, the Prince of Wales. The occasion was the match between the Tigers' unbeaten Rugby football team and their challengers, the Royal Horse Guards, who were the Army champions and twice our build. We won the game, and afterwards Their Royal Highnesses, accompanied by our Brigade Commander, Brigadier Smyth-Osborne, had tea with us.

Now, at Windsor, the King remembered the match, and asked: "Who was that smart little fellow you had at half-back?"

I replied: "Harry Coverdale, of Blackheath and England."

Tiger Squadron

The King then asked me from which part of Wales I came. When I told him that my home was in the village of St. Clears, Carmarthenshire, he said: "I wonder whether you know the officer in charge of my Household Troops. He comes from Carmarthen. I will send for him."

Imagine my surprise when I saw my gallant friend, Colonel Grismond Phillips,[1] smartly saluting His Majesty. We felt justified in shaking hands, laughing heartily, momentarily forgetting the presence of the King. It was a pleasant surprise.

I told the King that I had watched Flight Lieutenant (now Air Marshal Sir) A. Corrington teaching him to fly, and we recalled the days when he was Adjutant at Cranwell. Although that was back in the early 'twenties, His Majesty's memory of the period was excellent. We talked also of Sir Charles Longcroft, then the popular Commandant of the College; of Johnny Leacroft and his point-to-point efforts; of athlete Bones Brady; of John Alcock, who in 1919 was the first pilot to fly the Atlantic; of Jones-Williams, killed on his non-stop flight to India; and of many other famous men.

Then we came to the Battle of Britain. The King told me how much he admired Keith Park's fine leadership, and his habit of getting into his Hurricane at Northolt and flying over the battle area, wherever it might be—at Dunkirk or somewhere in the south-east of England. "You are about the same age, aren't you, Taffy?" he asked.

"Yes, sir," I replied. "About forty-five."

"You fly Spitfires, I hear."

I replied that I did.

Then, to my surprise, the King asked, with a smile: "Is it right that you have also been on sweeps over northern France?"

As I had had no permission for these trips, I stammered confusedly: "Only on one or two occasions, sir."

His Majesty laughed outright. "You're too old, Taffy. It's a young man's game," he said.

He then asked me the number of my old Squadron, and I replied: "No. 74—the Tiger Squadron. The best in France in 1918, and the best in the Battle of Britain." The King thought for a second. Then he said: "Yes; it's very good. That's Sailor Malan's squadron, isn't it?"

Sailor was a very proud man when I told him of this conversation.

I realised, as the King talked, how keen was the interest he had

[1] Knighted in the Coronation Honours List, 1953.

taken in the deeds of the Fighter Command squadrons and the successes of individual pilots. He reeled off the names of the aces in a manner which delighted me. Their Majesties chatted with each pupil in turn, and shook hands with everybody in the party before taking their leave at their private entrance to the Castle.

The Americans suddenly got in line abreast, sprang to attention and saluted smartly. As they walked away from the Castle, they waved fondly to the charming little Princesses, who, much to their delight, waved in reply. Little did those boys think they were waving to a girl who would, within a decade, become the reigning Queen of the Commonwealth, and possibly the greatest Queen in the long history of Britain.

It was a grand day for the young Americans, who came from all parts of the United States. Full of pride, they drove back to Heston. One of their biggest thrills, Lieutenant Greasley told me, had come when the band struck up "The Star Spangled Banner." The King had asked specially for it to be played.

It was a great day, too, for "Grandpa Tiger." As a member of the original 74 Squadron, I felt proud to have been selected to train those American pilots, and greatly honoured to have been chosen to introduce them to our beloved King and Queen in the surroundings of their most historic and favoured home.

In 1951, under a trans-Atlantic exchange scheme, Major George W. Milholland of the United States Air Force came to Britain to join the Royal Air Force, and two years later, at St. Faith's, Norwich, R.A.F. Station he received the Dacre Championship Trophy for weapon training on behalf of 74 Fighter (Trinidad) Squadron, R.A.F., of which he had become commanding officer. It was a happy climax to a friendship welded in the fierce fires of war.

Long may the partnership of the Tiger and the Eagle flourish!

WORLD WAR I BRITISH ACES

Name	Victories	Name	Victories
Major E. Mannock .	73	Captain Larkin . .	41
Colonel W. Bishop .	72	Captain J. I. T. Jones	40
Major R. Collishaw .	68	Major R. Dallas .	39
Captain J. McCudden	58	Captain J. Gilmore .	37
Captain D. McLaren .	54	Captain W. G. Claxton	37
Major P. F. Fullard .	53	Captain H. W. Wollett	35
Major W. G. Barker .	52	Captain F. G. Quigley	34
Captain A. W. Beau-champ-Proctor .	52	Captain F. R. McCall	34
		Major A. D. Carter .	31
Captain R. A. Little .	47	Captain J. M. M. White	31
Captain G. E. McElroy	46	Captain W. L. Jordan .	31
Captain A. Ball . .	43		

FIGHTER COMMAND PILOTS WITH MORE THAN TWELVE CONFIRMED VICTORIES

(Up to June 30th, 1941)

	Squadron No.	Day	Night	Total
W/Cdr. A. C. Malan, D.S.O. and bar, D.F.C. and bar . .	74 S	27	2	29
S/Ldr. R. R. Stanford Tuck, D.S.O., D.F.C. and bars .	257 H	24	2	26
P/O J. H. Lacey, D.F.M. and bar	501 H	23	—	23
S/Ldr. M. N. Crossley, D.S.O., D.F.C.	32 H	22	—	22
P/O E. S. Lock, D.S.O., D.F.C. and bar	41 S	22	—	22
F/Lt. H. M. Stephen, D.S.O., D.F.C. and bar . . .	74 S	21	—	21
F/Lt. G. Allard, D.F.C., D.F.M. and bar (deceased) . .	85 H	19	—	19
S/Ldr. R. G. Dutton, D.F.C. and bar	19 S	19	—	19
P/O H. J. L. Hallowes, D.F.M. and bar	122 S	17	1	18
F/Lt. F. H. R. Carey, D.F.C. and bar, D.F.M. . .	43 H (52 O.T.U.)	17	1	18
F/Lt. A. C. Deere, D.F.C. and bar	602 S	17½	—	17½
S/Ldr. M. H. Brown, D.F.C. and bar	1 H (58 O.T.U.)	17½	—	17½
S/Ldr. R. F. Boyd, D.F.C. and bar	54 S	17	—	17
S/Ldr. W. D. Davids, D.F.C. and bar	152 S (59 O.T.U.)	17	—	17
F/Lt. D. A. P. McMullen, D.F.C. and bar	151 D	13⅗	3	16⅗
F/Lt. C. F. Gray, D.F.C. (N.Z.)	1 H	16	–	16
F/Lt. J. G. Saunders, D.F.C. .	—	11	5	16
W/Cdr. D. R. S. Bader, D.S.O. and bar, D.F.C. and bar .	242 H	15½	—	15½
S/Ldr. N. Orton, D.F.C. and bar	242 H	15	—	15

Tiger Squadron

	Squadron No.	Day	Night	Total
F/Lt. J. W. Villa, D.F.C. and bar	92 S (58 O.T.U.)	15	–	15
S/Ldr. A. H. Boyd, D.F.C. and bar	501 S	$13\frac{5}{8}$	1	$14\frac{5}{8}$
F/Lt. R. F. T. Doe, D.F.C. and bar	66 S	$14\frac{1}{2}$	–	$14\frac{1}{2}$
S/Ldr. J. Ellis, D.F.C. and bar .	610 S (55 O.T.U.)	13	1	14
S/Ldr. J. I. Kilmartin, D.F.C. .	602 S	14	–	14
F/Lt. A. McDowall, D.F.C. and bar	245 H	13	1	14
Sgt. D. A. S. McKay, D.F.M. and bar	91 S	14	–	14
S/Ldr. T. F. D.-Morgan, D.F.C. and bar	43 H	10	4	14
S/Ldr. J. Cunningham, D.S.O., D.F.C.	604 Be	–	13	13
S/Ldr. C. F. Currant, D.F.C. and bar	605 H (52 O.T.U.)	13	–	13
S/Ldr. D. R. Edge, D.F.C. .	605 H	13	–	13
F/Lt. J. O'Meara, D.F.C. and bar	64 S	13	–	13
S/Ldr. J. W. Simpson, D.F.C. and bar	245 H	13	–	13
F/S. Thorne, D.F.M. and bar . ⎤ F/S. Barker, D.F.M. and bar ⎬ (A.G.) . . . . ⎦	264 D	12	1	13
F/Lt. J. C. Freeborn, D.F.C. .	74 S (57 O.T.U.)	$12\frac{1}{2}$	–	$12\frac{1}{2}$
F/Lt. F. W. Higginson, D.F.M. (missing)	56 H	$12\frac{1}{2}$	–	$12\frac{1}{2}$

Note: Malan kept the lead with thirty victories until August, 1944, when he had been off operations for two years.—(*Author*).

Explanation of initial after squadron number: Be—Beaufighter; D—Defiant; H—Hurricane; S—Spitfire.

INDEX

Italicised numbers refer to illustrations on facing pages

Index

Drake, W/Cdr. W. ("Billy"), *81*, 171, 197

Draper, Maj. Chris, 67 and *n*

Draper, P/O, 227, 228, 266, 271, 273, 277

Drossaert, P/O A. E., *81*

Dundas, F/Lt. H. S. L., *193*, 210

Dundas, F/Lt. John, *144*, 210, 275

Dunn, Sgt.-Maj., 71

Dutton, S/Ldr. R. G., 229, 287

EDGE, S/Ldr. D. R., 288

Edmonds, F/Lt. D. L., *224*

Eley, Sgt., 232, 236

Ellis, Lt., 61

Ellis, S/Ldr. J., 288

Embry, Air Marshal Sir Basil, 212, 216

Enright, Sgt. E. G., *81*

Ester, Sgt. J., *81*

Evans, Sgt., *129*

Evill, Air Vice-Marshal D. S., 40, 67

FALKENHAYN, General von, 44

Farqhar, W/Cdr., *177*

Farrer, David, 262

Faurot, Lt. R. L., *177*, 282

Ferrand, Lt. J., 167

Findlay, D. O., 210

Finucane, F/Lt. B. E. ("Paddy"), *193*, 210

Fish, Sgt., *129*

Flinders, Sgt., 190, 191, 202

Foggin, Capt., 63

Fokes, F/O, *177*

Fokker, Anthony, 41, 66

Fonck, Capt. René, 40

Ford, Sgt., *129*

Foster, Lt., 39

Franklin, F/O, *80*, 271

Frantisek, Sgt. Jozef, 202, *225*, 229

Freeborn, F/Lt. Johnny, *33*, 190, 191, 211, 213, 223, 227, 232, 233, 234, 240, 241, 244, 242, 257, 265, 266, 267, 273, 288

Freeman, Air Chief Marshal Sir Wilfred, 18, 263

Freese, Sgt., 271

French, Sir John, 17, 20

Fry, Clarence, 60

Fullard, Maj. P. F., 286

GAULD, Lt. George W. G., 143, 151, 155, 156-7, 158 and *n*, 159, 160, *192*

George V, King, *49*, 162, 163, 164, 166, 168-9

George VI, King, 223, 278, 283-5

Gibson, F/Lt. Johnny, *177*, 210

Giles, Lt. Wilfred B. ("Twist"), *49*, 59, 63, 66, 68, 73, 74-5, 77, 83, 84, 88-9, 96, 97, 99, 100, 102-3, 104, 105, 108, 111, 116, 117, 125, 126-7, 132-3, 137, 161, 164, 165, 230

Gilmore, Capt, J., 286

Glaser, F/O, *177*

Glendinning, Sgt., *80*, 271, 272

Glynn, Lt., 63, 90-1, 150, 161

Goering, Hermann, 48, 182, 192, 199, 206, 220, 226, 237, 255, 264, 275

Gordeau, Sgt., *129*

Gordon, Freddie, 140, 158 and *n*, 159, 160, *192*

Goudie, H. C., *192*

Grant, F/Lt. Reg, 252

Gray, F/Lt. C. F., 287

Gray, R. H., *192*

Greasley, Lt. P. H., *177*, 282, 285

Green, Lt. D. J., *177*, 282

Greenfield, Lt. W. D., *177*, 282

Grey, Lt., 149

Grider, Lt., 60, 124

Gross, Lt., *129*, *177*

Gunn, P/O, 232, 234, 236

HAIG, Earl Douglas, 19

Hallahan, Hal, 60

Hallahan, S/Ldr. P. J. H. ("Bull"), 197

Hallings-Pott, G/Capt., 232, 259, 263

Hallowes, P/O H. J. L., 229, 287

Halton-Harrop, P/O, 191

Hamer, Lt. H., *49*, 63

Hamilton, Sir F. H., 167

Hamlyn, Sgt. R. F., 202

Hanks, Prosser, 197

Hargreaves, Sgt. H. L., *81*

Harmel, Sgt. L. J. G., *81*

Harrington, General, 104

Harrison, L., *192*

Harvey-Kelly, Lt., 18

Hastings, P/O, 232, 239, 245, 257

Index

Index

Index

Library of Congress Cataloging-in-Publication Data

Jones, Ira, 1896-
Tiger squadron / Ira Jones.
p. cm. — (Wings of war)
Originally published: London : W.H. Allen, 1954.
Includes index.
ISBN 0-8094-9783-2 (trade)
1. Great Britain. Royal Air Force. 74 Squadron—History.
2. World War, 1939-1945—Regimental histories—Great Britain.
3. World War, 1939-1945—Aerial operations, British.
I. Title. II. Series.
D786.J665 1994   940.54'1241—dc20   94-7798 CIP

Cover photograph © Carl Purcell
Endpapers photograph © Rene Sheret/After Image

Printed in the United States of America.